POLICY-BASED NETWORKING

Architecture and Algorithms

Dinesh C. Verma

201 West 103rd Street,
Indianapolis, Indiana 46290

Policy-Based Networking: Architecture and Algorithms

By Dinesh C. Verma

Copyright © 2001 by New Riders Publishing

FIRST EDITION: November, 2000

International Standard Book Number: 1-57870-226-7

Library of Congress Catalog Card Number: 00-101491

05 04 03 02 01   7 6 5 4 3 2 1

Interpretation of the printing code: The rightmost double-digit number is the year of the book's printing; the rightmost single-digit number is the number of the book's printing. For example, the printing code 01-1 shows that the first printing of the book occurred in 2000.

Composed in Galliard and MCPdigital by New Riders Publishing

Printed in the United States of America

Trademarks

Warning and Disclaimer

PUBLISHER
David Dwyer

ASSOCIATE PUBLISHER
Al Valvano

MANAGING EDITOR
Gina Brown

PRODUCT MARKETING MANAGER
Stephanie Layton

PUBLICITY MANAGER
Susan Petro

ACQUISITIONS EDITORS
Karen Wachs
Leah Williams

DEVELOPMENT EDITOR
Lisa M. Thibault

PROJECT EDITOR
Elise Walter

COPY EDITOR
Gayle Johnson

INDEXER
Brad Herriman

MANUFACTURING COORDINATOR
Chris Moos

BOOK DESIGNER
Louisa Klucznik

COVER DESIGNER
Aren Howell

PROOFREADER
Debbie Williams

COMPOSITION
Suzanne Pettypiece

CONTENTS AT A GLANCE

CONTENTS

About the Author

Dinesh C. Verma manages the Policy and Network Control Research Group at the IBM T J Watson Research Center. He has worked in the area of networking for more than a decade, and he has been a member of research groups at the University of California, Berkeley, Philips Research, and IBM. Verma has written many papers and articles in various journals in the field, and he holds several patents related to networking technologies. He has been an active participant in various industrial forums such as the IETF and ATM Forums, and he acts as an advisor to the IBM and Tivoli product divisions in the field of networking. His current research interests include performance management and Quality of Service in IP networks, employing policies to simplify management of network performance and security, and using content distribution networks to improve dynamic application performance.

About the Technical Reviewers

The technical reviewers contributed their considerable hands-on expertise to the entire development process for *Policy-Based Networking: Architecture and Algorithms*. As this book was being written, these dedicated professional reviewed all the material for technical content, organization, and flow. Their feedback was critical to ensuring that this book fits our readers' needs for the highest-quality technical information.

Ed Ellesson is a Senior Engineer at Tivoli Systems, Inc., an IBM company. He is currently responsible for technical direction in the area of policy-based management, including the application of this technology to scalably manage service levels across networks and host systems. Ellesson chairs the Service-Level Agreement Working Group within the Distributed Management Task Force (DMTF), which has extended the Common Information Model (CIM) to support policy. He also cochairs the Policy Framework Working Group within the Internet Engineering Task Force (IETF). Ellesson has approximately 30 years of experience in a variety of voice and data communications technologies, and in a variety of engineering, architecture, and marketing roles with ROLM Corporation, TRW, and GTE, as well as with IBM and Tivoli. He is a member of the IEEE and the ACM. He did his undergraduate work in electrical engineering at Cornell University.

Dr. Dganit Amitai-Oreny is president and CTO of White.Cell Inc., a start-up company that develops and markets an end-to-end platform for management and security of data over cellular networks and cellular Internet access. Dganit is known within the Israeli industry as an expert in data networks and an able speaker.

Amitai-Oreny holds the position of senior lecturer at the Academic College of Tel-Aviv, where she is in charge of the data-communication laboratory. Her courses cover both theoretical and practical aspects of data networks. Dganit holds a Ph.D. in computer sciences from Tel-Aviv University.

Dedication

Dedicated to Paridhi, Archit & Riya.

Acknowledgments

Writing this book involved a tremendous amount of support from many people, and I would like to express my deep appreciation to all those who helped me in this process. I owe a big debt of gratitude to my wife, Paridhi, and kids, Archit and Riya, who had to put off many of their plans to give me time to write this book. Their support was crucial to my completing this book in a short amount of time.

A person owes most of his knowledge to his environment, and I am extremely lucky to have a fantastic team of colleagues at IBM. Those who have introduced me to different facets of network policies include Arvind Krishna, Bruce Dillon, Charles Kunzinger, Dilip Kandlur, Edward Ellesson, Gordon Arnold, Jay Aiken, John Tavs, Lap Hunyh, Lee Rafalow, Mandis Beigi, Mark Davis, Raymond Jennings, Reiner Sailer, Robert Moore, Roy Brabson, Vishal Bhotika, and William Pranger. The many discussions and debates with these colleagues over the years have had a significant impact on my thoughts about network policies.

Many people helped in the process of writing this book. Linda Engelman, Karen Wachs, and Leah Williams helped in navigating the publishing process, and Lisa Thibault, Elise Walter, and Gayle Johnson were a great help in improving the presentation and organization of the text. I also wish to acknowledge several New Riders editors and illustrators who worked behind the scenes to finish this book in its present form. But my biggest vote of thanks goes to the technical reviewers, Ed Ellesson and Dganit Amitai-Oreny, whose comments and revisions helped immensely in improving the contents of the book.

Tell Us What You Think

As the reader of this book, you are the most important critic and commentator. We value your opinion, and we want to know what we're doing right, what we could do better, what areas you'd like to see us publish in, and any other words of wisdom you're willing to pass our way.

As the Associate Publisher at New Riders Publishing, I welcome your comments. You can fax, email, or write me directly to let me know what you did or didn't like about this book—as well as what we can do to make our books stronger.

Please note that I cannot help you with technical problems related to the topic of this book, and that due to the high volume of mail I receive, I might not be able to reply to every message.

When you write, please be sure to include this book's title and author, as well as your name and phone or fax number. I will carefully review your comments and share them with the author and editors who worked on this book.

Fax: 317-581-4663

Email: nrfeedback@newriders.com

Mail: Al Valvano
Associate Publisher
New Riders Publishing
201 West 103rd Street
Indianapolis, IN 46290 USA

INTRODUCTION

A typical IP network consists of a large number of routers and servers running a variety
of applications that are used by a large number of users. Some of these applications (such
as the applications implementing the routing protocols) are needed for proper operation of
the IP networks, and other applications, such as Web servers or mail servers, are deployed
for a specific purpose. Although individual configurations of the IP network vary from
organization to organization, it is safe to assume that the different applications and users
in the network interact with each other in a complex and subtle manner. The applications
compete with each other to access network resources, such as the bandwidth on different
links, the buffer space in the routers, encryption facilities for secure communication, and
processing cycles at servers. Competition is not the only manner of interaction between the
applications. Some applications assist in the smooth operation of other applications. For
example, the Domain Name Service resolves machine names to IP addresses and is invoked
by many other networked applications.

In an ideal world, the network would have enough resources that the performance implications of these interactions among the users and applications could be ignored. Similarly, all
the users in an ideal world could be trusted to access only the applications they needed,
and all the applications could be trusted to use only the resources they needed.

Unfortunately, no real network comes close to this utopian dream. All networks typically
have one or more resources in short supply, such as the capacity of an access link, the number of IP addresses available within the network, or the processing cycles at a server, to
name just a few. Similarly, not all users can be trusted in the network, nor can all applications be trusted to behave at all times.

A policy is an administrator-specified directive that manages certain aspects of the desired
outcome of interactions among users, among applications, and between users and applications. The policy provides guidelines for how the different network elements, such as

routers, servers, and firewalls, should handle the traffic resulting from different users and applications. Policies can be applied to different aspects of a network, including (but not limited to) access to network resources by different users and applications, restricting the set of applications accessible by a user, or the support of different service levels in the network.

A framework within which policies can be defined in a standard way is being developed by the *Policy Framework Working Group* (PFWG) of the *Internet Engineering Task Force* (IETF). A detailed description of the representation schematic can be found in the book by Strassner [STRASS]. For the current documentation of the framework, see `http://www.ietf.org/html.charters/policy-charter.html`.

This book looks at some applications of the policy framework in the context of an IP network. I believe that one of the most important applications of policy is to simplify network management and operations for technologies that deal with network *Quality of Service* (QoS) and security. This book describes how the policy-based approach can be applied to simplify the management of *Service-Level Agreements* (SLAs) for a network or application hosting service provider or to manage secure communications in an IP network. This book also examines the different algorithms that can be used to apply a policy-based solution to the problem of managing SLAs or secure communications.

Who Will Benefit from This Book?

This book is intended for operators and architects of IP networks who want to understand how policy-enabled networking can be used to simplify the operations and management of their networks. If you are implementing business SLAs or offering *virtual private networks* (VPNs) on your networks and you want to understand how policy-based techniques can assist you in this venture, this is the book you want. Similarly, if you are an ISP hosting Web servers or other applications for your customers and you need to exploit policy-based techniques to support business SLAs, this book is for you.

If you are a network developer working on a policy-enabled product, this book will help you understand the different algorithms and techniques that can be used to efficiently implement the different components of a policy-based solution. Algorithms that are useful for policy management software as well as algorithms needed at routers and servers implementing policy support are included in this book.

This book is also beneficial to management consultants whose clients include operators of IP networks. If you are a management consultant and you would like to understand the technical issues associated with the use of policies in the network, this is the right book for you.

If you are a technical professional involved in areas of network management, traffic management, service-level management, or security management in an IP environment, and you want to understand how network policies can simplify your tasks, you will find this book very useful.

Finally, if you are a technical professional in the area of IP networks, with an interest in areas such as Quality of Service, IP network security, or traffic engineering, you might find this book of interest. If you want to understand the implications of policy in these different areas, this is the right book for you. (If these terms are new to you, you can find a brief discussion of these topics in Chapter 2, "IP Architecture Overview.")

Who Is This Book Not For?

If you are looking for a book describing government, enterprise, or legal policies related to IP networks, this book is not for you. This book describes the technical applications of policies regarding resource usage or access control in the network. It does not address any legal or business issues.

If you are looking for an introduction to IP network management, this book is not for you. This book addresses only aspects of network management that relate to policies.

Finally, if you are looking for specific details on how to deploy policies in a network using a specific vendor product, this book is not for you. The intention of this book is to describe the general techniques in this field, but it does not describe any specific product.

How This Book Is Organized

This book has 10 chapters.

Chapter 1, "Policy-Enabled Networking Architecture," introduces the concept of policies and the policy architecture developed within the IETF. It briefly overviews the standards being developed to represent policies and provides a brief history of the development of policy-based networking.

Chapter 2 provides a review of the technologies to which policy-based techniques can be applied. It briefly covers IP networks, QoS mechanisms for IP networks, and IP security protocol standards. Aspects of technologies related to policies are emphasized. The goal of this chapter is to provide the background information you need to understand the remaining chapters in this book.

Chapter 3, "The Generic Provisioning Problem," describes three sample environments in which we study the application of policy-based techniques. The environments examined include the operator of an enterprise IP-based intranet, an Internet Service Provider offering IP network connectivity, and a service provider that supports different IP-based applications for its customers. For each provider, the types of policies that are appropriate for QoS and secure communications are discussed. Two views of policies are discussed: a high-level view that addresses the business needs of the different environments, and a low-level view that deals with policies addressing specific networking technologies.

Chapter 4, "Technology Support for Business Needs," describes how the different business needs arising in the environments discussed in Chapter 3 can be satisfied by emerging technologies in the areas of QoS and secure communications.

Chapter 5, 6, and 7 provide details on specific components of the management tool.

Chapter 5, "Resource Discovery," describes how the policy management tool can obtain information about the different users, applications, and machines that constitute the IP network. The algorithms and techniques needed to obtain the state of an IP network are described.

Chapter 6, "Policy Validation and Translation Algorithms," describes how the different policies specified by an administrator can be validated and checked for inconsistencies, mistakes, or impossible targets. It also describes how high-level policies dealing with business needs can be translated into low-level policies that deal with supporting networking technologies that support those business needs.

Chapter 7, "Policy Distribution Mechanisms," describes how the precise policies generated by a management tool can be distributed to the different network devices. It describes the approaches that are being worked on in the IETF, as well as other solutions that might need to be used in a heterogeneous network environment.

Chapter 8, "Policy Enforcement Point Algorithms," describes how the different network devices can implement the policies that are distributed to them. This includes a description of the algorithms that are needed at the devices for efficient execution of policies.

Chapter 9, "Policy Application Instances," describes how the techniques discussed in previous chapters fit together to provide support for specific business goals. It describes how policies can be used to support business SLAs or to implement specific security targets within each of the environments described in Chapter 4.

Chapter 10, "Advanced Topics," discusses some advanced topics that are related to SLAs, including a discussion of policies across multiple administrative domains, policy monitoring, and dynamic and state-dependent policies.

1

Policy-Enabled Networking Architecture

At the time of its inception as a research network, the Internet took a very egalitarian approach toward networking. All the data packets in the network were considered equally important, and every node in the network was trusted to behave itself. Although there was some notion of the difference between data packets and packets required for control and network operations, data packets were all treated identically. As an academic network connecting universities and research institutions, this simple open model had several advantages. It led to rapid development of a very robust and reliable architecture, as well as several protocols performing a variety of functions.

As these advantages of the TCP/IP architecture became apparent to developers and enterprise operators, it came to be adopted as the preferred networking mechanism in many enterprises. Furthermore, much work was done in trying to support different types of applications, such as voice and video on the Internet. The rapid growth and success of the Internet posed significant challenges to the open egalitarian model. Unlike universities, which trusted each other to behave themselves, corporations did not have any confidence in the integrity of their competitors (or anyone outside their domain of control). Firewalls were developed to isolate the internal IP networks in the enterprise from untrusted users on the external network. Similarly, the demands of audiovisual applications were remarkably different from those of normal data traffic, and some level of discrimination was considered desirable within the network. As a result of these demands, several techniques for offering security and *Quality of Service* (QoS) in an IP network evolved. These techniques are described in more detail in Chapter 2, "Background Information."

Of course, multimedia applications and simple firewall security are not the only cases in which there is a need for the network to treat traffic flows in a different manner. An enterprise might want to differentiate between business-critical traffic and random Web surfing. An online store on the World Wide Web might want to treat traffic from surfers who are purchasing items using their credit cards differently from those who just "window shop" or browse through the information pages. A corporation might want to allow limited access to some servers and applications to its suppliers and contractors. A network administrator might want to allocate different sets of IP addresses to machines belonging to different organizations from a DHCP server, or implement different schedules for backing up the file systems belonging to different users in the network. You can add several other examples to this list.

As networks make the transition from the philosophy that "all traffic is equal" to the new model in which "some traffic is more equal than others," you need a way to specify how the different types of traffic are treated in the network. A network policy specifies which traffic should be treated differently, and how so. It is defined by a network administrator for the configuration and operation of the different network devices.

Network policies are an important emerging topic of research, and consortia such as the IETF and DMTF are working on standard ways to represent policies. This book examines some of the areas in which the policies can be applied and illustrates how policies can be used to simplify the task of managing a network's performance and security characteristics. Although policies can be used in many contexts, we will be studying them primarily in the context of network performance and security. As a first step toward this goal, I will provide a brief overview of the policy architecture around which the standards are evolving. A more detailed discussion of the architecture and information model can be found in the book on policy by John Strassner [STRASSNER].

The next section of this chapter discusses the different areas or disciplines that can benefit from such policies. The third section discusses the different levels at which policies may be specified in a network, and the fourth section provides a brief history of policy-related activities in the industry. The final section describes the policy architecture that has evolved in the different standard consortia.

Although the policy architecture and framework are independent of the area to which policies are applied, I will sometimes offer examples of policy usage in different technologies. If you are unfamiliar with any of the areas we discuss, you can refer to Chapter 2, which covers them in more detail.

Policy and Network Management

A network policy is a statement defining which traffic should be treated differently in the network, and how so. It is defined by an administrator and specifies the rules related to handling different types of traffic within the network. An example of a policy might be as follows: "All development engineers are permitted access to the servers which support the development applications, and no one else." Another policy might state that "Email traffic is only allowed from outside the company's servers only from a special mail gateway." Yet another policy might state: "All traffic between the accounting and finance divisions must be encrypted." Some other examples of policies can be found in Chapter 9, "Policy Application Instances." Policies provide a way to represent different things that the network elements can do.

Although different people working in the field have varying opinions about why policies are useful, I believe that an important part of the policy activity is to simplify the task of administration and management for different disciplines. The enterprise networks of today are complex and heterogeneous systems. Ensuring that the network operates smoothly is not a trivial task. If you add to this the different needs to support QoS or network security, the management complexity becomes magnified.

Policies provide a way to simplify the management of multiple devices deploying complex technologies. Let's illustrate the simplification with an example. Suppose you are working for the CIO's office in a small consulting company. The company has three locations in Manhattan, which are connected by means of three leased links and a core router at a fourth location. One of the company locations hosts the IT department and the data center, which provides the applications used by the employees. The other two locations host the accounting and consulting departments. The simple network configuration used by the company is shown in Figure 1.1. You are responsible for administering the four boxes, the three access routers, and the one core router shown in the figure. Most of the time, the network runs fairly well, except on the last day of each month. On this day, the accounting department balances the books and invariably complains that they are not getting adequate performance from the network. The cost of upgrading link capacities on the path from accounting to the data center is not justified by a requirement that arises only once a month.

Figure 1.1   A Simple Enterprise Network

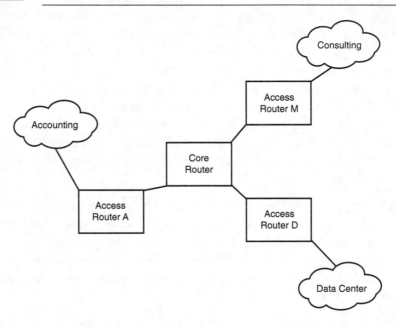

In this environment, you should give the traffic from the accounting department more importance than the other traffic for that one day each month. Although this requirement is easy to specify and understand on a network-wide level, its implementation requires that you, the network operator, configure all four routers so that the priority requirements can be satisfied on the last day of each month. You have to reconfigure them to the original state after that. Furthermore, if one of the routers supports simple priority queuing and the other one supports weighted round robin (these are different scheduling disciplines described in Chapter 2), you must determine the different limits to specify for the requirements of each router.

In a simple network of four routers, all this can be accomplished by a competent network administrator. However, in a typical enterprise network where the number of routers and servers runs into the hundreds (or even thousands), even the best system administrator would find it tough to configure the network to support such requirements manually.

A policy-based approach helps you simplify network management by means of two basic techniques:

- **Centralized configuration.** In a policy-based approach, the network configuration is specified not by configuring each device individually, but by specifying the policies for the entire network at a central location. The centralization point might be the console of a management tool that the network operator is using, or a repository where all the policies are stored. At the central location, where the configuration of all the devices is known, you can perform tests and checks to validate that the different configurations are mutually consistent. In the enterprise network example described earlier, the priority among applications is specified at a central location. You can look at the configuration of the different routers and ensure that the relative prioritization is set up correctly. Centralization of configuration helps in simplifying the job of consistency checking.

- **Simplified abstraction.** When you offer a simplified abstraction at a higher layer than the physical device configuration, the user is required to input policies in terms of day-to-day activities. This simplifies the task a user has to perform. As an example, the user specifies the priority among different applications, or the response time desired for an application, rather than specifying the exact marking or rates to be allocated to application flows.

In addition to these two techniques, the use of a policy-based management tool can generate policies optimized for specific devices. The simplified higher-layer abstractions can be satisfied by many different types of policy configuration information. A management tool can choose among these possibilities and determine the configuration that is optimal to support the desired objective. Similarly, not all policies are relevant to all the devices. A management tool can select the subset of policies that are relevant to each device, and configure the device appropriately.

Keep in mind that both centralization and simplified abstractions have associated overheads. A centralized configuration implies that you have to worry about the security and integrity of the configuration information, as well as determine the protocol to obtain the configuration information from the repository. And, although simplified abstractions are great for usability purposes, the simplification comes at the cost of reduced flexibility.

Despite these overheads, policy-based techniques provide a method that can automate the specification and enforcement of the network-wide criteria. In the policy-based environment, an automated tool accepts the simple network-wide policy that one type of traffic is given higher precedence than the others and translates it into the individual configuration required for the various routers in the network.

Policy Disciplines

The notion of policy or different behavior can be applied to many different areas of an IP network. It can also be applied to many areas in other types of networks, or in non-networking-related fields. I refer to each area in which policy can be applied as a *policy discipline*.

The two areas that receive the majority of the focus within the network are QoS and security. These are described in more detail in the following sections and in Chapter 2.

Some other disciplines in which policies can be successfully allocated are address allocation of IP subnets, done by means of DHCP (Dynamic Host Configuration Protocol, described in Chapter 2), and the routes taken by IP packets in the network.

Although policies might apply to many different areas, many of the operations needed for enforcing and managing the differences use similar techniques. Therefore, it makes sense to examine policies as a technology that can be applied to several different disciplines.

Within the broad areas of network QoS and security, many techniques can be used, as discussed in the next two sections.

Quality of Service

The broad category of QoS has three different technologies that have emerged for IP networks in the late 1990s.

The first technology is that of traffic shaping. Many companies offer traffic shapers, which are devices that can be placed in front of a congested link. These devices employ buffering and other techniques to control what share of a link's capacity goes to different applications within the network.

The second technology is that of *differentiated services* (DiffServ). This technology relies on the ability of some devices to classify and mark IP packets belonging to different classes. The marking is done by reusing one of the header fields in the existing IP packet structure. Such a marking device might be an access router or an end station. After the packets are marked in the right fashion, a router in the network can interpret the IP header and give the packet the desired priority in forwarding.

The third technology involves reserving network capacity along specific paths by using a signaling mechanism. An example of this approach is support of Integrated Services in IP networks using the RSVP protocol for signaling. This allows you to pin down paths for traffic flow with a reserved capacity. Packets that belong to the flow that has reserved capacity are likely to experience better network latency than ones without such a reservation.

Each of these technologies and their relative merits are discussed in more detail in Chapter 2. Within each of these three areas, different behavior has to be accorded to different types of traffic. Thus, each of these three can be considered independent policy disciplines.

IP Security

The broad area of IP security has three techniques for secure communications: traffic filtering, session layer encryption for security, and network layer encryption for security. If you are operating a computer connected to the Internet, you can protect the system using one of the following three techniques:

- **Install a packet-filtering firewall between the computer and the Internet.** The firewall looks at the traffic coming in from the Internet and allows only the subset you choose to reach your computer. Which subset of traffic you allow in is up to you. You might want a partial set of applications running on the firewall to be accessible to the outside. You might want to restrict all communication in through the firewall to the set that was initiated by an application on the protected computer. All these functions can be provided by an intermediate box looking at different incoming and outgoing traffic at different levels of granularity.

- **Use the *secure sockets layer* (SSL) protocol suite to encrypt the data before you send it out on the network.** A firewall does not prevent anybody lurking outside the firewall from inspecting your packets and collecting information about you. SSL and similar techniques encrypt the data before sending it so that no one can understand the content being sent out.

- **Perform the encryption as the network layer using the *IP security protocol*** (IPsec). IPsec performs encryption within the operating system of a machine transparently to the applications running on the machines.

A more detailed discussion of these protocols can be found in Chapter 2.

Policy Definition

In order for policies to be active in the network, an administrator needs to define them, and the devices need to enforce them. For a smooth operation of the network, the policies must satisfy several requirements:

- **Precision.** A policy must be precise and specified to a level of detail that can be understood by a network element. There should be no ambiguity regarding a policy's interpretation. From the point of view of a network element, the policy must be specified with all the requisite details that might be needed for the enforcement of a policy. For example, a policy might dictate that a subset of traffic on the network be encrypted. In order to implement it, a firewall must receive details specifying the type of encryption to use, the algorithm to use, the set of secret keys to be used for the specific encryption, and details regarding how soon the secret keys should be refreshed. The detailed information depends heavily on the function that the network element is performing.

- **Consistency.** The set of policies that is given to a network element or to all the network elements in the network must be consistent. If two firewalls are encrypting secure traffic among themselves, they must be configured to use a set of algorithms and keys that both can use to interoperate. Similarly, if a subset of traffic needs to be carried at a higher priority, all the routers handling that traffic need to be configured so that they give it the right priority in their operations.

- **Compatibility.** The set of policies that is given to a network element must be compatible with the capabilities that the network element can support. Many routers in the network look at only the network layer header in a packet. The policy must be specified to such a network element in terms that include a network layer header field. Specifying policies that depend on interpreting information that cannot be interpreted by the router would be useless. For example, consider a policy that requires that all packets belonging to the accounting department be handled at high priority. In order for a network router to implement this policy, it must be specified in terms of constructs it can interpret—that is, in terms of the IP addresses of the machines used by the accounting department.

- **Mutual consistency.** If multiple policies are specified for a network element, they must be consistent with each other. The network element should be able to apply these policies in an unambiguous manner. Specifically, for each packet passing through the network element, it should be possible to identify precisely the set of policies that is applicable to that packet. Furthermore, this set of policies should not specify that conflicting action be taken. As an example of an inconsistency, one policy might specify that all packets from accounting should be handled with high priority, while another may specify that all traffic to the human resources database server be blocked. If a packet from accounting to the human resources database is encountered, a router would not be able to determine whether to accord it the highest priority or to discard it.

At the very least, if conflicting policies are found, the network element should be able to determine unambiguously the policy that should be selected among all the possible choices.

- **Ease of specification.** In order for a network administrator to specify policies, a policy must be simple and easy to specify. A network operator must be able to specify the policies with the minimum effort required to specify a consistent and precise set.

- **Intuitiveness.** In order for the network operator to specify policies, policy definition must be done in terms that are familiar to the network operator. These terms might require that policies be defined in terms of the business processes or concepts that are commonly used within an organization. A network operator might find it much easier to specify a policy in terms of an application, such as payroll processing, rather than in terms of the machine addresses and header fields that are used by the payroll application.

It should be apparent that all these requirements cannot be optimally satisfied together simultaneously. For a specification that is intuitive, the policy must be specified in terms of familiar business concepts. In other words, a policy may define how applications used by the accounting department should be handled. However, the compatibility requirement states that just the opposite be done—that is, the policy must be specified in terms that can be handled by the routers and servers in the network. Similarly, ease of use requires that much of the detail of the operation of the network elements be hidden from the network operator. This is in direct contrast to the preciseness requirement.

The reason for this apparent conflict is that there are at least two different levels of policies:

- One that a human operator would like to enter and specify

- One that the devices would actually be capable of enforcing

Each of these levels imposes a different set of requirements on the policy definition and specification. The human operator uses a higher-level policy to express his/her objectives, which are then translated into a lower level of policies that are interpreted by each of the devices. The next sections take a closer look at these two levels of policy.

Low-Level Policies

In order to become effective, the policies must be specified precisely and consistently for each device in the network. Also, these policies must state in detail what actions need to be taken by each device. The policies must be specified to match the device's capabilities.

This view of the policy needs to be geared toward the individual configuration of a specific device. This policy would specify in unambiguous terms the exact operations that the device must undertake.

The low-level view of policies is very specific to the discipline to which policy is being applied. The low-level policy view for a network with rate control boxes describes the various rate allocations made to different applications. The low-level policy view for a network with service differentiation specifies the mapping of traffic to different types of packet marking. The low-level policy view for a network with resource reservation capabilities describes the amount of bandwidth to reserve for specific types of applications. Similarly, for secure communications, the types of low-level policies depend on the security technology deployed in the network, packet-filtering firewalls, secure sockets layer, IP security protocol-based encryption, and so on. For a more detailed discussion of these technologies, refer to Chapter 2.

High-Level Policies

As mentioned, the view of policy from a human operator perspective must be easy to specify and intuitive. A human operator must be able to specify the policies without significant effort. This implies that the policies be specified in a format that is intuitive to a human operator.

The definition of high-level policies depends on the end goal of the network operator. If a network operator wants the network to operate so as to satisfy specific service-level objectives, he specifies those objectives as the high-level policies. To a large extent, this specification is independent of the underlying technology deployed in the network, rate control versus service differentiation versus resource reservation. Similarly, if a network operator wants to set up private communication groups in the network, enable remote accesses of employees to its corporate network, or permit limited access by its suppliers to its network, he specifies the high-level policies in terms of those goals. These various goals are realized to a different extent by the different secure communication technologies, viz, packet filtering, SSL, IPsec, and so on. However, the high-level policies are relatively independent of the underlying technology that is used to implement the goals of the network operator.

A high-level policy is usually relatively static compared with the state of the network. The configuration of a device within the network can change more dynamically as compared to the policy definition. Policy definitions are entered by human operators, and are therefore modified at the human time-scale. However, one might deploy adaptive techniques within the network that can change the configuration of the network devices in accordance with those policies. As an example, a network policy may classify all traffic coming into a site into high-priority and low-priority. The low-priority traffic is not regulated at a router if the utilization of access link to the site is less than 50%. However, if the utilization exceeds this threshold, the access link bandwidth is shared in an 80-20 ratio between the high priority and the low priority traffic. There are two possible device configurations that can satisfy this policy, with the current utilization of the network determining the correct configuration. However, the policy description controlling the behavior of the network remains the same regardless of the exact configuration. Thus, device configuration can change at a dynamic rate while the policy within the network remains fairly static.

How Many Levels of Policies Does a Network Need?

I have presented two levels of policies in the network. Of course, opinions differ regarding whether there are more or fewer levels of policies in the network.

At one extreme is the opinion of many developers I have met in the various disciplines. In their view, there is only one level of policy in the network—the per-device configuration that is used by the devices. These policies are the ones that are configured by an expert administrator. Other layers of policies are simply abstractions that hide necessary details and make the administrator unaware of what is happening in the network.

On the other side, some researchers in the field have proposed an architecture with four levels of policies:

- **Business-level policies.** These policies are input by a human administrator.

- **Network-level policies.** These policies correspond to network-wide abstractions specified in a precise format. This format is used to communicate the network policies among different devices within the network.

- **Abstract device-level policies.** These policies are specified on a per-device basis. However, these are specified in a generic format that needs to be mapped to a specific device configuration.

- **Device configuration.** This corresponds to the exact machine configuration of a specific device.

The difference between the abstract device-level policies and the device configuration is mainly syntactic. The same configuration information is being specified in two different formats, but no new information is being added. For example, the abstract device-level policy can use the schema proposed by the IETF policy framework working group to specify that all traffic to and from the accounting department be given high priority. For a Cisco router, this translates to a specific command line with the same effect. However, the information contained there does not change.

continues

Similarly, it is difficult to distinguish between the business-level policies and the network-wide policies. From the discussion viewpoint of algorithms related to network management/configuration, business-level policies and network-wide policies are one and the same. While one can explore a higher level of policies, one describing business processes at an abstraction higher than the network, the description and automation of these policies are still at a very early stage (see a discussion on this topic in Chapter 10, "Advanced Topics"). This book groups the first two levels into the high-level view and the latter two into the low-level view.

Because the policy field is still fairly new, it is unclear how many layers will eventually emerge in common implementations. I believe that it probably will be more than one because higher layers of policy tend to simplify management tasks. The exact number of policy levels supported by a real management product depends on the design choices made by the architects.

Policy Application Examples

As an example of a policy application, consider the case of enterprise network performance. An enterprise wants to put into effect specific performance targets for its communication network. The performance objectives become the high-level policies for the communication network. By the use of capacity planning tools, these objectives are converted into the specific allocations of rates to different traffic flows. The rate allocations become the low-level policies enforced by different devices in the network. If the underlying network supported some notion of service differentiation, appropriate mappings of the traffic into different classes would also be part of the low-level policy definition.

As another example of policy application, consider an enterprise that wants to set up extranets that connect its servers to different vendors over the Internet. In order to do so, it must set up authentication and a secure (encrypted) communication infrastructure. It has opted to use IPsec protocols to achieve this goal. The high-level policy would specify the structure of each extranet—the access that different vendors have to the different applications or servers. The low-level policies would specify the IPspec controls that should be enabled in order for the extranet access to occur.

Policy Activity: A Historical Perspective

Policy work in the industry has been occurring in various consortia and standards bodies through the years. The first use of the term *policy* in the context of IP networks was for specifying routing policies in the Internet. The Internet is composed of many subnetworks, each independently administered by various ISPs and interconnected via various exchange points. A scheme for describing what types of packets each ISP would accept for forwarding was needed at the exchange points. This led to the specification of routing policies and a language for specifying routing policies. This work is described further in Chapter 10.

Although the routing policies fall within the purview of policy as I have defined it, work in that area remains very specific to the routing domain, and I am unaware of any effort to move that in the direction of a general specification.

The next step in the area of policies was done in the context of resource reservation policies. This work began within the IETF in 1996 and led to the development of a protocol called *Common Open Policy Service* (COPS). Soon, the developers of the protocol realized that this could be used for more functions than the original objective. Since late 1998, there has been a lot of activity to insulate COPS from its close ties to resource reservations, and to use it as a general-purpose policy protocol.

The biggest boost to policy activity was obtained through the *Directory Enabled Networks* (DEN) Initiative in 1998, led by Microsoft and Cisco corporations. With the dominant position of Microsoft in the workstation operating system marketplace, and that of Cisco in the Internet router space, this initiative aroused a lot of interest within the industry. The goal of DEN is to build a networking infrastructure that is easier to manage and operate than traditional ones. The ease of management was obtained by driving the networks from a central repository originally based on a directory.

A *directory* is an application that is typically used to store the names, addresses, and other properties of human users in the networks. Almost every enterprise has a directory of its employees. In addition to the common storage of information about people, the directory server can be used to store information about other entities, such as applications or services available in the network, or different types of devices available in a building (such as printers). The basic approach of DEN was to store different types of information related to different network devices and applications in a directory and to use that to manage the network.

Directories have always been capable of storing this information. However, different applications and vendors have tended to use different types of information to store their properties in the directory. The major thrust of DEN is to define a standard format (or a schema) by which the properties relating to network devices are defined. In other words, the information stored in the directories had to correspond to a specific model that DEN specified. More information on the DEN initiative can be found in the books by Goncalves [GONCAL] and Strassner [STRASSDEN]. A Web site with DEN-related information is also available [DENWEB].

Although DEN had a very good goal, it was viewed with some apprehension by several vendors in the field as an attempt to develop a proprietary schema by couple of dominant vendors. In order to get a more open standard, the companies involved in DEN decided to migrate the work to the DMTF by the end of 1998. DMTF is an industry consortium formed in 1992 by several computer companies with the goal of developing a common method for managing personal computers. The acronym DMTF originally stood for Desktop Management Task Force, but in 1999 the organization decided to rechristen itself the Distributed Management Task Force. DMTF defines a common information model that was originally intended to be used to describe the characteristics of a computer. It was extended to apply to networks of computers and other devices. These specifications form the *Common Information Model* (CIM) for systems and network management.

Although the DMTF was a suitable forum for carrying out many DEN and policy activities, the DMTF working groups had traditionally been PC-focused and did not have much expertise in the area of networks. Since the early 1990s, the dominant networking protocol has been TCP/IP. Most of the technical activity related to TCP/IP happens in another industry consortium—the IETF. At the same time that the DMTF activity started, an activity within the IETF was started with the goal of obtaining feedback from the networking community for policies related to networking. The goal of the IETF activity was to define a framework that could be used to specify policies across various disciplines, and to show that it could be used in the context of QoS disciplines. In order to keep the activities within the two standard bodies (DMTF and IETF) from diverging and producing two incompatible standards, the working groups in both organizations were headed by the same set of people.

The outcome of these activities resulted in the common policy architecture described in the next section.

Policy Architecture Overview

The policy architecture as defined in the IETF/DMTF consists of four basic elements (as shown in Figure 1.2):

- A policy management tool
- A policy repository
- A *Policy Decision Point* (PDP)
- A *Policy Enforcement Point* (PEP)

Figure 1.2   The IETF/DMTF Policy Architecture

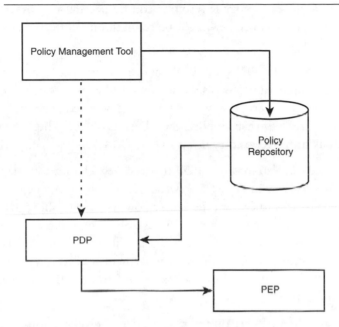

The *policy management tool* is used by an administrator to input the different policies that are active in the network. The policy management tool takes as input the high-level policies that a user or administrator enters in the network and converts them to a much more detailed and precise low-level policy description that can apply to the various devices in the network. The devices that can apply and execute the different policies are known as the *Policy Enforcement Points* (PEPs).

The preferred way for the management tool and PEPs to communicate is through a policy repository. The *policy repository* is used to store the policies generated by the management tool. The repository can be used to store both high-level and low-level policies. In order to ensure interoperability across products from different vendors, information stored in the repository must correspond to an information model specified by the *Policy Framework Working Group* (PFWG).

Instead of communicating directly with the repository, a PEP uses an intermediary known as the *Policy Decision Point* (PDP). The PDP is responsible for interpreting the policies stored in the repository and communicating them to the PEP. In some devices, the separation between PEP and PDP is a logical one. In other words, the PEP and the PDP could be two different functions in the same device, or even the same process running on the device. However, in the case of some resource-constrained devices, or devices that are *policy-unaware,* the policy consumer might be running on a different box than the policy target.

The management tools, the PDPs, the PEPs, and the repository can communicate with each other using a variety of protocols. Which protocol is used to communicate with the repository depends on the type of repository selected. The preferred choice for the repository is a directory that supports the LDAP protocol. Thus, the management tool and PDPs talk to the repository using LDAP. LDAP is described further in Chapter 2.

A management tool can also inform a PDP that policies relevant to it have changed. This is shown by a dotted arrow in Figure 1.2 between the policy management tool and the PDP. The dotted arrow (rather than the solid arrow) is used to show that the IETF realizes that this notification mechanism is not necessarily done using an established protocol. The solid arrow is used to denote protocols that are standardized. One common way for this notification to occur would be for the management tool to run a remote command (such as the UNIX rsh command) that sends a signal to the PDP process, asking it to reload policies from the repository.

When the PDP and the PEPs are on the same device, they can communicate in a manner designed by the implementor. When they are on separate devices, they can communicate using a protocol such as COPS or SNMP. Both of these protocols are described further in subsequent chapters.

Policy Management Tool

The policy management console interacts with the human administrator and allows high-level policies to be input into the network. It needs to perform the following functions:

- Present a user interface to the human administrator that is optimized for ease of use, using appropriate graphical techniques to depict the structure of the policy information being entered at a level that is (hopefully) more human-friendly than that represented in the policy repository, which is optimized for distribution of the policy and for unambiguous interpretation by heterogeneous PDPs.

- Validate the syntactic and semantic correctness of user input. This includes checking that proper and acceptable values are specified for the different parameters that constitute the high-level policies. Also, any relationships that must exist between the different parameters of the policies must be validated.

- Validate that the high-level policies are specified consistently. Policies are considered inconsistent if they specify different conflicting actions to be taken for the same traffic flow. For example, a policy that specifies that all traffic from accounting be given higher-priority service is inconsistent with a policy that specifies that all traffic to a Web server be given a lower priority. Either of these two policies can apply when a user in accounting accesses the Web server. The policy management console must identify these inconsistencies and resolve them. The resolution can be done in various ways, the simplest option being to ask the user to select which of the two policies should be applied in case of a conflict.

- Validate that the policies can be satisfied given the network's resources and constraints. A policy that asks that a traffic flow be encrypted using DES algorithm cannot be satisfied if the firewalls in the network do not support that algorithm. The *Digital Encryption Standard* (DES) is one of the most popular encryption algorithms in use today. Similarly, there might be physical limitations that can prohibit the implementation of certain policies. A policy that states that the delay of an application must be less than 100 milliseconds is not feasible in a network where the round-trip time is 200 milliseconds.

- Validate that the policies specified cover all the important scenarios that might be required for a specific application. This is especially important for policies related to security.

- Determine the association between the set of policies specified by the users and the different devices in the network. In other words, the management tool needs to determine which policies are applicable to which set of policy targets (or policy consumers).

- Determine which low-level policies can be used to support the high-level policies specified by the user.

- Store the policies in the policy repository and detect when the stored policies are modified. In the case of policy modification, the management tool may choose to notify the relevant policy consumers of a change in the policies using a notification mechanism, as illustrated by the dotted arrow in Figure 1.2.

Policy Repository

The policy repository is where the policies are stored by the policy management tool and retrieved by policy decision points or policy enforcement points. The repository provides the central location that drives the operations of the entire network.

An example of a policy repository is an LDAP directory that contains both the high-level and low-level policies required for network operations. Of course, other types of repositories can also be used. Instead of a directory, you can use a database server. You can also use a Web server, where different files represent the policy information stored for the various devices and for each low-level device-specific policy. Among the various alternatives, the LDAP-accessible directory is the major contender and is the focus of most working group activities.

Regardless of the type of repository selected, the policy stored in the repository needs to conform to specific conventions. These conventions are specified as the information model for policy specification. The details of the information model proposed within the standard bodies are discussed in Chapter 8, "Policy Enforcement Point Algorithms."

What Is an Information Model?

The focus of the standardization activities in the field of policy is related to developing a common information model for policies. When designing software systems, you often need to use a data repository—an entity that stores different types of information. Examples of data repositories are databases, directories, files, and programming constructs such as arrays and lists. An information model (or a data model) is simply an abstract way of describing the type of information that may be in a data repository.

Suppose you are developing software for an online book shop. The software has to include a catalog of books. The information model for the catalog would describe what type of information must be stored for each book. In addition to the records that are used to describe the books, the catalog might also contain other types of records, such as information about a book's authors. The model would also contain the relationships that can exist among the different types of records. For example, each author must have authored a book, and each book should have one or more authors.

It is typical to follow paradigms of object-oriented analysis in describing the information model. The information model would thus identify the types of objects that are stored in the data repository, the attributes that make up each type of object, and the relationships between the different objects. An object may be derived or inherited from other objects. For example, if you decided to have two types of objects—one describing generic books, and the other describing networking books—the description of networking books would include all the attributes that make up generic books, plus other attributes.

When you develop a real system, this abstract information model must be mapped to a real system. If the data repository is a relational database, you have to map it to descriptions of specific types of records in a database, specifying the fields in each record, and so on. If the data repository is an array that is kept in the program's memory, the implementation has to describe the attributes as the structures that describe the fields of the abstract information model. For LDAP-based directories, the information model must be expressed in terms of a directory *schema,* which enumerates the types of objects and fields that can be stored in the directory.

Policy Decision Point

The PDP is responsible for the following functions:

- Locating the set of rules that is applicable to any PEP it is managing, and retrieving the rules from the repository.

- Transforming the set of rules it retrieves from the policy repository to a format and syntax that is understood by the PEP function.

- Checking the current state of the network and validating that the conditions required for the application of any policy are satisfied. An example of such a check might be that the current time is within the time period during which the policy is applicable.

- Keeping track of the changes in the policies that might take place by monitoring the repository or by listening to any notification from the management tool.

A PDP could be a software application on a server that retrieves the policies from the repository and configures the local networking stack to comply with the specified policies. Another example of a PDP is a COPS server that configures many routers to conform to a specific policy.

Policy Enforcement Point

The PEP is responsible for executing the policies as defined by the PDP. It is also responsible for monitoring any statistics or other information relevant to its operation and for reporting it to the appropriate places.

The PEP is often the components that are invoked along the path of the packets flowing through the traffic. Common examples of PEPs are network routers, firewalls, and the TCP/IP processing stack in end hosts, proxies, and SOCKS gateways. Any of these entities can be relied upon to deliver the requisite functions as specified by the policy, which are input to the policy management tool.

An Implementation of the Architecture

Figure 1.3 illustrates one of the ways in which the policy architecture can be realized. The environment consists of a network with two campuses. One campus hosts a server, and the other campus hosts several clients that access the server. The server runs two types of applications—a Web server and a database server. You need to ensure that requests to Web servers complete within 100 milliseconds for downloading a 100KB Web page and that a typical database transaction is completed within 500 milliseconds.

Figure 1.3   An Implementation of Policy Architecture

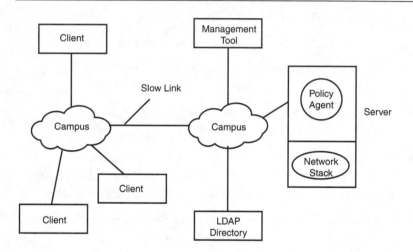

The policy architecture within the network is realized by means of some components shown in Figure 1.3. A policy management tool determines the bottleneck resource in the network from the network topology and the performance requirements. Let's assume that the tool determines that the bottleneck is network bandwidth, and it decides that sharing the network bandwidth in the ratio of 80:20 for Web pages and the database transaction is sufficient to meet the required performance parameters. It then publishes this information to an LDAP-based directory. The LDAP directory is the policy repository. The management tool can update this ratio periodically by monitoring the mix of database and Web server traffic.

On the server is a policy agent that retrieves the information from the repository and interprets it. The policy agent talks to the networking stack in the server's kernel and configures it to enforce the corresponding rate limits. In terms of the IETF architecture, the policy agent is the PDP, and the networking stack is the PEP.

With only one server, having a separate management tool and a policy directory would definitely be overkill. However, in a typical installation where there could be many more servers, such an implementation would be a reasonable one.

Further Information

More information on the policy information model and the policy architecture can be obtained by means of the various Internet drafts and RFCs pertaining to the policy working group of the IETF [POLICYWG]. A description of the CIM model defined by the DMTF can be obtained from the Web site of the DMTF [DMTFCIM]. A more detailed description of the information model can be found in the book by Strassner [STRASSNER]

CHAPTER 2

IP Architecture Overview

In order to understand the various applications of policies and how they help in network management, you need to be familiar with the basics of various protocols and applications related to IP. This chapter provides a brief overview of aspects of IP and related technologies of QoS and security that are required as a background for the rest of the book.

It's quite likely that you are familiar with many of these basic techniques. If that is true, I recommend that you simply skip the relevant sections. However, if one of the topics is new to you, this chapter will provide a quick overview.

Keep in mind that this chapter provides just a brief overview of the material and techniques related to policies. In order to keep the description to a reasonable size, I emphasize aspects that are related to policies and gloss over many of the other details in the protocols and technologies described. In each section, I attempt to provide references to books and papers that provide a more detailed description of the relevant topics.

I also cover the basics of TCP/IP networking technology and describe how the different protocols at various layers operate. This is followed by a section in which I discuss the various topics related to QoS, including capacity planning, rate control technologies, DiffServ, and resource reservation. The third section of the chapter discusses topics related to secure communications in an IP network, including packet filtering firewalls, SSL, and the *IP security* (IPsec) protocol.

IP Overview

The term *TCP/IP architecture* refers to the networking architecture used in IP networks. It's much broader than just the two named protocols. *IP* or the *Internet Protocol* is the glue that keeps the Internet together. This section provides a brief overview of this architecture. For a more comprehensive overview, consult Comer's book on TCP/IP [COMER]. It is one of the standard references for learning about IP and associated protocols.

Like most networking architectures, the TCP/IP protocol suite is designed in layers (see Figure 2.1). Each layer provides a language that lets two machines talk to each other. Each layer uses the layer that is immediately below it, and is independent of the details of actual implementation of the lower layer.

Figure 2.1   TCP/IP Protocol Layers

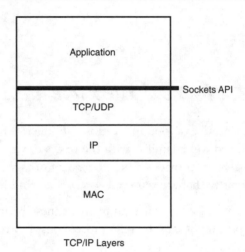

TCP/IP Layers

The layers are as follows:

- The *Media Access Control* (MAC) layer provides access to physical hardware that connects machines, such as a LAN or an access link. Ethernet and Token Ring are examples of MAC layers.

- The IP layer provides connectionless delivery of packets in a best-effort manner.

- The Transport layer includes the TCP and UDP protocols, which provide reliable end-to-end connections and unreliable message delivery, respectively.

- The Application layer includes anything an application may do to communicate across a network, over and beyond the functions provided by the other three layers.

A common MAC layer lets two machines communicate with each other across a shared physical network. Machines connected on the same ethernet can communicate with each other using the ethernet protocol. Also, a common physical layer has serious limits as to the geographical distances it can span.

Machines that share the same network layer (that implement the IP layer) can talk to each other across multiple physical layers. In order to do so, some machines that are connected to different numbers or types of physical networks have to take on the role of forwarding packets from one physical network to another. Such machines are typically referred to as *routers*.

Processes and applications, running on a pair of machines communicating via a network, can use the transport protocol to get additional functions that simplify their task associated with communication. With TCP, two communicating applications get the semantics of a reliable byte stream where bytes put into one end are spl received by the other end. With UDP, the applications get the semantics of an unreliable message system, where messages are delivered in one piece across multiple IP layers. However, the message delivery is unreliable, so messages may be lost. Both with UDP and TCP, the information may be split into multiple IP packets for transfer within the network. However, the packet splitting and reassembly is invisible to the application.

The sockets layer has traditionally defined the boundary between the transport layer and the application layer in TCP/IP. However, some transport protocols are implemented above the sockets layer. A notable example is *Real-time Transport Protocol* (RTP), commonly used in *Voice over IP* (VoIP) applications. Another notable protocol implemented above the sockets layer is the *Secure Sockets Layer* (SSL), which provides support for the exchange of encrypted data. In most UNIX-based implementations, layers below sockets are implemented within the operating system kernel, and layers above sockets can be implemented as normal applications. This has been one of the motivating factors in the development of the transport protocols above the sockets layer in recent years.

Consider Figure 2.2. It shows a Web browser running on machine A. It needs to talk to a Web server running on machine B. In order to communicate with another machine, the browser calls the sockets interface and sends information to its local transport layer (in this case, TCP) via the socket calls. The transport layer forms one or more IP packets and sends them to the local network (IP) layer. The IP layer forms MAC packets (also known as MAC frames) and sends them to the MAC layer (let's say an ethernet), which gets them across a local network to router C. The router C IP layer receives the MAC packets from the local ethernet layer, re-creates the IP packets from it, and determines that the packets need to be forwarded along the T1 link to router D. The IP layer in router C then forms MAC packets that can carry the IP packets via the T1 interface. Similarly, the IP layer in router D forwards the packets received from the T1 MAC layer to the Token Ring MAC layer. The Token Ring MAC layer in router D sends the packets to the MAC layer in machine B. The Token Ring layer forwards them to the IP layer in machine B, which re-creates the IP packets. The IP packets are passed up to the TCP layer, which re-creates the TCP messages. Finally, they are passed to the Web server application via the sockets interface.

In Figure 2.2, the thick lines show the path taken by the data for the end-to-end flow. The end result of this communication is the virtual communication (shown by the dotted line) between the browser and the server applications.

Figure 2.2   IP Communication Mechanism

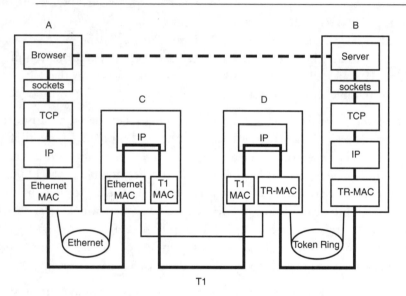

IP Network and Transport Layers

At the network layer, IP offers a best-effort connectionless packet delivery service. From the perspective of IP connectivity, the entire universe consists of millions of machines, each one uniquely identified by a number called the *IP address*. The IP address is 32 bits long and is usually expressed in a dotted notation. The dotted notation divides 32 bits into four groups of 8 bits each and separates them by periods. The machine address of 9.2.22.16 refers to the machine whose address has the first 8 bits containing 9, the second 8 bits containing 2, and so on.

To communicate with another machine using IP, a machine needs to generate IP packets. An IP packet consists of a standard header and the user data. The routers that are present in the IP network look at the header fields to decide where to forward the packets. The user data consists of information that is not supposed to be seen by the routers in normal usage. The information contained in the header is shown in Figure 2.3. It shows the header layout along with the width of each field in bits (labeled at the top of the figure).

Figure 2.3   Internet Protocol Header Structure

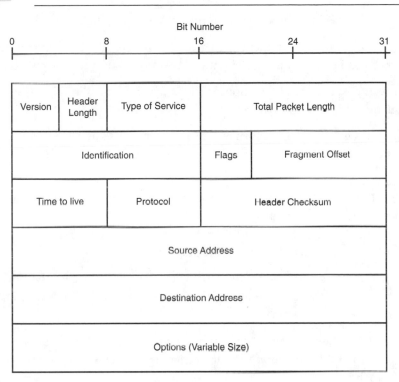

The header includes the following fields:

- Version number identifies the packet as using the IP protocol and also specifies the version of the protocol. This book deals only with version 4 of IP.

Note

The IP that forms the basis of the present Internet is IP version 4. The next generation of IP, version 6, has a different header format. However, version 4 is expected to be the predominant version for quite a while. In case you're wondering about the missing fifth version, it was assigned to an experimental protocol, ST-II. IPv4 was developed in the 1970s. Its current form is defined by an RFC published in 1981 [POSTEL]. IPv6 was defined by an RFC published in 1998 [DEERING], and the RFC for the version 5 experimental protocol was published in 1990 [TOPOC].

- Header Length states how many bytes of information are contained in the header.

- Type of Service was intended to state how important the packet was. This is essentially ignored in most conventional IP networks, but these bits are redefined and reused in differentiated services networks (see "DiffServ").

- Total Packet Length states how long the packet including user data is.

- Identification contains an identity that can be used to identify and reassemble packets that need to be broken up in the network. A broken-up packet is called a *fragment*.

- Flags can contain special directions, such as that a packet should not be fragmented in the network.

- Fragment Offset contains information to identify the sequence in which fragments should be ordered when reassembling. Reassembling is done only at the receiving machine.

- Time to Live contains information that indicates when the packet is running in circles instead of making progress toward its destination. It is a number that is decremented for every node in the network traversed by the packet, with the packet being discarded if the value reaches 0.

- Protocol specifies what should be done when the packet reaches the destination. More precisely, it specifies which protocol should be used to process the user data in the packet at the destination.

- Header Checksum contains a checksum over the contents of the packet header to detect any possible corruption in the header. The checksum algorithm can be found in [COMER].

- Source Address contains the 32-bit IP address of the machine that generated the packet.

- Destination Address contains the 32-bit IP address of the machine that is to receive the packet.

In addition to these fields, the IP header can also contain a variable number of options. These options can include directions regarding special processing that needs to be done for the IP packets—such as if a specific route needs to be followed, or if a record should be kept of the path taken by the packet in the network.

IP packets are forwarded in a fairly simple manner. Each node in the network determines the identity of the next node that should receive the packet and forwards it to that node. If that node is the final receiver, it passes the packet to the correct local entity for further processing.

The forwarding of a packet over a single "hop" (LAN or link) is done using the MAC layer mechanisms. In order to forward the packets, a protocol called *Address Resolution Protocol* (ARP) is used by the IP layer to determine the MAC address of a machine on the local LAN from the machine's IP address. The reverse function, determining the IP address from the MAC address, is done using a protocol called *Reverse Address Resolution Protocol* (RARP). When the MAC address of the other machine is known, a MAC packet can be formed and sent to the physical hardware for delivery.

TCP and UDP Headers

The user of the IP layer functions is the transport layer. The two predominant transport protocols today are TCP and UDP. They use headers as shown in Figure 2.4.

Figure 2.4 TCP and UDP Header Structure

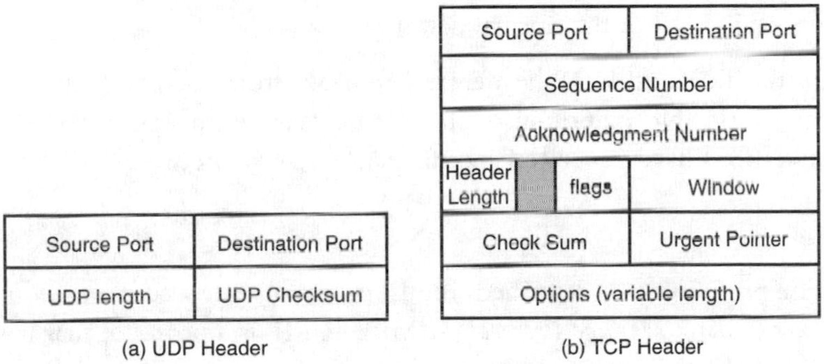

(a) UDP Header

(b) TCP Header

The UDP header consists of only four fields. The first two are the port numbers being used at the source machine and the destination machine involved in the communications. *Port numbers* are 16-bit integers that are used to distinguish among multiple applications on the same machine (you'll read more about this topic in the next section). The third field states the length of the UDP packet, including the 8 bytes of header. The final field is a checksum over the UDP header fields to guard against packet corruption.

TCP header format is relatively complex compared to UDP because it provides more functions. It begins in the same manner as UDP, with the source and destination port numbers. The next field is a sequence number. The sequence number is needed so that TCP segments can be reassembled at the receiver in the order in which they were transmitted. The acknowledgment number tells the other side how much data has already been received. Acknowledgments are needed for reliable delivery of data. When a TCP user (for instance, A) transmits packets to another user (for instance, B), the receiver uses the acknowledgment number to tell the sender how much data it has received. This acknowledgment number is carried on the TCP header for packets in the opposite direction—packets being sent by B to A.

Because TCP headers can be variable-length, a Header Length field is included. There are several flags in the TCP header. These flags are set in special conditions. For example, the first segment that establishes the TCP connection would have one of the bits in the Flags field set to 1 (this bit is called the *SYN bit*). Similarly, a *FIN bit* in the Flags field marks a segment that indicates the end of data transmission. If a fast machine is sending data to a slow machine, the sender can overflow the buffers at the receiver. TCP provides for the receiver to set upper bounds on the amount of data a sender can transmit. The Window Size field provides information is the field that specifies this additional limit. A checksum is used for reliability purposes. The urgent pointer is used to point to the location of urgent data in the TCP segment. The urgent data is some information that the sender might want the receiver to obtain ahead of the normal data.

The structure of the TCP and UDP headers is important from the perspective of policy support in the network. Information in the header fields allows network devices to determine which applications have generated specific packets in the network.

ICMP

In addition to the protocols just described, the IP protocol suite also uses a control protocol called *Internet Control Message Protocol* (ICMP). ICMP is a protocol that runs above the IP layer and uses IP as the transport mechanism across different machines. However, it is a dedicated protocol that is used by different IP machines to notify each other when they encounter some situation that they do not expect. For example, a router will send an ICMP message to the origin of a packet if it sees a packet with TTL field of 0. During normal operation, such a packet should not be encountered. In addition to notifying exception conditions, ICMP is also used for other types of operations, such as to check if a machine is alive within the network. It is done by sending an ICMP echo request message to the target machine, which would respond with an ICMP echo reply if it sees the request message.

IP Applications

On top of the sockets API, a large number of applications have been written with their own protocols for exchanging data among the machines. Some of the commonly used application protocols include *FTP*, which is used to transfer files; *Telnet*, which enables terminal emulation; *SMTP*, which is used to transfer email between machines; and *HTTP*, which is used to transfer documents on the World Wide Web.

At the end hosts, there may be several applications, so you need some way to identify the application toward which a specific piece of information is headed. In the Internet, each end host supporting the TCP and UDP protocols is required to support the notion of *ports*. A port is like a mailbox for each tenant in an apartment complex. Each tenant is assigned a mailbox in the apartment complex where he or she can receive letters. For outgoing mail, the tenant can simply leave the letters in an outgoing mailbox (corresponding to the source port in our example), and the mail carrier will take them from there. The source and destination ports provide this "mailbox" functionality in the computer.

The ports are identified by a number at each machine. Each application must reserve the port it will use. When an application wants to communicate with another one, it simply needs to send the message to the right destination IP address and the right destination port. Some applications always run on well-known port numbers. Other applications use a *dynamic port number*—that is, they use any port number that is available when they need it.

Communication using TCP transport typically occurs in the following fashion: The application consists of two parts—a client part and a server part. The server part of the application reserves a port number that is known to the client and waits for clients to send messages to it (you could say the server is "listening" on a specific port). The client typically uses a dynamic port and sends an initial message (a connect request) to the server with the identity of the client's receiving port. The server now knows the port number assigned to the client and can accept the request for the connection. Data can now be exchanged.

Communication using UDP can occur in this manner, although the connect operation is not always necessary. An application can send messages using UDP to any other application on a known port without necessarily invoking a connect step.

Client applications can know the port number of servers using one of two techniques:

- They know the port number due to an established convention of standard usage

- They are given the port number by a user

When you use a browser to access a document on the Web, the browser (an HTTP client) assumes that the server is listening on port 80. However, you can also specify another port number. The document identified by a URL like `http://9.2.13.4:8080/index.html` tells the HTTP client to talk to a server on machine 9.2.13.4 listening on port 8080 and to get the file index.html from it. If you specified the URL as `http://9.2.13.4/index.html`, the browser would use the convention with HTTP servers to assume it is talking to a server listening on port 80.

Packet Routing and Routing Protocols

Let's examine how packets are routed within the IP network toward the final destination. Consider a packet that is to be sent to a destination. IP addresses are 32 bits long. The 32-bit length permits billions of machines to be active at the same time. Most of these machines are many hops away from the destination. For each destination address, each network node just needs to determine which next hop to send the packet toward. Because it is impractical to maintain a table in every node that contains a mapping of all possible IP addresses to the next hop, there are ways to group IP addresses for the purposes of routing and forwarding.

To reduce the size of routing and forwarding tables (and for various other reasons), addresses are clustered into networks. A *network* in this context is a group of contiguous IP addresses. The first few bits of an IP address represent the network, and the last few bits represent the machine address within the network. The first few bits of the network address identify the class of the address. This part of the address could be 8 bits, 16 bits, or 24 bits long, resulting in what are called *Class A, Class B*, and *Class C addresses*, respectively. Routing entries in a routing table are maintained only for every network, not for every address. Each routing entry contains the network address and the next-hop router.

Although maintaining routing entries at the level of networks reduces the size of the routing table, each router still needs a large number of entries for Class C networks. There can be up to two million Class C networks. It is useful to combine multiple routing table entries into one wherever possible. This is the idea behind *Classless InterDomain Routing* (CIDR), which does away with the notion of classes and attempts to combine routing table entries wherever possible. CIDR also comes with recommendations for hierarchical address assignment in the Internet that can improve the efficiency of CIDR. Each network is identified by the starting address in the network and the length of the CIDR prefix, which is the number of bits indicating the network address. An address of 148.2.8.0/21 would cover all the possible addresses which have the same 21 bits from the beginning as 148.2.8.0; in other words, all addresses from 148.2.8.0 to 148.2.127.255, the equivalent of all 128 Class C networks in that range. If the next hop to all these networks is the same, a single routing table entry can replace 128 equivalent entries for Class C addresses.

Which next-hop router to send a packet to is determined by looking at the routing table entry with the longest prefix that matches the destination address of the packet. If no such entry is found, the packet is sent to a preconfigured default router. As an example, consider a router which is connected to three other machines. It has three routing table entries, entry one stating that subnet 9.2.8.0/21 be forwarded to machine A, entry two stating that subnet 9.2.0.0/16 be forwarded to machine B, and entry three stating that subnet 9.0.0.0/8 be forwarded to machine C. The default router is machine C. In this case, packets destined 8.2.3.4. have no match and are sent to machine C. Packets destined to 9.2.3.24 match entries two and three, but 16 bits are matched in the prefix of entry two while only 8 bits with the prefix of entry three. Therefore, it is sent on the basis of entry two and sent to machine B. Similarly, a packet destined to 9.2.8.16 matches all three entries, but entry one would be most precise, and the packet is sent to machine A.

The next-hop information in the routing table depends on the network's topology. Because this topology can change as new machines are added or existing links are dropped, schemes are needed to keep the routing table information current. These protocols (commonly called *routing protocols*) work as follows:

The entire IP network is divided into several *autonomous systems* (ASs). All routers within an AS are in the control of a single network administrative domain. An AS is defined just for the purpose of routing table exchange. An ISP can have more than one AS, or the operator of an intranet can have multiple ASs inside the intranet. All routers within a single AS exchange routing information using an *Interior Gateway Protocol* (IGP). Different ASs exchange routing information with each other using an *Exterior Gateway Protocol* (EGP). The EGP determines the most appropriate point to exit from the AS for each network entry outside the AS.

Note

A *gateway* is an alternative name for a router. Almost all routing protocols use the gateway nomenclature.

RIP and OSPF

Two examples of an interior routing protocol are RIP and OSPF. *Routing Information Protocol* (RIP) was commonly used in the 1970s. It was implemented as a distributed algorithm to compute the shortest paths among all the routers within an AS. The current trend is toward the use of *Open Shortest Path First* (OSPF) The OSPF protocol exchanges information about link lengths among all the routers within the same AS domain. Each router can construct a snapshot of the graph representing the entire AS of which it is a part. A shortest-path computation is done on this graph to determine which route needs to be followed for each network address. For network addresses that are not in the AS domain, OSPF can use the information about the next AS to come up with the routing table entry.

Routing protocols such as OSPF, in which link length is sent to all routers in the administrative domain, are called *link state routing protocols*. In link state routing protocols, each router maintains the topology of the network. In contrast, protocols such as RIP and IGRP are *distance vector routing protocols*. In distance vector routing protocols, each router maintains a table with shortest known lengths to all destinations. Adjacent routers exchange tables with each other periodically.

RIP computes shortest path in terms of numbers of links traversed to a destination. Each router maintains a table of hop count and the next-hop router toward different destinations. In addition to the periodic exchange, table exchange is triggered on events such as links coming up or down. When an update from a neighbor is received, the shortest-path information contained in the new message is combined with the current table information to determine the new table contents. The tricky part of RIP (or any distance vector routing protocol) is to ensure that this combination does not result in a routing loop. RIP uses several techniques for loop prevention, which are generally based on sending a different version of the table to different neighbors. The RIP standard specifications define 16 as the maximum number of hops which implies that RIP (at least in its standard form) cannot be used in networks where the path between two routers may involve more than 16 hops.

IGRP

Interior Gateway Routing Protocol (IGRP) is a routing protocol developed by Cisco that addresses some of the limitations of RIP. IGRP and its enhanced version, EIGRP (Enhanced IGRP), are commonly deployed in many enterprise networks. Instead of a single hop count, IGRP keeps a set of sophisticated path metrics comprising the sum of transmission delay to the destination, the lowest-capacity link along the path, the accumulated error rate (a measure of link reliability) of the links along the path, and a measure of load on the links along the path. The hop count and the maximum packet size of a path are also maintained in the tables. Each router uses a combination of the metrics to determine the shortest length path toward the destinations.

IGRP also supports multiple paths toward the same destination and supports the case of multiple parallel links between two routers. IGRP implements loop prevention algorithms that are similar to the ones in RIP, with some variations. One big win over RIP is that IGRP does not have the 16-hop restriction and can be deployed in larger enterprise networks. EIGRP implements a sophisticated loop-prevention algorithm called the *Diffusion Update Algorithm* (DUAL). The details of DUAL and other loop-prevention algorithms can be found in the book by Huitema [HUITEMA].

BGP

An example of an exterior routing protocol is *Border Gateway Protocol* (BGP). BGP routers communicate with each other using TCP connections. A program (the routing daemon) implementing the BGP protocol typically runs on each of the access routers at the border of the AS. The routing daemons at an access router communicate with daemons on other access routers within this AS, as well as with routing daemons on any immediately attached router belonging to a different AS. The BGP protocol requires that each routing daemon exchange the list of network addresses it knows, as well as the sequence of ASs that are needed to reach each network address. Each of the BGP routers then computes the best AS to take for each of the network addresses thus exchanged.

Routing decisions made by BGP are done in conjunction with routing policies. *Routing policies* allow an AS to specify whether it is willing to act as a transit point for packets originating from other AS domains. For example, a corporation might not want to deal with any packets except the ones that are sent to and from machines in its domain. An ISP might want to accept packets from only adjacent ISPs with whom it has peering agreements. Restrictions on routing are specified by means of routing policies, which can be specified using a policy specification language [RPSL].

More information on routing in the Internet can be found in the books by Comer [COMER] and Huitema [HUITEMA].

Domain Name Service

Keeping track of IP addresses as a number is fairly tough for us, even when they are expressed in the dotted format. As a convenience to human users, the TCP/IP architecture permits applications to identify machines using a character string.

The string name is defined in a hierarchical manner. A name consists of a machine name and a domain (just like people have a first name and a surname). The domain itself may be further deconstructed into another subdomain, and so on. The machine with the IP address of 198.81.209.108 has the string name domino.watson.ibm.com. The name of this machine is domino, and it belongs to the domain watson.ibm.com, which is a subdomain within a larger domain of ibm.com, which in turn is a subdomain with the larger domain of .com.

For the purpose of resolving domain names to IP addresses, name servers are used. The entire domain name space is divided into multiple zones, each zone having a domain name server. The zones would usually (but not necessarily) be organized along the same hierarchy as the domains. Each zone has a primary domain name server and possibly some secondary name servers. Each domain name server knows the name servers of its child domains and its parent. Thus, the domain name server of the com domain would know the child name servers that could resolve any names ending with ibm.com, or cisco.com, and so on. The name server responsible for ibm.com is the parent of the name servers responsible for watson.ibm.com, almaden.ibm.com and so on. It would know the identity of these name servers. The name server responsible for Watson.ibm.com knows the name of all machines within that prefix. The translation of string names to IP addresses occurs through an application called the *Domain Name Service* (DNS). To translate the domain name to an IP address, a local translation file is first checked for the definitions; otherwise, a configured DNS server is contacted. If the DNS server does not know the answer to the query, it contacts another DNS server to obtain the answer. A DNS server would first check whether any of the name servers in the child domain might be able to resolve the name. It does so by comparing the domain name being looked up and the set of names contained in each of the child domains. If the name can be resolved by one of the child name servers, it is passed to that name server. Otherwise, the name is passed to the parent domain name server, which applies the same algorithm recursively.

Responses obtained from other DNS servers are cached for a limited period of time in order to reduce the number of queries.

IP Network Management and SNMP

Network management refers to the technologies and protocols that are needed to monitor an operational network, identify problems in its operation, and configure various devices. The prevailing method of doing management in an IP network is via *Simple Network Management Protocol* (SNMP).

The model assumed by SNMP is fairly simple. All nodes (routers, servers) in the network run an application called the *SNMP agent*. The agent listens on port 161 and waits for requests from an SNMP manager, and also provides information to the SNMP manager about the node in which it is running. The *manager* is a process that runs on a host in the network and is used to obtain management information. The machine on which the manager runs is called the *management station*. The manager and agent communicate with each other using the SNMP protocol. A network may have more than one network management station.

The SNMP manager exchanges management information with the SNMP agents. The management information depends on the type of elements being managed. In order to manage an Ethernet interface, you need to know about its MAC address, its IP address, the size of the maximum transmission unit, and so on. Statistics collected about the interface include items such as a count of packets sent on the interface, or a count of errors in the transmission on that interface. On the other hand, the information needed to manage an open TCP connection would include the IP address and port numbers of both points of the connection and the state of the connection. Management information about these two different types of managed elements has many differences.

The basic type of management information is called an *object*. Generally speaking, an object describes an attribute variable or a set of attributes that is useful for the purpose of network management. These objects are collected in a *Management Information Base* (MIB). Thus, all information needed to manage an Ethernet interface would form an MIB for an Ethernet interface. Each type of SNMP agent would support a specific group of MIBs, depending on the types of network elements that it is providing management information for. The object description for each attribute variable would typically consist of a unique name for the attribute, its syntax (whether it is an integer or a string, and so on), The unique name for the object/MIB is determined in a hierarchical manner.

A set of standard MIBs is defined that must be supported for specific types of managed objects. For example, an SNMP agent that supports the management of an Ethernet interface must support a standard MIB for an Ethernet interface. The list of standard MIB definitions can be found in Internet RFCs. The original MIB-II was defined in 1991 [MIB2], and its definitions have subsequently been updated with revisions to the type of information related to IP [IPMIB], TCP [TCPMIB], and UDP [UDPMIB].

Adding new types of items for network management is relatively easy. You have to define the new MIB using the SMI notation. *Structure of Management Information* (SMI) [SMIREF] is a set of conventions used to define the contents of a MIB. Most network management tools (such as OpenView from Hewlett-Packard) can read the SMI specification and parse it to understand the composition of the MIB. The tool can then obtain and manipulate the MIB through any SNMP agent. The agent must understand the semantics of the MIB and ensure that the proper actions are performed.

The SNMP manager can obtain the current value of all the objects that are defined in the MIB by querying the SNMP agent on an SNMP-managed node. It can also change those values. Manipulation of the MIB contents by the SNMP manager is the bulk of the SNMP protocol. Usually, an SNMP manager polls all the SNMP agents at a slow rate to retrieve (or modify) the MIBs. However, agents also have the ability to send an asynchronous message (called a *trap*) to a configured list of managers. The trap is sent in case the manager needed to look at something urgently. Upon receipt of a trap, the manager obtains the MIBs from the agent generating the trap. This mode of operation is called *trap-directed polling*.

The SNMP protocol in itself is fairly simple. Here are the main types of messages it supports:

- `get-request` allows a manager to read an attribute from the agent.

- `get-next-request` allows a manager to read the next attribute from the agent.

- `get-bulk-request` allows a manager to read a group of attributes in one operation.

- `set-request` allows a manager to change the value of an object.

- `trap` contains a message from the agent to the manager.

Each of these messages has an associated response message. There is also an `inform-request` message that can let a manager inform another manager about the set of local MIBs it is managing.

Three versions of SNMP are in operation today. The most commonly deployed version is SNMP version 2. Version 3 has also been standardized. It is currently in the early stages of deployment. It puts in features that would make the communication between the SNMP manager and the agents more secure. In the earlier two versions, this communication occurred in the clear, with a simple password mechanism used by the agents to authenticate that they are talking to the right manager. Further details on the different versions of the protocol can be found in the book by Stallings [SNMP].

IP Configuration: Dynamic Host Configuration Protocol

A DHCP server is quite often deployed in IP networks for automated configuration of IP workstations. When the IP architecture was originally developed, it was assumed that all machines would have IP addresses statically assigned. It did not account for mobile machines, such as a laptop computer, which might need to be moved across multiple networks. DHCP allows network addresses to be assigned dynamically to the hosts. Of course, DHCP can be used to provide full configuration information to the host, not just the IP address.

During bootup, a machine sends a broadcast to all the machines connected to its physical network looking for a DHCP server. Each physical network has a DHCP server or a relay agent that can relay the requests to DHCP servers on another LAN. The closest DHCP server, which obtains the request, replies to the client. When the DHCP server has been identified, the client can communicate with it to obtain the IP address and other configuration information.

DHCP servers are usually configured to give out blocks of addresses to machines belonging to specific subnets. In other words, all machines in a certain LAN will always be assigned addresses that start with 142.1. Thus, although the individual addresses of machines might change, the IP network to which the machine belongs would not change. This prevents the need to change IP routing tables whenever addresses are assigned dynamically.

Quality of Service Overview

A network's *Quality of Service* (QoS) refers to the properties of the network that directly contribute to the degree of satisfaction that users perceive relative to the network's performance. QoS can be considered good or poor on the basis of many factors, such as network delay, loss rates in the networks, load on the servers, and so on.

The perceived QoS depends on the type of application the user is running. For example, a network might have poor quality for listening to real-audio on the Web, but it might be sufficient to download a text file relatively quickly. Different applications that are running on a network make different assumptions about the environment and the network. The field of QoS deals with the mechanisms that can meet the performance requirements of different applications.

There are two aspects to having a network operate at the desired level of performance:

- You must design the network with links of sufficient capacity and routers and servers that have sufficient processing speed to handle the normal operational load on the network. However, networks often operate at loads that are much higher than the planned capacity. This is a natural outcome in an environment where the number of users and applications in the network grows rapidly.

- In those overloaded conditions, you need to have mechanisms that ensure that a preferred subset of applications continues to receive its desired performance, even at the expense of other applications. Such assured performance can be obtained by a variety of mechanisms. They are described in the following sections.

Network Design and Capacity Planning

The aim of network design is to determine the most appropriate topology for meeting a specific traffic load on the network. Most network design problems are formulated in terms of finding the lowest-cost graph to connect a number of sites, where the estimated traffic generated at each of the sites is known. The cost depends on the links selected to connect the different sites, as well as the capacity selected for the different links.

The design problem might be specified with constraints on network performance, or it might be specified without any such constraints. The former case is the constrained network design problem, and the latter one is the unconstrained network design problem.

The immediate question is, "What is the best graph?" The usual definition of the best graph is the one that minimizes the cost of the resulting network. The cost of the graph is the cost of the telecommunication links represented by the edges connecting nodes in the graph. If you or your organization has fiber-optic cable, this is the cost of digging the trenches and laying the fiber. More commonly, you or your organization will lease bandwidth. In this case, the cost of the graph is the recurring or monthly fees paid to the provider.

The cost might measure the monthly charges associated with operating a direct line between the sites (perhaps including an amortized term dependent on the one-time expenses of creating the site). The cost would depend on many factors, including the distance between the sites, the amount of traffic to flow between the sites, and the location of the sites. Determining the traffic, especially if the sites being connected are in two different countries, is not a trivial task. However, commercial tools that estimate the costs of creating a line are available.

It is usually common in network design problems to come up with not only the lowest-cost graph, but also a few enumerations of possible network topologies that would meet the specific performance constraints and traffic loads. As a matter of fact, nobody knows how to design the best network. Each design tool does its best to solve a problem.

The choice among these designs is made using subjective trade-offs between the cost, the performance, and the reliability achieved among the different designs. For example, the network operator might want the lowest-cost network but might be willing to pay 10 percent more if an alternative topology reduces network delay by 50 percent.

The typical formulation of a network design problem consists of a description of participating sites, a traffic matrix, and a cost matrix. The participating sites are the sites that need to be connected. These sites would be the nodes of the graph resulting from the design. For the sake of brevity, I will assume that we only need to consider the specified nodes to generate the final graph. In the general network design problem, other secondary nodes might also need to be introduced for a better solution. For example, it might be cheaper to connect three sites located in the northern, eastern, and western U.S. by getting a fourth location in the central U.S. and connecting them, rather than restricting the graph to direct connectivity among the three sites.

In many cases, you are looking for a tree network. This is true if you are designing an access network for an ISP. In other cases, you are looking for a mesh design that need not necessarily be tree-structured. Mesh design is common in ISP backbone networks and the wide-area component of corporate intranets.

Typical tree network design algorithms are based on variations of algorithms that compute the minimum spanning tree among the selected sites, with modifications that accommodate the capacity constraints needed by the traffic matrix. The two common algorithms used for this purpose are Prim's algorithm and Kruskal's algorithms. The basic approach is to start with all sites disconnected. The first step is to form a partially connected tree by selecting the lowest-cost link that can connect two sites and that has the minimum capacity needed. You can select the minimum among all possible links or start with a selected root node to make the first link selection. At each stage of the algorithm, the partially formed tree is augmented by adding new links that meet the minimum link cost and capacity constraints. These steps are repeated until all sites are connected. A detailed description of these algorithms can be found in the text by Kershenbaum [KERSH]. It has also been shown that the tree algorithms are a special case of a generic spanning tree computation algorithm [KCHAO].

Multiple mesh design algorithms are available. I have chosen the MENTOR [MENTOR] algorithm as a typical example. MENTOR divides all the nodes in the network into two sets—edge nodes and backbone nodes. The nodes are divided into clusters, each cluster consisting of one backbone node and several edge nodes. The nodes are connected in a tree network with the constraint that edge nodes can only connect to one of the backbone nodes, preferably to the backbone node in their cluster. Then capacities on the links are calculated to meet the expected traffic load distribution in the network. Additional links are introduced to balance the traffic load on the different routers between a source and a destination using a routing protocol such as OSPF.

If during the operation of the network you find that the capacity of a network link or router is inadequate, the link can be upgraded to higher speeds. In general, links that are subject to higher traffic utilization compared to the others in the network are likely candidates for upgrading.

In order to design a network with performance constraints, you typically follow the approach of designing a network without performance constraints. Then, the network's resulting performance (in terms of end-to-end delays and network reliability) is analyzed using mathematical models. Additional links may be introduced in the network to meet the performance requirements. The process of adding new links or removing old links is usually an iterative process based on heuristics customized for the specific network being designed.

Note

A heuristic is an algorithm that provides an efficient approximate solution to a problem whose exact solution may require too much time.

For more thorough coverage of the issues involved in network design, many excellent books are available, such as the ones by Cahn [CAHN], Kershenbaum [KERSH], and Schwartz [SCHW2].

Network capacity is only one aspect that can affect the performance perceived by an application. Another aspect of the performance is the capacity of the servers and clients that are used to run the applications themselves. The capacity of servers is usually the more critical component, because a server tends to deal with multiple simultaneous users, and the clients (in the current days) are typically single-user machines.

When the fastest-possible machine you can deploy is inadequate to meet the processing capacities required at the server, you can resort to the following techniques for having additional capacities:

- **Name service round robin.** In this approach, multiple servers are placed at different points in the network. When a client needs to communicate with the server, it usually needs to contact the domain name server to determine the location of the server (as described earlier). The domain name server can be configured to return the address of one of the many redundant servers in the network on each client request in a round-robin fashion. This distributes the load from the clients to different servers in a uniform manner. If one of the servers becomes unavailable, the domain name server can exclude its address from the list.

- **Front-end dispatcher.** The front-end dispatcher approach does not rely on a modified domain name service to distribute the requests. It relies on the efficiency of a fast processor that acts as a front-end interface for the servers. The front-end dispatcher selects one of the servers with which a client must communicate and dispatches those messages to the appropriate server. The front-end dispatcher needs to process requests at the combined rate of all the servers. However, because it is only dispatching requests to one of the servers rather than processing the message completely, the goal can be achieved by an efficient software design.

Good capacity planning is critical for smooth operation of the network. However, there might be instances where the network planning underestimated the load on the network. When an upgrade to the higher-capacity link is not feasible, either because it costs too much or because the high utilization occurs at only certain times, you have to resort to other mechanisms to meet the performance goals of one of the applications at the expense of the others.

Rate Control

Rate control (or Traffic Shaping) can be described as the ability to divide the capacity of a link in the network into multiple logical links. Each logical link operates at a specific bandwidth, or at a fraction of the physical link bandwidth. Let's assume that a company's transatlantic link between New York and London is congested. The network administrator wants to ensure that a set of applications (identified as business-critical) gets 80 percent or more of the link capacity on the transatlantic link, while the other set of applications are allowed to use only 20 percent of the link capacity in the presence of business-critical applications. Of course, if the link capacity is unused, this set can use the full bandwidth. Devices that provide such rate control mechanisms are available from many different vendors.

A scenario in which rate control can be used effectively is shown in Figure 2.5. It shows several servers that share access to the wide area network through a slow link. A rate control device is placed at the access point to the wide area network. It acts as the arbitrator of the bandwidth on the slow link. The rate control device can operate using packet shaping or by manipulation of TCP headers, as described next.

Figure 2.5   Rate Control Usage Scenario

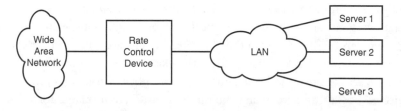

Rate Control by Packet Scheduling

The rate control device can dictate what percentage of link bandwidth can be used by any class of applications in the network. In order to do so, it needs to do the following:

- Identify the class to which an application belongs

- Implement mechanisms so that rate control constraints are enforced

The first step of classification is typically done by looking at an IP packet's network and transport header fields. The intermediate box typically uses four fields from the IP and TCP header for this classification—namely, the source and destination addresses contained in the IP header and the source and destination port numbers contained in the TCP (or UDP) header. Many applications run on well-known port numbers. For example, the Web server typically runs on port 80. The IP addresses can be used to distinguish users coming from different organizations (assuming that the organizations use distinct IP addresses) or to identify the specific server that the packets are destined for (or originating from).

Some applications use dynamic port numbers and cannot be classified simply by looking at the transport and network headers. A rate control device might look at higher-layer protocol information to obtain this information. In some cases, a rate control device might implement a full application stack. This application acts as a proxy for the real application parses the headers contained within the higher layers in the stack, and determines the appropriate class for a packet based on these headers.

As soon as the correct class has been determined, scheduling and rate control mechanisms can be used to restrict the rate that a specific class of traffic is allowed to use.

Token Bucket Rate Control

One of the ways to implement rate control is to use a *token bucket*. This mechanism requires that every packet at the rate control device be assigned a specific number of tokens before it can be sent out into the network. Tokens are allocated for each class of traffic and are kept in a "bucket" assigned to the class—hence the term "token bucket." Each time a packet is transmitted, the appropriate number of tokens is removed from the aforementioned bucket, thus reducing the number of tokens available for subsequent packets of that class. The bucket is refilled in the background with tokens at a rate determined by the amount of bandwidth to be allocated to the class in question. If there are insufficient tokens in the bucket to allocate the appropriate number to the next packet ready to be sent, the packet must wait until that number of tokens is present. It is replenished via the refill rate.

For example, let's assume that you want to keep an application from using no more than 8Kbps worth of link capacity. Each byte from that application that is to be transmitted on that link needs to be allocated a token in order to be transmitted into the network. A packet that is 200 bytes long will need 200 tokens in the bucket in order to be sent into the network. Packets have to wait until there are sufficient tokens in the bucket (200), which allows the packet to be transmitted into the network. Tokens are generated (that is, go into the bucket) according to the desired rate. In order for the application to be able to use 8Kbps, for example, tokens need to be generated into the bucket for this application at a rate that will support an 8Kbps stream. This is usually done by assigning an appropriate number of tokens at periodic intervals. For example, a rate of 8Kbps (or 1Kbps) can be obtained by generating 100 tokens (one for each byte) every 100ms (milliseconds).

If an application is quiet (does not send any packets) for an extended amount of time, this can cause the number of tokens in the bucket to build up significantly. This can, in turn, cause surges of traffic at high rates (up to the link speed) into the network, when the application "bursts" a relatively large number of bytes at one time and the bucket is full of tokens. To prevent this, the total number of tokens that can be accumulated in the bucket has a limit. This limit is the *bucket depth*. The bucket depth thus limits the number of bytes and, therefore, packets that can be sent into the network at the peak rate of the link.

When a sufficient number of tokens is unavailable, packets have to wait. Each waiting packet will occupy a buffer at the router. If too many packets arrive and wait for tokens, the available buffer space might be exceeded, and packets would need to be discarded.

A rate control scheme can also follow the scheme that packets not finding the required number of tokens are discarded, rather than delayed until a sufficient number of tokens are available.

Time Stamp-Based Rate Control

An alternative way to implement rate control is to use *time-stamp-driven rate controllers*. These operate in a different manner than the token bucket. This approach exploits the ability of many current machines to measure time very accurately using hardware timers.

To keep an application flow from using a rate in excess of a specific limit, such as 8Kbps, you can compute the time that would be required to transmit a packet on the link. The difference in time stamps between consecutive packet arrivals can be used to determine if packets are conforming to the rate limit.

For example, consider a flow of packets that is not to exceed 8Kbps (1Kbps—or, in other words, 1 byte per ms). Suppose a packet 200 bytes long is to be transmitted. At the rate of 8Kbps (1 byte per ms), this implies that no other packet can be transmitted for another 200ms. You can determine the times when packets are arriving and use that to determine how long the packets need to wait before being transmitted.

As with token bucket rate control, each delayed packet requires a buffer at the router. If not enough buffers are available, the packet might need to be discarded. Typically, a time stamp-driven rate controller would have an upper limit on how long a packet can be delayed. If it is determined that the packet needs to wait longer than the time interval, the packet is discarded.

Time stamp rate controllers perform their operations one packet at a time and are appropriate for performing rate control/traffic shaping operations in interrupt handlers that are invoked on the arrival of a packet at a device.

Scheduling

In addition to the mechanisms just described, the rate-control device would implement a scheduling mechanism that differentiates between the classes of packets. *Scheduling* is the process of determining which packet gets transmitted when more than one is waiting for access to a link. Most routers implement the *First In First Out* (FIFO) scheduling policy, in which the packets that are received first at the node are the first ones to be transmitted.

The FIFO queue treats all packets as equal. However, most rate control scheduling processes treat packets belonging to different classes differently. A variety of other queuing disciplines have been proposed to deal with different classes of service.

A simple variation available on many devices is a *static priority scheduler,* which consists of multiple FIFO queues. Each queue is assigned a static priority. All packets belonging to the highest-priority queue are serviced first. When the highest-priority queue is empty, the next queue is serviced. A queue gets serviced only when all higher-priority queues are empty. The static priority queues can give good performance to the packets in the higher-priority queues. However, the packets in the lower-priority queues might see a significant degradation in their performance. When this happens, the lower-priority queues are said to be "starved" by the higher-priority queues because they are denied access to the link.

An issue related to priority is that of packet preemption. Suppose a router has two priority levels, and there are currently no high-priority packets. A low-priority packet is selected for transmission on the outgoing link. Halfway through the transmission of the packet, a high-priority packet arrives. The router has two choices: It can delay the high-priority packet for the low-priority packet, or it can abort the current transmission once and transmit the high-priority packet immediately. When the transmission is aborted, the scheduling is called *preemptive;* otherwise, it is called *nonpreemptive.* Most routers implement nonpreemptive scheduling only. The extra delay experienced by the high-priority packet is small compared to the waste of bandwidth associated with aborting the current transmission.

Another common scheduling discipline is *Weighted Fair Queuing* (WFQ). In WFQ, each class of packets is served round-robin by the scheduler, each one being visited with a frequency that is determined by the weights assigned to each of the different classes. If all the queues are assigned equal weights, one packet from each queue is serviced in each round. When the link capacity is being fully utilized, this results in an equal division of the link capacity among the different queues. When each queue is assigned a different weight, a different number of packets are transmitted from each queue during each round of the scheduler. This allows the queues to share the link speed in a different proportion than equally while avoiding the "starvation" problem with static priority schedulers.

As a simple example, consider two queues that are being served with round-robin weights in the ratio of 2:1. The scheduler serves up two packets from the first queue on every round and only one packet from the second queue. When several packets are waiting at the router, this gives two thirds of the link bandwidth to packets in the first queue and only one-third of the link bandwidth to packets in the second queue. When there is little traffic on the link, the classes can typically get the full link capacity when they have packets to send.

Rate Control by TCP Header Manipulation

Scheduling packets for rate control comes at a price: The packets have to be queued at the rate control device, and they use up buffer space. The management of the buffers and different queues can add a lot of complexity to the rate control device. An alternative is to manipulate the TCP headers at the rate control device to control the rate that a specific session is getting. The limitation is that it applies only to TCP traffic, not to the UDP traffic. Depending on the intended application, this may or may not be a limitation. TCP comprises over 80 percent of the traffic in the Internet. However, some important applications, such as voice-over IP, run over UDP.

To understand how transport header manipulation can help in rate allocation services, let's examine how TCP regulates packet transmission in the network. The TCP protocol requires that the receiver acknowledge the bytes it has received. The number of bytes that have been sent but not acknowledged by the other side is the amount of data in flight. TCP also keeps track of the round-trip delays experienced by the packets on a connection. These round-trip delays are tracked by a time-stamp option that is carried in the TCP header for packets and acknowledgments.

The amount of data in flight is controlled by two main factors:

- **The size of the receiver's buffers.** Both sides of a TCP connection inform each other about the amount of data that they can receive without overflowing their buffers. The sender ensures that the data in flight never exceeds the value advertised by the receiver.

- **Congestion in the network.** The sender tries to maximize the amount of data in flight (up to the limit requested by the receiver) as long as it does not cause an overload at any of the intermediate nodes in the network. The amount of data in flight is increased when packets can be successfully transmitted and is reduced when TCP detects that there has been a loss of packets in the network.

The maximum amount of data that can be received, as well as the acknowledgment of packets, is calculated using byte sequence numbers. Each byte of data exchanged has a byte sequence number, which is obtained by adding the actual location of the byte from the beginning of the data stream with a starting number which is selected randomly. Within TCP, a receiver sends the byte sequence number (acknowledgement number in Figure 2.4) of all data that it has received, and also the maximum byte sequence number of the data (sequence number field in Figure 2.4) that it can contain within its buffers. The difference between the two fields is the advertised buffer, the available buffer space that the receiver is allowing to the sender. The sender keeps track of the maximum byte sequence number it has transmitted so far. After receiving an acknowledgment, he can send data up to the maximum byte sequence number specified by the receiver.

The round trip in TCP is computed by including the time when a segment was transmitted as one of the TCP options. The acknowledgments carry the same time stamp back to the sender. The sender uses the difference to compute the round-trip time for the connection. This round-trip time is used to determine the time-out periods for the connection.

The amount of bandwidth received by a connection is determined by the amount of data in flight as well as the round-trip time of packets. An intermediate box can offer different service levels to different connections by manipulating TCP headers in one of the following ways:

- **Modifying the size of the receiver's advertised buffer.** By decreasing the maximum sequence number advertised in TCP's acknowledgement, an edge device can reduce the number of window buffers for applications that are to receive a lower throughput. It can also increase the size of the receiver's advertised buffer (although caution must be exercised in doing so) for preferred applications, provided that the characteristics of the end hosts are taken into account and that buffer overflow at the receiver is avoided. When a smaller window buffer is advertised, a smaller number of packets are outstanding in the network, and the rate received by the connection is reduced accordingly. When a larger window buffer size is advertised, thus increasing the number of outstanding packets in the network, the sender can increase the sending rate, provided that the buffers at the receiver are not overrun.

- **Modifying the byte-sequence number of acknowledged packets.** Because the byte sequence numbers of acknowledged packets are the key determinant of the amount of data in flight, reducing this information can cause applications to reduce the amount of data in flight and thereby affect the bandwidth available to the set of applications to be reduced. The intermediate box can subsequently generate acknowledgments with larger byte sequence numbers (up to the sequence number acknowledged by the final receiver) at a constrained rate so as to force the flow of data to occur in a much smoother fashion. Instead of sending a large packet of 1024 bytes in the network, this method can ensure that four packets of 256 bytes (excluding TCP/IP headers) are being sent.

Modifying the acknowledgment byte sequence numbers and time stamps can definitely increase the share of bandwidth for one class of packets at the expense of another class of packets. However, this scheme suffers from a few disadvantages:

- Looking into the transport header fields and modifying them requires a significant amount of state information to be kept at the rate-control device.

- If encryption is used to protect the contents of a packet, the transport header information might not be available for manipulation. You should keep in mind that this problem arises only when IPsec is used to encrypt packet headers. Encryption at the transport layer using *Secure Sockets Layer* (SSL) does not encrypt the TCP headers—they can still be manipulated.

Note that rate control by TCP manipulation can also be done at the end server. Suppose you want to restrict a connection to a rate of 1Mbps. The connection has a round-trip time of 200ms. The round-trip time is determined as part of normal TCP processing. A simple way for the server to control the rate of the connection is to simply not allow more than 1Mbps × 200ms, or 200 kilobits (that is, 25 kilobytes) of data in flight—data that is sent out by the server but not received by the other party. Such control mechanisms are implemented in some severs, such as the IBM OS/390, but unfortunately are not available on all operating systems.

DiffServ

The basic schemes deployed in rate control mechanisms, such as scheduling, token buckets, and so on, form the basis of providing different levels of services in the network. However, each rate control device effectively operates by itself, performing the classification function repeatedly. One obvious improvement would be to include the classification information as a field in the IP header. DiffServ is an IETF standard that offers a way to provide different service levels in the network.

The main idea behind the DiffServ approach is that the information about the QoS of a packet should be encoded in a single byte of the IP header, and that this should be used to provide a limited number of different classes of service in the network.

Figure 2.6 shows the model of a DiffServ network. The network shows a single administrative domain with two types of routers—access and core. The access routers connect the network to different customer networks or other ISP networks. The core routers provide connectivity among the other routers in the same administrative domain and are not connected directly to any customer network.

Figure 2.6   DiffServ Network Architecture

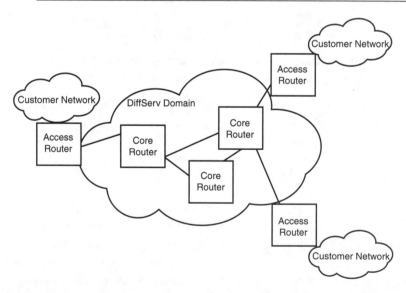

The core routers in the network can handle packets differently, depending on the contents of the *Type of Service* (ToS) byte contained in the IP header. This is essentially reusing the ToS for its original intended purpose. Instead of the full 8 bits in the ToS byte, only 6 bits are available for service differentiation. The other 2 bits are reserved for future use in explicit congestion notification for TCP. These 6 bits constitute the DS field in the IP header (DS stands for DiffServ).

Each of the 32 possible combinations, with the 6 bits of the DS field, signifies that the packet be handled differently by the core routers. Each different type of processing that can be provided to the packet is called a different *Per-Hop Behavior* (PHB). Currently, four types of PHBs are specified for use within the DiffServ network: the class selector PHBs, expedited forwarding, assured forwarding, and the default set of PHBs. These PHBs are described in more detail in the next section.

The access routers in the network have the responsibility of classifying the packets marked for processing by one of the PHBs that are supported within the DiffServ network. They can also implement rate control for different classes of traffic. The one additional function they perform is mark the DS field in the IP header with the correct value for the PHB. In addition, they may collect statistics for billing and accounting purposes.

Packets can be classified in one of two ways, depending on the connectivity of the access router. Some access routers are connected to customer networks (that is, these customers are not themselves network operators), and others are connected to other network operators (ISPs).

An access router that is connected to a customer network is expected to use one or more of six fields in an incoming IP packet to determine the PHB that the packet should receive in the core networks. These six fields are

- IP source address
- IP destination address
- Transport protocol
- DS field in the incoming packet header
- Source ports in the transport headers
- Destination ports in the transport headers

Other types of access routers could simply use the DS field in the incoming IP packet to determine the PHB for their network. An access router would simply change the DS field to some other value that corresponds to a specific PHB at the core routers. This type of classification would be the one expected at the exchange points of other ISPs. The other ISP domain might have been using a different set of PHBs, or it might use different DS field values to represent the same PHB.

DiffServ, as presented above, is applicable only for portions of a network flanked a set of access routers with DiffServ capability. The DiffServ functions are available on many servers, and that support can be used to implement DiffServ almost anywhere inside an IP network.

The specific DS field value that corresponds to a PHB is called a *DS code point*. The DiffServ specifications state that code points must be assigned by means of configuration by an ISP operator.

DiffServ PHBs

The DiffServ PHBs represent the different types of processing that a packet can receive in the network. Four types of PHBs are currently defined in the network:

- Default behavior
- Class selector
- Expedited forwarding (EF)
- Assured forwarding (AF)

The default (or best-effort) PHB corresponds to the default best-effort packet forwarding in a network. Packets belonging to this PHB can be forwarded in any manner without any restrictions. The recommended code point for best-effort PHB is 0x000000.

The class selector PHBs define up to eight classes in the network. These class selector PHBs are required to have a DS field that takes one of the following eight values: 000000, 001000, 010000, 011000, 100000, 101000, 110000, or 111000. This PHB uses only the first 3 bits of the DS field; the last 3 bits are zeroed out. The first 3 bits form a numeric number from 0 to 7. A packet with a higher numeric value in the DS field is supposed to have a better (or equal) relative priority in the network for forwarding than a packet with a lower numeric value. A router need not implement eight different priority levels in the network to support the class selector PHBs. It can claim compliance with the standards by supporting only two priority levels, with the eight numeric values mapping to one of the two classes. The DS field of 000000 in the case of class selector PHBs is the same as that for default forwarding.

The EF PHB has a rate associated with it. This rate must be configurable by the system administrator. An upper limit as well as a lower limit may be specified for this rate. Packets belonging to the EF PHB must be serviced at a rate that is between the two specified limits. The rate limits must be obeyed independent of the load on the queue from other types of traffic. The recommended code point for expedited forwarding PHB is 101110.

The AF PHB defines a set of four classes that have to be assigned individual bandwidth and buffer allocation at each router. The classes are independent of each other. The classes are to be served at the assigned bandwidth on average. Within each class, three loss priorities are defined. The loss priorities may be collapsed into two loss priorities. Packets within the same class with a lower loss probability should be less likely to be discarded than the ones with a higher loss probability. The recommended code points for AF are as follows:

	Class 1	Class 2	Class 3	Class 4
Low drop precedence	001010	010010	011010	100010
Medium drop precedence	001100	010100	011100	100100
High drop precedence	001110	010110	011110	100110

The different PHBs are implemented in the core router by mapping each PHB to a specific queue in a multiqueue scheduling system. Weights assigned in scheduling disciplines such as WFQ are computed to ensure that traffic characterized by the EF or AF PHBs meet their target rate requirements.

For a more detailed discussion of DiffServ, refer to the book by Kilkki [KILKKI].

IntServ/RSVP

Integrated Services (IntServ) is the Internet standard for specifying the quality of service parameters signaled by *Resource ReSerVation Protocol* (RSVP), as well as the network element services controlled by these parameters, and the resultant end-to-end behaviors. Readers familiar with design of integrated services networks like ATM will find many parallels in the design of IntServ/RSVP and ATM resource reservation.

The approach used in IntServ/RSVP to ensure smooth operation of the preferred set of applications is to reserve specific bandwidth for them. The bandwidth reservation is made when applications signal their requirements to the network and the network responds as to whether the desired amount of bandwidth is available. When the reservation is established, data communication can begin with an assured level of performance. Of course, you can take a slightly more aggressive stand and start sending packets before the reservation process has completed, expecting that the reservation is likely to succeed.

The Internet standard protocol for signaling reservation is RSVP. In order to support reservations, a router in the network must understand RSVP and implement an admission control function. The admission control function verifies that the performance requirements of existing flows are not violated when new flows are added. In addition to satisfying performance requirements, other kinds of limits on reservations might be required. You might only want to permit the reservation of flows from specific applications, or from specific hosts.

RSVP Signaling Protocol

The reservation model that RSVP follows is based on simplex flows. The flow is identified by the destination IP address, the transport protocol used by the application, and the port number used by the application.

Within RSVP, a sender of data starts the reservation process by sending out PATH messages. The PATH messages are addressed to the destination and follow the normal route in the network to reach the destination. Each PATH message is sent with a special IP option called the Router Alert option. This option causes the PATH messages to be trapped and processed at each intermediate router along the path of the PATH message. The path traversed by the packet is recorded in the PATH message as it progresses between the routers.

The PATH message carries a specification of the traffic (Tspec) as it is generated by the sender, as well as the identity of the sender (IP address and port number). The *traffic specification* is a statement made by the sender to the network that it will be generating a packet flow that requires, or could benefit from, the reservation of resources according to the parameters specified. Furthermore, the traffic specification represents a statement to the effect that the application will not generate packets at a rate that exceeds the traffic rate specified by these parameters. The traffic specification consists of terms such as the peak and average rates that will be used by the connection.

The PATH message also carries a description of performance characteristics of the path along which the message is being sent. This description is called an *advertisement specification* (ADspec) because it advertises the characteristics of the path to the receiver. The sender initializes the ADspec, and each of the intermediate routers updates the ADspec as it receives the PATH message. The ADspec may contain information such as the number of hops along the path and the minimum available bandwidth along any link traversed so far.

When the receiver obtains the PATH message, it responds to the PATH message by sending a RESV message. The RESV message travels hop-by-hop using the reverse path accumulated in the PATH message. Each reservation message carries a flow specification and a filter specification. The flow specification contains a *reservation specification* (Rspec), which is the rate the receiver would like to reserve along its path, as well as a Tspec. Each router examines the Rspec and can modify it before passing it upstream. The modification of the Rspec is mostly needed for combining reservation requests from multiple users, such as when group communication is being used. The filter specification describes the set of packets that are to benefit from the reservation.

The path and reservation messages are repeated at periodic intervals by the sender and the receiver. If a router does not receive the PATH message or RESV message for a specific amount of time, it deletes the reservation and information about the flow. If packets get rerouted along the network, the PATH and RESV messages automatically follow the new path and thereby establish a new reservation along the new path.

IntServ Service Classes

The IntServ standards define two types of services that can be offered in an IP network. The first type of service, *guaranteed service*, guarantees quantitative upper bounds on the communication delays seen by the application. The second type of service, *controlled load service,* offers no quantitative guarantees, but it makes a qualitative assurance that network performance will not be much worse than the performance of the application on an unloaded network.

Guaranteed service is easy to understand from an application's perspective. However, it can be quite wasteful in its use of network resources. The controlled load service does not offer an easily understood service from an application's perspective, but it can achieve better utilization of network resources.

The remaining traffic, which does not need RSVP signaling, constitutes the best-effort traffic, which is supposed to be delivered at a lower priority than the guaranteed or controlled load services.

Guaranteed delays are provided within RSVP by modeling any delay in a router as a function of the network bandwidth reserved. Each router offering guaranteed service is required to compute two parameters, C and D. If a flow has a reserved rate of r bytes per second in the network, the variable delay of a packet in the flow at the router should be between 0 and D+C/r microseconds. As an RSVP PATH message flows through the network, the routers in the path add the value of their parameters to the values already carried in the ADspec. On receiving the accumulated characteristics along the path, the destination can determine the bandwidth to be reserved in order to meet the required delay guarantees. The reservation is then requested by the RESV messages that flow back along the path.

The controlled load service leaves open how the routers implement or perform the reservations. They are allowed to use any admission control technique as long as they can be reasonably sure that the performance of the network would not be much worse than that of an unloaded, uncontrolled network. For example, a router might decide that its performance is acceptable as long as the sum of peak bandwidth of all the flows does not exceed 125 percent of the link's capacity. It could use this heuristic to refuse reservations beyond a certain level of loading.

In addition to the admission control criteria, routers might want to include other criteria for accepting or refusing reservation requests, or for determining how much to reserve for them. These decisions could be made by the router itself, or it might outsource this task to another box in the network. When it needs to, it talks to another box in the network by means of a protocol called COPS. COPS is described further in Chapter 7, "Policy Distribution Mechanisms."

For a more detailed description of RSVP, refer to the book by Ferguson and Huston [FERGUSON].

A Comparison of RSVP and DiffServ

One of the strengths of the IntServ/RSVP approach is that it can provide an assured QoS. If the RSVP reservation is successful, a connection is assured a certain level of end-to-end performance from the network. Furthermore, it automatically adjusts to routing changes in the network. The PATH and RESV messages automatically follow the routes taken by normal IP packets and reserve/release capacity as needed. Furthermore, RSVP has been optimized, to a large extent, to support multicast communication in IP networks.

Despite its strengths, RSVP has some limitations. It suffers significant scalability problems, especially in backbone networks. Another aspect related to scalability is that of the signaling load on the network. Because each application flow has to generate periodic PATH and RESV messages that need to be processed by intervening routers, the routers might need to process a large number of messages per reserved flow. The reservation process adds an inherent latency to the communication process if you want to wait for a reservation to succeed before sending packets. Furthermore, any reservation approach faces efficiency issues when handling traffic flows with highly bursty or variable-rate characteristics.

The DiffServ architecture is much simpler than that of RSVP, so its functionality is also less than that of IntServ/RSVP. However, DiffServ has significantly better scaling characteristics. Another advantage of DiffServ is that it can coexist with IP security protocols because ToS markings can be modified without interfering with IP security authentication and encryption headers. RSVP requires filter processing at each router and faces problems when transport layer information is encrypted.

In the backbone networks, it is much more likely that DiffServ will be deployed rather than RSVP. RSVP still might have a role to play in signaling reservations at the edges of the network, especially for applications such as digital audio and video, which would benefit from reservations for relatively long-lived, high-bandwidth flows.

Multicast Communication in IP Networks

IP address between 224.0.0.0 and 239.255.255.255 are *multicast group addresses* or *Class D addresses*. These addresses identify more than one destination machine in the network. For example, a packet addressed to the address 224.0.0.1 would reach all the systems on the local LAN. Other multicast addresses are created and managed in a dynamic manner.

Any application can join a group address by contacting a router capable of supporting multicast. The multicast capable routers exchange group information among each other periodically using a protocol called *Internet Group Management Protocol* (IGMP). For each group, trees (one tree per source sending to the group) reaching all known members in the multicast group is maintained. When a message is received from a source on one branch of the tree, it is forwarded to all the other branches.

On the Internet, routers capable of supporting multicast form an overlay network which runs over all the unicast-only routers in the network. This network of multicast capable routers is called the *MBONE*.

IP Security Overview

The goals of IP security include preventing information contained in traffic flows from falling into the wrong hands, as well as addressing such security threats as unauthorized use of network resources, denial-of-service attacks, and unauthorized or unintended modification of information content, including information that controls the operation of the network. These goals are satisfied in many ways. At the network level, you need to introduce various safeguards to make sure that only traffic that is not permitted to be on the network is blocked. Furthermore, the data that is used to communicate can be transformed (or encrypted) in a such a manner that only the intended recipient would able to understand it. You also need to ensure and authenticate the party with which you are communicating.

These mechanisms are provided by a large array of technologies. This section briefly reviews the relevant security techniques. They are divided into three categories. The first category includes techniques that are used by intermediate devices to detect and prevent unauthorized traffic in the network. This is followed by a brief description of cryptographic techniques, which are widely used to enhance security and privacy. Then the two prevalent modes for communicating using encrypted traffic are discussed: Secure Sockets Layer and the IP security protocol. The final subsection covers techniques related to validating the identity of anyone who wants to communicate on the network.

Basic Packet Filtering and Application-Level Gateway

The Internet was originally designed for an academic/research setting in which all machines were trusted and accessible to every other machine. When Internet technologies are used to build enterprise networks, security and privacy concerns become more important and must be addressed. The global network can be modeled as having many subnetworks, with only limited access from one subnetwork to another. For example, suppose the accounting department of an investment banking company in a banking concern trusts its own accounting subnetwork but doesn't want to permit access by other people in other parts of the bank's network. Accounting needs to be connected to the bank's overall network because it might want to allow access to some applications (such as expense reimbursement requests) to all of the bank's employees. Similarly, that same department needs to be connected to the Internet so that its employees can access the network for electronic mail, current news, or other accounting practices, but it doesn't want anyone outside to connect to any of the servers inside the network. The accounting subnetwork needs to be connected to a partially trusted network on one end and the totally untrusted network on the other end, as shown in Figure 2.7.

Figure 2.7   Hypothetical Department Network

Remember the application communication process in IP networks. One end, the server, listens on a well-known port and waits for someone to connect to it. The other end, the client, initiates the connection to the server. Accounting applications are running as server applications on the machines in the accounting network. If there are no safeguards in place, anyone from the Internet can connect to any application on the accounting department's server machines. You need to protect the network by placing firewalls at points A and B, as shown in Figure 2.7.

The simplest type of firewall can enforce these safeguards by looking at IP packets and determining which packets to allow in and which ones to discard. For example, suppose that the only accounting department application that the bank's employees need access to runs on a machine with the IP address of 15.12.2.36, using TCP on the well-known port of 3040. The bank has an IP network in which all addresses belong to the network 15.0.0.0/8 (which stands for all IP addresses that have the first 8 bits the same as the specified address), and the accounting subnetwork has the network address 15.12.2.0/24. The firewall at point A will be told to allow packets in to the accounting subnetwork only if the packet's source address is in the network 15.0.0.0/8, the destination address is 15.12.2.36, the transport protocol is TCP, and the destination port number is 3040. Similarly, it would allow packets to go out from the accounting subnetwork into the bank's network only if the source address is 15.12.2.36, the destination address is

15.0.0.0/8, the protocol is TCP, and the source port is 3040. By deploying the firewall with specific rules (called filter rules), the accounting department has restricted the rest of the network to use only one application within its network. There might be other applications running on other ports in the accounting subnetwork, but they are accessible only to the accounting department employees. Machines that look at transport and network headers and allow only a selected subset of packets are referred to as packet-filtering firewalls.

A similar packet-filtering firewall at point B can be used to connect the accounting department to the Internet. Suppose the department has a mail server that needs to be accessed by outside machines. The packet-filtering firewall can be configured to allow connectivity to the mail server, and also for the mail server to connect to any machine outside the network. This allows access for the mail server but prevents anyone else inside the accounting network to access the Internet. Suppose, however, that you want to permit inside customers to access the external Web servers. In that case, the firewall can put in a rule that says that access to external boxes to port 80 is allowed. However, this leaves two problems unsolved. The first one is that many Web servers run on ports other than 80, and access to them would be denied. The second one is that a knowledgeable attacker could use a client program running on an external machine using port 80 and could connect to the machine 15.12.2.36 on port 3040. The firewall would not be able to distinguish this flow from a browser on machine 15.12.2.36 trying to access an external Web server.

The next type of firewall is one that implements filtering on the basis of connections. With this technique, you do not permit any of the boxes in the accounting network to connect directly to the Internet. All connections to the Internet must be routed to an application running at the firewall at point B. The application will allow connections that are created by clients inside the accounting network to go to the server on the Internet and will only allow data to flow back and forth on these connections. A limited set of inbound connections can also be permitted. For example, connections can be permitted to machine 15.12.2.36 on port 3040, but only if it is from a machine in the bank's domain.

In order for such an application to run, machines in the accounting department must use a protocol to tell the firewall which machines they want to connect to. The dominant standard in this area is the socks protocol [SOCKSREF]. The application in the firewall is called a socks proxy. The socks proxy is responsible for validating the legitimacy of the connection request, authenticating the client who made the connection request, and forwarding data along that connection.

In addition to connection filtering, you might need to devise other protection mechanisms. A socks proxy will not prevent all attacks. For example, someone on the Internet could try to send a carefully contrived mail message that will bring the mail server on the accounting department down, or in a worse mode, try to take over control of the mail server itself. These things can be filtered out by a special-purpose application that would be specific to mail servers and that would validate that all mail messages are well-formed and do not contain any viruses or malicious programs. Similar checks can be devised for other applications. Firewalls with safeguards designed for specific applications are usually called application-level gateways.

Cryptography and Encryption

Filtering firewalls or application-level gateways prevent specific types of traffic flows from happening. However, they do not prevent anyone from looking at the packets that are flowing into the network. The accounting department has many employees, and only some of them should be able to see the details of expense reimbursement accounts. However, nothing prevents an employee from setting up a packet snooper and looking at the details of the packets. In order to prevent it, the packets must be encrypted. Encryption and related technologies are used in many places in secure communications. This section presents a brief overview of them.

The goal of encryption is to transform the original digital message into an encrypted version that can be understood (decrypted) only by the two communicating parties. The methods to encrypt digital data can be roughly classified into two categories: those based on a shared secret (also called a private key) and those based on a public key.

When encrypting data using a *shared secret,* both parties involved in the communication have some information that can be used by the sender to encrypt the data and by the receiver to decrypt the data. A simple (but relatively easy-to-break) scheme would be to shift all the letters of a message by a known amount. For example, the sender and the receiver agree to shift all letters by 2—that is, to change all As in the message to Cs, all Bs to Ds, all Ys to As, all Zs to Bs, and so on. The message would make sense to the sender and receiver but would look like garbage to everyone else.

Practical digital encryption using a private key uses more sophisticated schemes. The *Digital Encryption Standard* (DES) is such a shared secret scheme. It involves performing a series of numerical operations, such as bitwise exclusive ORing, and shifting in a number of stages with the secret key for encryption and decryption. The shared secret information is commonly called the *key.* The key would be a long bit pattern. The number of bits in the pattern determines the difficulty in trying to decrypt the message without the key. The main issue in using shared secrets is to exchange the secret between the communicating parties in a secure manner.

In many cases, you might not want to encrypt the message. You might simply attach enough information to the message to ensure that no one has tampered with the contents of the message. Such an attachment is called a *message digest* or a *hash*. The algorithms to compute the hash functions are designed so that it is easy to compute the hash from a document but is computationally hard to generate two different documents with the same hash. Common algorithms to generate the message digest include *Message Digest 5* (MD5) and *Secure Hash Algorithm* (SHA).

A *digital signature* validates that a document originated from the sender. A hash using MD5 or SHA is computed for the document. This hash is then encrypted with a private key, and the result is included with the document. The receiver can recompute the hash and check it with the private key to validate that it was sent by the sender, the only other party who knows the secret private key. Digital signatures are also known as *Message Authentication Codes* (MACs).

In the case of public-key encryption, each party has a private key and a public key. The private key is kept secret, and the public key is made known to everyone. In order to send a secure message to the recipient, anyone can find the recipient's public key and encrypt the message with the public key. The recipient would be able to decrypt the message with the private key. Usually, the private and public keys are the inverse of each other. In other words, if a message encrypted with the private key can be decrypted with the public key, a message encrypted with the public key can be decrypted with the private key.

The most common algorithm used in public keys is the *Rivest Shamir Adleman* algorithm (RSA), named after its inventors. It is based on a public key that is the product of two large prime numbers and a private key that is the primes themselves.

Digital signatures using a public key follow a scheme similar to that in signatures formed using a private key. The sender computes a hash of the document and encrypts it using its private key. The encrypted hash is attached, along with the document as the signature. The receiver recomputes the hash and validates it with the sender's public key.

With a public key, the challenge for the sender is to ensure that the public key indeed belongs to the recipient. The public key information is often provided in the form of a digital certificate. The *digital certificate* is usually structured in a format defined by the OSI standard X.509. The digital certificate contains the identity of the recipient (name, address, and so on), the public key of the recipient, and the signature of a *certificate authority* (CA), covering the recipient's name and public key. The CA is a party whom the sender and receivers trust and whose public key is widely known.

On an intranet, a corporation can set up its own certificate authority. For communication on the Internet, two common certificate authorities are VeriSign [VERIS] and Thawte [THAWTE].

Public-key algorithms usually require more computational resources to compute than private-key algorithms. As a result, they are most commonly used to negotiate a shared secret for communication, while the actual data flow is encrypted using a private-key algorithm and the negotiated secret.

Details on DES, RSA, SHA, MD5, and many other cryptographic algorithms can be found in the book by Schneier [SCHNR].

SSL

SSL is a protocol suite commonly used to secure communications over the Internet. The SSL protocol suite operates above the transport layer (more specifically, using TCP as the transport). In most implementations, applications need to invoke the sockets library to access the transport layer functions. When using the SSL protocol, they access another library that sits on top of the native sockets library to access the transport layer.

The SSL protocol suite operates in two stages. In the first stage, the client and server authenticate each other and exchange with each other so as to establish a shared secret key that will be used to encrypt the traffic flowing between themselves. In the second stage, the actual data flow occurs. At any time during the data flow, the handshake protocol can be invoked to change the security parameters between the client and the server.

The SSL protocol suite contains two types of specifications: one that defines the format of the data records that will be exchanged, and another that defines the type of messages that will be exchanged to perform the different functions. The former is called the *SSL record protocol,* and the latter constitutes the different protocols that make up the SSL protocol suite.

Note

SSL was the name used when the technology was initially introduced by Netscape. As part of its standardization, it has been renamed *Transport Layer Security* (TLS). However, I will continue to refer to it as SSL, the name by which it is more widely known. There are subtle distinctions between TLS and SSL. These can affect interoperability, but they are too detailed to be described at the overview level I am presenting.

The SSL record protocol specifies the format of messages that are to be exchanged between the client and server. The record protocol takes messages to be transmitted, fragments the data into blocks, optionally compresses the data, includes a message hash, encrypts, and transmits the result. In its basic specification, the record protocol can carry four different types of records. Each type corresponds to one of the different protocols that make up SSL. They are as follows:

- The handshake protocol consists of an exchange of messages to establish a shared secret for communication of application data.

- The alert protocol consists of the messages that are used to notify the other party of an error or exceptional condition.

- The change cipher protocol consists of the messages exchanged by the client or server to change the shared secret or encryption parameters during communication.

- The application data protocol is used to transport the encrypted application data.

The record protocol is designed so that new types of records can easily be added to it.

The change cipher protocol consists of only one message and is used during the handshake protocol. It tells the other party that it should start using the new algorithms and keys that are negotiated during the handshake protocol.

The alert protocol consists of multiple types of messages. Each message can be sent to the other party to describe an error condition, such as if there is an error decoding a message, or if an illegal parameter was passed in a previous message.

The handshake protocol is used by the client and server to authenticate each other and to establish a shared secret, as described in the following list of steps:

1. To initiate the handshake protocol, the client sends a client hello message to which the server must respond with a server hello message, or else the connection will fail. The client hello contains a set of encryption and compression algorithms supported by the client in the order of its usage preferences and a random number. The server hello contains the algorithms that the server deems acceptable and another random number generated by the server.

2. Following the hello messages, the server sends its certificate to the client. The client can authenticate the certificate that the server sends and verify that it is indeed communicating with the intended server. The certificate contains the server's public key.

3. If the public key cannot be used to communicate the shared secret for any reason (such as if the server wants to use a stronger algorithm with longer keys), the server can send a key exchange message in which it tells the client about the public key to be used for that purpose. This key-exchange message is signed with the key contained in the certificate so that the client can validate it. At this stage, the server may also ask the client to send its certificate, which can be validated by the server.

4. The client computes a master secret using its random key and the server random key, encrypts it using the server's public key, and sends it to the server. If the server has asked for the client's certificate, the client must also provide its certificate for validation by the server.

5. At this stage, the client sends a change cipher message to the server, and the server responds with a change-cipher message. The change-cipher message tells the other party that the newly negotiated master key ought to be used.

6. The server also responds with a finished message that is encrypted using the newly computed master secret. When the client receives the change-cipher message, it also sends a finished message to the server. When the party receives the finished message, it knows that it is okay to proceed with data communication using the newly negotiated master secret.

The application data protocol is the method used to transmit the actual application data over the wire.

The Right Layer for Encryption

Security functions such as authentication and encryption can be performed at different layers. The SSL layer provides security above the transport layer, and the IPsec protocols (AH and ESP) provide it at the network layer. Standards such as S/MIME provide this function as part of the application processing. A natural question would be to compare the pros and cons of each approach.

The advantage of IPsec protocols is that they can be introduced transparently to the end applications. A machine or firewall can provide secure tunnels without modifying any applications. However, the fact that IPsec protocols do not permit source and destination addresses to be modified implies that there would be a problem dealing with devices such as network address translators. Plus, it does not work well with QoS mechanisms that depend on looking at transport header data (port numbers or higher application-level data) for their operation.

SSL and mechanisms that operate at the transport layer typically require applications to be modified to call the new transport layer. This is a hit to the application. However, SSL can pass transparently through the network address translators and poses no problem to QoS devices. Of course, the fact that transport headers are exposed makes SSL give out more information to a potential bad guy.

One issue with security protocols is that they are expensive in terms of the computing required at the machines. IPsec, which requires a kernel modification, can easily utilize hardware assistance for some of the encryption functions. SSL is written at the application level, so the platform-independent code is harder to modify for hardware assistance, but it can be done with effort.

Application-level security mechanisms provide the best assurance that true security is maintained end-to-end. However, in addition to requiring new standards and modifications to all algorithms, they are typically the hardest ones to modify to use hardware assistance for encryption.

IP Security Protocol

IPsec is similar to SSL in many ways, but it operates at the network layer rather than at the application layer [IPSEC]. Like SSL, the IPsec protocol operates in two phases. In the first phase, a master secret and set of compression/encryption algorithms are negotiated, and in the second phase, actual data flow occurs. The keys can be renegotiated at periodic intervals. However, because the protocol operates at the IP layer, the format and the types of messages exchanged are quite different from that of SSL. For a discussion of the merits of doing things at the IP layer versus the transport layer, see the preceding sidebar, "The Right Layer for Encryption."

On the Internet, there is no way for a receiver to determine if the IP packets it receives are indeed originating from the machines whose IP address is in the source field of the header. The IPsec protocol allows the receiver to authenticate the identity of the machines generating IP packets. In addition, it allows the contents of the IP packets to be encrypted so that no third party can examine the contents of the packets being exchanged on the network.

The authentication is done by means of including extra information in the IP packets. This extra information forms the authentication header that is contained in the IP packet. Similarly, the encryption is done by means of an *Encrypted Secure Payload* (ESP) header. When an ESP header is included, the contents of the IP packet are encrypted. The goal of IPsec is to create logical secure tunnels between a pair of machines. These secure tunnels are called security associations in IPsec terminology. A security association is identified by the keys and policies associated with it, so two machines can have more than one SA between them, protecting the various forms of information.

As opposed to SSL-based communication, which occurs between two applications, IPsec-based communication can occur in one of two ways. The authentication (or encryption) can occur between firewalls that protect two different sites, or it can occur between the end machines that are communicating. When IPsec protocols are used to secure communication between firewalls, they use an extra layer of IP headers to include the authentication information. As an example, consider a packet flowing from machine A to machine B over an insecure network, as shown in Figure 2.8. Part of the network from machine A to firewall C is considered secure. The packet flows on a secure IP tunnel established between the firewall at C and B. The IP packet generated by machine A includes the original IP header and the data payload. When firewall C receives the packet, it includes the IPsec headers (either AH or ESP). It then puts the IPsec header and the original IP packet into an extra IP header that is sent to destination B. When IPsec headers are carried inside an additional IP header, they are said to be in tunnel mode. The tunnel mode with an additional IP header is useful when the packets are encrypted/authenticated at points different than the source or destination carried in the original IP header. The extra IP header can be used to route packets to a firewall which can decrypt/authenticate the packet and forward the inner IP packet to the original destination.

Figure 2.8   Tunnel and Transport Modes of IPsec

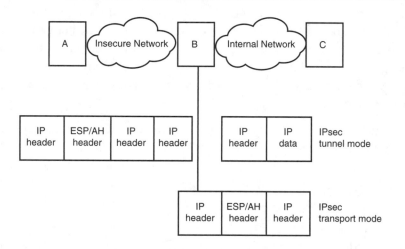

There could be cases where machine A might want to implement its own IPsec functions rather than relying on firewall C. This was done by machine B in the example just cited. In that case, the inclusion of a second IP header is not necessary. The originating machine A can simply include the AH or ESP header along with the data payload in the original IP header. In this case, IPsec headers are said to be carried in transport mode. Basically, IPsec is acting as a transport protocol between the TCP/UDP protocols and the IP protocol.

The IP authentication header consists of five main fields:

- The payload length indicates the length of the AH header.

- The next protocol indicates what type of protocol follows the AH header. This would be IP in tunnel mode and the original transport (TCP/UDP) header in transport mode.

- The Security Parameter Index identifies the security association that is to be used for this packet.

- A sequence number field is a count of packets transmitted by the sender of the security association to the receiver.

- Authentication data consists of a MAC over the original payload. This validates the contents of the payload.

The sequence number is used to guard against someone's collecting traces of IP packets and replaying them later. These messages would pass the authentication codes. Sequence numbers always begin at 0 for a new tunnel and are not supposed to wrap (that is, repeat starting from 0). Every new packet increments the sequence number by 1. If a sequence number wraps, the sender and receiver exchange a message to reset the sequence number. Each receiver at the end of an AH tunnel (or security association) maintains a window of valid sequence numbers that it would receive. The window is updated on every packet received, and duplicate packets are discarded.

AH authentication is performed over selected fields of the original IP header. Fields that change as part of normal IP processing, such as Time to Live, are assumed to be 0 when the AH MAC is computed.

When ESP is used to protect an IP packet, the contents of the IP packet consist of the following fields (in addition to the external IP header):

- The Security Parameter Index identifies the security association for the packet.

- A sequence number field operates in the same manner as for AH.

- The payload data consists of the encrypted version of the original packet (tunnel mode) or the original IP payload data (transport mode).

- Padding bytes are needed to make the encrypted version a multiple of block sizes over which encryption algorithms are performed.

- The length of the padding bytes.

- The next protocol header would be IP in tunnel mode and the original transport (TCP/UDP) header in transport mode.

- Authentication data consists of a digital signature over the rest of the ESP header.

Further details can be found in the RFCs for the authentication header [IPAUTH] and the ESP [IPESP].

The security associations on which packets using the AH or ESP header are transported are established using the *Internet Key Exchange* (IKE) protocol [IKE].

Internet Key Exchange

The Internet Key Exchange protocol is used to establish the security associations needed for IPsec-based communication. IKE is based on a combination of a general purpose key management protocol [ISAKMP] with specific types of message exchanges defined in [OAKLEY]. IKE operates in two phases.

In the first phase, two entities (such as two firewalls) authenticate each other and agree on how to protect further negotiation traffic between themselves, establishing a security association between themselves, which is then used to protect further IKE traffic. The second phase of negotiation is used to establish security associations for security protocols, such as for AH traffic or ESP.

Let's take the situation of two firewalls that want to communicate securely. They first exchange messages using IKE protocol to establish a security association. This set of message exchanges follows IKE phase 1 specifications. During this exchange, they authenticate each other's identity. After the security association is established, they use this secure communication channel to negotiate parameters for a new security association. The exchanges for establishing the new security association follow the IKE phase 2 exchange specification. This newly established association is then used for communication using the AH or ESP protocol.

There are three distinct methods of authentication in phase 1 of IKE:

- Authentication with preshared keys

- Authentication with digital signatures

- Two methods of authentication using public key encryption

One of the firewalls (or machines) must initiate the exchange. This firewall is called the initiator, and the other firewall is called the responder. The initiator sends a message to the responder that contains a proposal for different encryption algorithms that can be used to establish the phase 1 tunnel. The proposal consists of many groups, each of which contains items such as encryption algorithms, hashing algorithms, authentication methods, and the maximum number of bytes or the maximum time a generated key would be used for. The responder selects one of these proposed groups and sends it as a counterproposal back to the initiator. After the set of algorithms is determined, the initiator sends back a message containing a random number and a key exchange message that contains some information related to how the keys for secure communications should be generated. The responder sends back a message with another random number and similar information for key generation. The third message sent by the initiator to the responder is encrypted and includes the security parameters for the IKE phase 1 security association. Depending on the authentication method, this message can include the initiator's digital certificate. The responder sends an encrypted response back for this message, and the phase 1 security association is established after the six message exchanges.

The six message exchanges comprise what is known as the *main mode* for IKE negotiation. It is possible to reduce the message exchange to four for this negotiation. When four messages rather than six are used for IKE negotiation, this is referred to as the *aggressive* mode.

On phase 2 security negotiations, the negotiation used is called *quick* mode. The message for quick mode negotiation flows on the phase 1 security association. Either of the two nodes involved in the phase 1 security association can initiate the phase 2 negotiation. The initiator's message contains a number of proposals for establishing a secure phase 2 connection, and the responder selects the ones that it finds acceptable or most appropriate for it. After receiving the response, the initiator sends a confirming message to the responder. All the exchanges are encrypted because they travel on the phase 1 security association.

Other Security Protocols

In addition to the SSL and IPsec protocols, various other mechanisms can be used to provide security in an IP environment. Some applications, such as electronic mail, have a method by which the contents of a mail message can be encrypted. These encrypted messages can be carried in a standard mail environment using S/MIME encoding.

Other protocols provide secure tunneling across different insecure networks to a point across the network. An example of such a protocol is L2TP. It provides a method by which a dial-in user can access a remote firewall securely.

Another key aspect of security is authentication. A variety of authentication techniques are found in the networked environment. These range from simple password-based mechanisms to more complex schemes based on digital certificates. They are described in most books on Internet security.

Further Information

I have provided a very broad overview of TCP/IP networks. An excellent detailed overview of the architecture can be found in a series of books by Comer [COMER]. A good general overview of network protocol and architecture can be found in the text by Tannenbaum [TANNEN].

There are also a few books written explicitly on the topic of QoS in the network. A good overview of QoS approaches using RSVP is given by Ferguson [FERGUSON]. A book describing DiffServ in detail [KILKKI] is also available. Other books discussing QoS include ones by Armitage [ARMI] and by Iseminger[ISEM].

Several excellent books describe the issue of network security and the different security protocols. The book by Cheswick and Bellovin [CHESWICK] is considered a classic in the field of Internet security. Similarly, the book by Schneir on cryptography [SCHNR] provides very good coverage of cryptography and various algorithms such as RSA, SHA, and DES. Information about SSL (or rather its standardized version) can be obtained [TLSREF].

I have mostly concentrated on IP version 4, which is the one most commonly deployed in current networks. A newer specification of IP, version 6, is also available. It addresses many of the issues with the current version of IP. Both RSVP and DiffServ can be used with IPv6 networks. More information on IPv6 can be found in the books by Thomas [THOMAS] or Loshin [LOSHIN].

3

The Generic Provisioning Problem

Chapter 2, "IP Architecture Overview," looked at some of the technologies and standards that are being developed within the Internet community. However, the deployment of these technologies is usually a complex and difficult undertaking. The rollout of the technology within a network requires configuring the different devices within the network that support those technologies. Policy-based techniques can help alleviate the management issues associated with the rollout of these technologies.

The configuration and provisioning of new technologies is complex for a variety of reasons. One of the challenges is that deployment requires configuring a large number of devices in a typical-sized network. Another challenge is that the technologies are often developed without adequate attention to the issues of management and deployment. As a result, there is often a mismatch between the technology specifications and the reason a network operator might want to deploy a given technology within the network.

The administrators and operators of most networks do not want to deploy technology for the sake of the technology. Very few enterprise CIOs would choose to deploy Differentiated Services within their network just because it has been standardized or because it is readily available from the different router/server vendors. The reason for deploying any technology is to satisfy a business need. For example, if a CIO determines that it needs to satisfy a network performance SLA put in place for an important customer, and Differentiated Services is the best approach to satisfy that SLA, the CIO might choose to deploy the relevant technology within the enterprise.

As described in Chapter 1, "Policy-Enabled Networking Architecture," there are two types of policies: high-level (operator view) and low-level (device view). The business needs of the deployers drive the high-level policy definitions, and the details of the technology drive the low-level policy definition. A policy management tool bridges the gap between the two views and simplifies the job of technology deployment. This chapter takes a closer look at the high-level and low-level policies that can be used in different types of network environments.

The organization of this chapter can be explained through the policy application matrix shown in Figure 3.1. The vertical axis of the matrix shows the different business needs that can arise in the various types of network environments. The horizontal axis shows the different technologies that can be used to satisfy these business needs. A shaded box indicates that the corresponding technology can be used to satisfy the matching business needs within a specific environment. Not all technologies are appropriate for each business need, and the ones that are not suitably matched have an X. An overview of the technologies shown on the horizontal axis is provided in Chapter 2.

The reader must keep in mind that the entries in Figure 3.1 are shown mainly for the purpose of illustration. In any organization, one may find business needs that are not captured by the items shown on the vertical axis. Similarly, in certain cases, some of the business needs may be better satisfied by mapping to a technology that is different from the one shown in Figure 3.1. As an example, an *Application Service Provider* (ASP) may want to have a business SLA covering privacy and security needs of its customers. In this case, SSL would be useful for satisfying these SLAs, even though it is not shown as an appropriate technology in the figure.

Figure 3.1   Policy Application Matrix

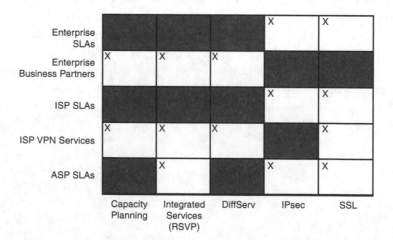

The next section of this chapter takes a closer look at three different types of network environments that are common in current IP-based networks. Then I will describe the two axes of the policy application matrix. Specifically, I will discuss the high-level policies that are most appropriate for the business needs of the different network environments. After that, I will describe the low-level policies that are appropriate for each of the technologies that can be used to satisfy those business needs. Finally, I will describe the structure of a generic policy management tool that can be used to map the policy representation along the vertical axis into the policy representation along the horizontal axis.

This chapter focuses on the generic principles that can be exploited to build a policy management tool. The details of how a technology can be used to satisfy the various business needs are described in Chapter 4, "Technology Support for Business Needs."

Business Environments

The high-level policies within the network reflect the business needs that motivate the deployment of a specific technology. An organization's business needs include items such as the services it provides to its customers, its internal requirements for smooth operation, or compliance with any regulatory or legal statutes that might apply to that organization.

The business needs of each organization depend on the organization's nature and characteristics. In order to study these business needs, we will look at three types of organizations, each with a different set of networking needs: an enterprise, a networking services provider, and an application hosting services provider. The enterprise environment is a corporation with its own network and computational infrastructure. The networking services provider, an *Internet service provider* (ISP), offers network connectivity services to its customers. The application hosting services provider hosts applications, such as Web sites or mail servers for its customers.

This section describes the different business environments in more detail. The following section examines their business needs.

The Enterprise Environment

The enterprise environment represents the typical network of a large corporation. Such a corporation typically has many branches that could be geographically separated by large distances. Depending on the size of the enterprise, the branches might be a few miles away, or they could be distributed across the globe.

Such an enterprise is typically managed by an IT department, which is responsible for the operation of the networking and computing infrastructure. The IT department needs to operate the network at required performance levels and enforce adequate security in networked communication. The management and operation of such a network can benefit tremendously from a policy-based approach.

A typical enterprise environment consists of several local campus networks that are connected by a WAN. Campus networks typically are based on LAN technologies, such as Ethernet, Gigabit Ethernet, FDDI, and token ring. Each LAN connects to the WAN by means of one or more access routers. The WAN typically consists of leased lines obtained by the enterprise from a telecommunications company or an ISP. Such an environment is shown in Figure 3.2.

Figure 3.2   Enterprise Environment

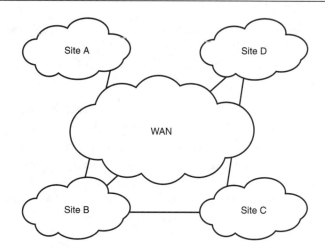

In most cases, the enterprise has adequate bandwidth on the LANs for its purposes. Current LAN technologies are cheap enough to offer gigabits of local bandwidth at relatively low costs. Even at the relatively old technologies of ethernets operating at 10Mbps and token rings operating at 16Mbps, LAN bandwidth is an order of magnitude faster than access links to WAN, which are predominantly T1 (1.5Mbps) links. New technologies of Fast Ethernet and Gigabit Ethernet are significantly faster than T3 access links (45Mbps), which are becoming more widespread.

The reasons that deployed LANs are significantly faster than wide-area access links are most likely business-related rather than technical. There is no technical reason why a wide-area link can't be as fast as or faster than a LAN. Speeds in excess of 1Gbps can be achieved quite readily over optical fiber. However, the cost of operating a LAN is significantly different from the cost of operating a wide-area link.

The installation of a LAN is dominated by a one-time lump-sum cost associated with the purchase of equipment and any building infrastructure updates that might be needed. Although this cost might be a substantial one-time expense, relatively few recurring monthly costs are associated with LAN bandwidth. Amortized over the typical life span of a building LAN (which is usually a few years), the cost per unit of bandwidth per month of LAN is fairly small. However, wide-area access links are available only through the telecommunication companies and are priced on a monthly basis, which easily dwarfs the expenses associated with the one-time equipment installation costs over one year. Unless there are fundamental shifts in the way wide-area links are priced, it is safe to assume that the bottlenecks associated with network communications are more likely to be in the WAN rather than the LAN.

As far as security, different corporations vary widely in the trust model that exists among campuses in the enterprise network. Most companies tend to have an open internal access approach, whereby almost anyone can have network connectivity (such as being able to ping the computer) to any computer on the internal corporation network. This is not to say that access controls at the application layer are not needed. In most companies, files and documents should be given only to those employees who really need them. However, no firewalls or other network-layer security devices are commonly deployed between the different departments.

Enterprise networks do have to contend with a different type of security issue. There is an increasing need for employees to gain remote access to the company's network from external locations. In many cases, the external location is the residence of an employee working from home. However, there might be employees who are accessing the network from their hotel rooms or over the Internet. Their access needs to be supported as well.

It is in the backdrop of such an enterprise that we will look at the requirement for the high-level and low-level policies necessary to manage the performance and security of an enterprise network. The high-level policies need to be defined in terms of functions that are used in daily operations of the companies, and the low-level policies need to be defined in terms of the technology deployed within the network (such as configuration of access server and routers).

The Network Services Provider (ISP) Environment

The network services provider is an organization that operates a network on behalf of its customers. I refer to such an organization as an ISP because many Internet service providers essentially offer such a service to their customers. Examples of some companies that provide network connectivity are UUNET, Sprint, and AT&T Global Networks. These companies offer WAN connectivity to their customers.

A simplified view of the computer network environment for a typical network provider is shown in Figure 3.3.

Figure 3.3   A Typical ISP Network

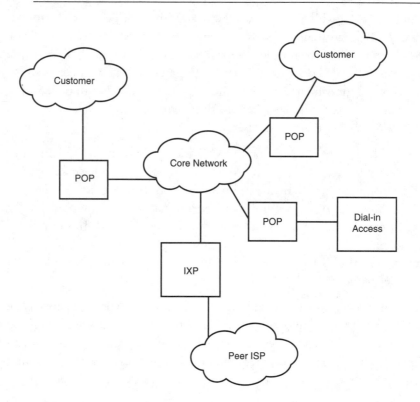

The oval shown as the core network is the domain of a single network operator or ISP. An ISP would have multiple *points of presence* (POPs) at various cities. The POPs are sites that could be used to access the ISP network. Customers may connect to POPs using leased lines or dial-up lines. Dial-up access requires modem banks that terminate in a local office of the ISP and are connected to the POP using high-speed links (typically T1). For access to other customers, the ISP may place a router on the customer's premises (CSR: Customer Site Router) and connect it to the POP using a metropolitan-area network or a leased line. In addition to the POPs, the ISP needs to partner with other peer ISPs in order to connect to the Internet. These peering points are known as *Internet Exchange Points* (IXPs). An IXP can connect a regional ISP to a national ISP or act as conduit among several ISP networks. Different ISPs have peering agreements among themselves as to which traffic they will accept from other ISPs at an IXP. Very large service providers also have private peering arrangements with each other.

> **Note**
>
> An exchange point is also known by several names other than IXP. Common equivalent terms include NAP (Network Access Point), MAE (Metropolitan Area Exchange), and FIX (Federal Internet Exchange).

The POPs and IXPs supported by the ISP are interconnected by its core network. The ISP's core network consists of several routers connected by means of high-bandwidth circuits that may be owned by the ISP or leased from other bandwidth vendors.

> **Note**
>
> The public Internet consists of all the ISP networks and the different servers provided by the ISPs or their customers. The IXPs provide the gateways by which a user on an ISP network can access servers provided by a customer of a different ISP.

The Application Hosting Provider Environment

An *application hosting provider* is a company that hosts and supports different types of servers on behalf of their customers. Such companies are commonly referred to as *Application Services Providers* (ASP), which is the acronym I will use in this book. The most common of these providers are Web-hosting companies that provide servers to operate Web sites for individual companies. Examples of such companies are Exodus and IBM Global Services. Exodus primarily provides location services to its customers. For example, it offers space and power supplies to its customers close to one of the major ISP's exchange points. IBM Global Services offers a more comprehensive service, which includes ensuring that the applications and services are up and available. In addition to these major players, many small companies provide services for hosting Web sites as well as Lotus Notes database servers. In 1999, Intel announced a move into a similar business with a plan to open large application-hosting locations.

The most common type of servers outsourced for support and operations are Web servers. However, it is also common to find other types of application servers being hosted. Typical types of application services that are hosted are Web servers, electronic commerce transaction servers, mail servers, groupware servers, and directory servers.

Figure 3.4 shows a simplified configuration of a hosted site. It shows the service provider accessing the Internet through one access router. The access router is typically followed by a firewall that restricts public access from the Internet to only the servers that are intended for this access. The firewall also prevents denial-of-service attacks and otherwise validates access to the server farm. The figure shows two customers, of which Customer 2 has the simpler configuration. Each customer has its own separate LAN on the premises to which a number of servers are attached. Each customer might also have a back-end connection to this LAN through a firewall to one of the customer's intranet campuses. This connectivity is provided so that the customer can administer or update the applications running on its servers. Customer 1 has a somewhat more complex configuration that involves a load balancer. The load balancer is a device that can spray connection requests across multiple machines running the same applications. Several such types of load balancers are available on the market. This customer also has a back-end connection to its intranet for the sake of easy administration.

Figure 3.4   A Simplified Model of an Application Hosting Environment

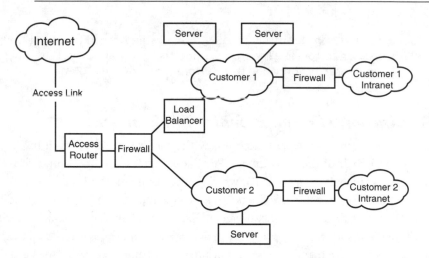

In this figure, many variations are possible. Instead of a dedicated connection to the customer's intranet campus, the connectivity might be via a secure VPN over the Internet connection. Similarly, the figure shows a firewall insulating the customers from the Internet as well as from each other. In practice, you might have multiple layers of firewalls. For example, one layer might protect the customers from the Internet, and the other layer protects the customers from each other. Layering firewalls in this manner simplifies the filtering rules to be configured at each layer and helps in checking inadvertent security loopholes. Other variations might include replicating many of the functions, such as access routers and firewalls, in order to ensure some level of tolerance of failures of individual boxes.

High-Level Policies

Within each of the environments described in the previous sections, different types of business needs motivate the deployment of the different technologies. This section looks at some of the business needs that can arise in each of the different environments.

The Enterprise Environment

Within the enterprise environment, the most common needs are that of satisfying the business SLAs that exist between the different parts of the enterprise. For security purposes, an enterprise might need to ensure that access to its network is secure and is accessible only to the employees or other entities that are authorized to have access to specific enterprise resources.

Note

These business needs in this section are intended as illustrative examples for use in subsequent chapters of the book. These examples are not intended as an exhaustive enumeration of all the business needs that can arise in the enterprise environments.

Business SLAs

It is a common practice in many business organizations to have SLAs in place among their different divisions. An SLA is an explicit statement of the expectations and obligations that exist in business relationships between a service provider and its customer [SLAREF]. In the case of an enterprise, the SLA defines the details of the services that an IT department in an enterprise is expected to provide to the other departments that use the computing/networking infrastructure.

Many enterprises choose to outsource the operation and maintenance of their computing infrastructure to another company. This is often the case when the enterprise does not consider running and operating a computer network to be its core skill. The subcontracting company is usually responsible for satisfying an SLA that specifies the performance objectives that are expected from the other company.

An SLA typically contains the following:

- Description of the type and nature of service to be provided

- Expected performance level of the service

- Process for reporting problems with the service

- Time frame within which a response or resolution of a reported problem is expected

- Process for monitoring and reporting the service level

- Credits, charges, or other consequences for the service provider in not meeting its obligation

- If applicable, any escape clauses describing the conditions under which the SLA might not be valid

Although a significant part of the SLA deals with business aspects, such as the process for reporting problems, service-level compliance, the terms of credits, or escape clauses, I will focus more on the technical aspects of SLAs, such as how you meet the performance objectives outlined in the SLA.

Note

As a matter of terminology, some organizations differentiate between an SLA and an SLO (Service-Level Objective). The SLA refers to the overall business agreement and consists of multiple SLOs that need to be satisfied. One of these SLOs is a performance objective that must be satisfied.

A service's expected performance level has two major aspects: reliability and responsiveness. *Reliability* includes availability requirements, such as when the service is available and what bounds on service outages may be expected. *Responsiveness* includes how soon the service would be performed in the normal course of operations. In the context of a computer network, reliability is usually measured in the network's uptime, and responsiveness is measured as bounds on round-trip delays between two customer sites. In order to meet its SLA, the operator of an enterprise network needs to ensure that applications running on the network are available and are performing at the desired level for the target.

The goal for an enterprise IT networking provider is to ensure that the applications supported by to it have a performance that is good enough to meet specific response-time criteria. The performance would be the end-to-end response time of the applications running in the enterprise network.

Chapter 4 describes how business SLAs can be supported effectively by technologies such as capacity planning, Integrated Services, and Differentiated Services.

Extranets

Although the security needs of many enterprises are quite diverse, we will look at a security scenario that often arises in an enterprise environment. This scenario relates to the provisioning and configuring of extranets among different enterprises.

In an era where all enterprises are connected to the Internet, there are many reasons to move many common business-to-business functions to an Internet-based infrastructure. For example, a company might require that its suppliers conduct business with it electronically. Consider a soft drink bottling company that needs to procure various types of containers from its suppliers. Examples of such containers include plastic bottles, metal cans, and glass bottles. A large bottling company typically procures the containers from a variety of suppliers. Other items supplied by a contractor include labels, bottlecaps, and distilled water. Different bottling plants that are located in different geographic locations might have requirements for different quantities of each type of container or other supplies.

When the bottling company wants to obtain the containers or other supplies, it typically sends a bid out to its list of approved suppliers, who send back quotes and terms for providing the supplies. The bids might be accepted by the company according to a variety of criteria. Although this negotiation is typically done via paper contracts in a traditional fashion, the cost savings that can be realized by migrating the process to an electronic one are significant.

One of the ways in which this system can be realized is by having a bidding server that runs an application that manages the bids received for any specific component, such as containers. The bidding server would be placed so that it is accessible to the suppliers contracted by the company over the Internet. However, for security purposes, the bidding server must be accessible to only a selected subset of suppliers through the Internet.

Such an extranet can be supported and established using the network-level mechanisms of *Internet Key Exchange* (IKE) as well as the transport-level mechanisms of SSL or TLS. The details of how to exploit these technologies to support the notion of extranets are described in Chapter 4.

The Network Connectivity Provider

Within the context of the network connectivity provider, we will look at the business needs of supporting business SLAs and the creation of a VPN service.

Business SLAs

In the networking services provider environment, customers may use the ISP network in one of the three manners:

- To access the Internet
- To interconnect two or more of its sites
- To access proprietary, industry-specific networks

Most customers in the real world probably want to do a combination of these methods. One of the business objectives of any ISP is to support the communication needs of its customers at a reasonable performance level. These target performance levels are often specified as part of an SLA between the customer and the service provider.

When a customer uses the ISP to connect two or more of its sites, SLAs can be defined to ensure some performance level on the network communication between the pair of access routers that connect those two sites. When accessing the Internet, the customer is present at one of the access routers but can communicate with any of the IXPs in the network. The end objective of the customer communication on the Internet is quite likely to be outside the administrative domain of the ISP. Although the ISP cannot honestly offer any assurances about the performance level of the network outside its domain, it can provide some assurances about the performance of the communication within its own domain.

The SLAs provided to the customer are often specified in terms of the delays that can be provided among the different access points within the ISP network. For example, the ISP might provide connectivity among two private campuses of its customer. It might offer an assurance about the maximum latency a packet would experience in the network between the two campuses. An example of such an SLA is the one offered by UUNET to its customers with leased-line access [UUNETSLA].

Another common performance metric used within SLAs relates to the maximum amount of bandwidth than an ISP will accept from the customer for transport across the network. The ISP promises to transfer the specified amount of bandwidth across its network without a significant loss rate.

The terms specified in the SLA might be the same for all the customers, or they might be different for different customers. The former is the more prevalent case in most ISP environments. However, there are many cases where the SLAs would be defined differently for different customers. A customer trying to distribute real-time stock quotes over the network is likely to demand tighter bounds on network latency from its ISP than a customer dealing primarily with storing and forwarding electronic mail.

As in the case of the enterprise environment, the SLAs within the network may be supported by a variety of techniques, including traffic capacity planning, rate control devices, or the deployment of Differentiated Services.

Virtual Private Networks

The most attractive customers for an ISP are enterprises that need to interconnect their campuses. Quite often, these enterprises have their own private network—their intranet. A typical enterprise network (such as the one shown in Figure 3.2) consists of several campuses with their individual LANs and a WAN connecting the campuses. The WAN usually consists of serial links, such as T1 or T3 links, or where bandwidth demands are not that intense—56Kbps dialed or leased lines. Other techniques used for WAN connectivity are frame relay and ATM connectivity services, which gained popularity in the 1990s. You typically run routers where the IP protocol treats the underlying frame relay or ATM links as a lower-layer protocol. The cost of leasing the links with the right bandwidth is usually the most important factor in the cost of operating the private network.

Because of the growing popularity of the Internet, most enterprise campuses (at least the large ones) are connected to the Internet. The Internet is an open IP network that connects a large part of the world. This results in any pair of enterprise campuses having two paths between themselves—one through the WAN that forms the corporate intranet, and the other one through the Internet. Of course, the intranet path is more secure than the open Internet and is also likely to have much better performance characteristics. As a result, most large corporations maintain their own private corporate networks.

To the ISPs that provide Internet-based connectivity to the enterprise corporations, the emerging scenario provides an attractive option to provide virtual private networks. An ISP can give an enterprise customer the option of eliminating its intranet and replacing it with a virtual network that has comparable performance and security. Such an offering is the *virtual private network* (VPN).

A VPN provides logical connectivity among the different sites of an enterprise while insulating them from each other. Basically, only the sites involved in the VPN should be allowed to communicate with each other. The only exception to this rule is that every campus needs access to the public Internet through some security device, such as a firewall.

The cheapest VPN is obtained if the campus sites simply connect to the Internet and use encrypted tunnels to carry their traffic across the Internet. However, given the wide variety of threats that exist on the open network, as well as the wide performance fluctuations, it is much more likely that the VPN service would be offered on a private network physically separate from the one that the ISP uses for Internet connectivity. A customer network would get access to both the Internet and the ISP-private network. Several customers would be multiplexed to the ISP-private network. This would reduce the overall cost to the ISP of maintaining its network. The ISP would also be able to offer VPN access to the customer at a reduced cost instead of the customer's having an intranet.

Such a scenario is shown in Figure 3.5. An ISP offers VPN services to two customer enterprises on an ISP-private network. The first customer (Customer A) has three sites connected to the network. The second customer (Customer B) has two sites connected to the network. The ISP connects to other peer ISPs at an exchange point, but it typically supports the private connections from the customers within its own network. The customer sites are connected to both the ISP-private network and through firewalls to the ISP-public network. The firewalls connecting the customers to the Internet typically belong to the customer. At the access routers connecting the customer to the ISP-private network, the ISP has the onus of making sure that the customers are protected from each other. For the sake of brevity, the figure shows access routers and firewalls only at the first campus of both customers. It's implied that a similar structure needs to be in place at each campus.

Figure 3.5   A VPN Deployment Scenario

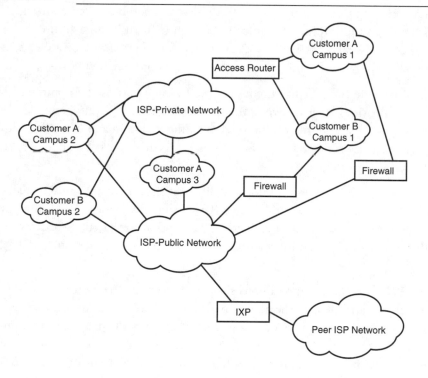

The high-level policies for deployment—in this case, for the ISP—would be to define the proper set of VPNs and to enable access among its customers in the environment shown in Figure 3.5. Such a solution may be obtained by using IKE and IPsec-based encrypted communication.

Application-Hosting Provider Environment

Within the ASP environment, we will look at the problem of supporting business SLAs and access control as examples of business needs.

Business SLAs

In an application-hosting environment, a service provider can provide its customers with assurances about the availability and reliability of its hosting service. Most service providers promise a 24×7 uptime. In other words, the sites and systems are always operational. From a performance perspective, the application-hosting service provider needs to ensure that the service is running properly and adequately. The service provider also needs to provide SLAs regarding the performance of the applications that will be hosted on the site.

The SLA between the service provider and the hosted customer can be defined in many ways. The simplest and most intuitive way to specify the performance would be to define a response time for a hosted application. The system's response time depends on a variety of factors, including the application design as well as the amount of load in the system. The goal of an application-hosting provider is to ensure that the application operates with specific response targets.

Note that the response target for an application is different from the end-to-end response time that a user of the application service might see. The application-hosting provider has no control over the network that is used to access the application. The network, if congested, can degrade the throughput and end-user response time significantly. However, the application-hosting provider can provide assurance on the part of the server reaction time, which is the time that elapses between the arrival of a request and the beginning of the servicing of the request by the server.

A more typical SLA in the service provider environment might provide the hosted customer with limits on the network bandwidth or server capacity that the customer can use. The limits on network bandwidth can be specified in terms of the absolute bandwidth required, offering a specific customer a slice of bandwidth that connects the application hosting provider site to the Internet. Such an SLA might specify that a customer will receive a performance equivalent to the performance it would have received if it has a dedicated leased line of equivalent bandwidth. Similar rates can also be specified on the connection rates that are supported by the server.

The two most important factors comprising service provider SLAs are the total amount of access bandwidth and the server capacity (the rate of connections that the site can support) allocated to a customer. The fulfillment of business SLAs by an ASP typically involves allocating adequate amounts of these two resources to different customers.

Access Control

From a security perspective, the most complex task of a service provider is to manage the many different types of firewalls that typically exist in a server farm environment. These various firewalls are required to protect the different parts of the server farm from each other. Here are the security functions that need to be implemented in a server farm:

- Protect the customer's applications from hackers on the Internet

- Protect the different customers from each other

- Secure each customer's access into his or her network

- Secure the administration and management applications within the server farm from the customers

These functions are usually implemented in different firewalls. The goal of these multiple firewalls is to ensure that each customer has the right access to its own part of the server farm. Therefore, the best representation of the security policies in the server farm is provided by specifying each customer and the section of the ASP network that it is allowed to access.

Low-Level Policies

The different business needs outlined in the preceding section are satisfied by a variety of techniques. Many of these techniques can be used interchangeably. The choice of scheme depends on the specifics of the particular environment.

In order to support business SLAs, you can follow the approaches of capacity planning, Differentiated Services, or Integrated Services.

The basic idea behind supporting SLAs using capacity planning is fairly simple: Provide enough link bandwidth and processing capacity that the SLA requirements are satisfied. If an SLA is feasible at all (if it can be met on an unloaded network with unloaded servers), it should be possible to determine the link bandwidth and processing capacity that satisfied the performance objectives under normal operating environments. When the appropriate network has been designed, it can be operated as a best-effort network. Of course, the network needs to be monitored to ensure that the SLAs are being complied with.

There are many cases in which capacity planning might not be adequate. An example is the case in which loads on the network are not readily predictable or show a sudden spurt of growth. Situations in which capacity planning has failed are quite common on the

Internet, where many companies have launched an advertising campaign or hosted an event that caused their servers to become overwhelmed. In these cases, QoS techniques can help ensure that the performance of a subset of the users in the network can be maintained.

As described in Chapter 2, there are two main approaches to support QoS in IP networks—Integrated Services/RSVP and Differentiated Services. The RSVP approach can be loosely described as a signaled approach, and DiffServ is a provisioned multiclass approach. In a signaled approach, applications communicate (or signal) their QoS requirements to the network routers and remote workstations. Each router that is signaled reserves enough local resources (link bandwidth or buffer space) to support the application's QoS requirements. The other approach is to support multiple preprovisioned and differentiated classes of service in the network. These multiple classes are provisioned so as to deliver different levels of average performance. Different service classes have different expectations of average network delays and loss rates. With the provisioned multiclass approach, the network decides to map an application's packet flow into one of these preprovisioned differentiated classes of service and schedules them appropriately. A subset of Differentiated Services capabilities can also be used to provide rate control within the networks. Rate control devices can also be used to effectively control SLAs within the network.

In order to support the security needs in the different environments, you can use the protocols associated with IPsec or use the analogous transport layer scheme of SSL. Both of these technologies were described in Chapter 2. Either of these approaches can be used to support the different security needs within the different environments.

The next few sections take a closer look at the policy requirements of the different devices within each of the technologies.

Policy Issues with IntServ

The main issue with policy in an integrated services network is to try to answer these questions:

- Who is entitled to signal a reservation request using RSVP?

- Which requests should be honored by a router, and which ones should be rejected?

Because QoS mechanisms are intended to provide an assured performance level for a set of specific applications, their goal is to provide preferential treatment to those applications. These applications can obtain the desired performance by means of reservation. However, nothing prevents other applications in the network from invoking RSVP to reserve bandwidth to improve their own performance. Any application can signal that resources be reserved for it. If no internal charge-back is associated with any reservation, there is no incentive to not ask for the maximum possible reservation that you can extract from the network. Obviously, a free-for-all reservation architecture is not likely to perform any better than a best-effort service. It can even perform worse. A user who is relatively sloppy at ending reservations might hog a large amount of bandwidth and never give any of it up.

The policy control module in RSVP decides who should be allowed to make reservations and also limits the number and duration of reservations that can be made. When reservation requests are received by the routers, they check the policy control module to ensure that the reservation should be honored. Thus, an enterprise can allow only reservations invoked by some key applications to succeed. Furthermore, it can also determine the amount of bandwidth that should be reserved by each flow belonging to the particular application.

Some routers in the network might not be capable of making policy decisions on their own. In that case, the routers can obtain policy decisions from an external policy server using a protocol called COPS.

When signaling for the reservation using the PATH message or RESV message, the endpoints involved in an RSVP flow can include a policy object as part of the message. This policy object can (among other things) identify the user, organization, or application requesting the reservation. The policy server can thereby enforce policy decisions at various levels of granularity.

Policy decisions can prevent someone from hogging resources or allow reservations to be made only by specific applications that are considered business-critical.

Policy Issues with DiffServ

A DiffServ network consists of two types of boxes—access routers and core routers. The access routers classify the various packets depending on the contents of the packet headers. This classification is marked into the DiffServ field of the IP header. An access router must know the rules which determine how different packets should be marked.

In addition to the marking, DiffServ access routers also can implement various types of rate control, limiting the amount of network bandwidth to be used by a particular type of traffic to specific limits. The policy definition for an access router needs to specify any such limits if they exist.

The core routers interpret the DiffServ field according to the set of PHBs defined for them. Thus, the policy definition for core routers must specify the type of queuing behavior that corresponds to different packet markings. Such a behavior can indicate the queuing priorities of the different network devices, as well as the rate limits or bandwidth shares that can be allocated to the different classes of traffic.

With the availability of any level of differentiation, you have to decide who or what gets which class of service. The answer to this question constitutes policy in DiffServ networks. In order to manage the performance of a DiffServ network, you must obtain the configuration information for all the DiffServ access routers so that the classifiers and rate controllers at DiffServ boundaries can be managed to meet expectations. Similarly, the core routers that make up a DiffServ network must be configured to have the correct configuration corresponding to that of different applications.

Communication in any network is bidirectional, and improving the quality of communication requires improving performance in both directions. Thus, trying to improve the performance of a specific application session would require configuring at least two access routers (plus the core routers that lie along the path). Coordinating a consistent configuration of multiple access routers is not a trivial task. The goal of the policy management tools described in Chapter 5, "Resource Discovery," is to ensure such a consistent configuration in the various network configurations.

Policies and Device Configuration

There is a subtle but important distinction which needs to be made between the notion of a device configuration and the low-level policies associated with a technology. The low-level policy definition for DiffServ consists of the rules that determine the behavior of the network and devices in a manner that is independent of the details of a specific device. These rules are represented in a format that can be understood and interpreted by any of the devices within the network. As an example, such policies may be represented in an LDAP directory using a commonly accepted schema. Also, these policies may be specified for a group of devices (or for the entire network), rather than for each device individually.

Corresponding to the policy specification, each device can generate its configuration which implements the set of policies which are relevant to it. The semantics of the configuration must match the semantics of the low level policies.

Thus, there are two important differences between the low-level policies and device configuration: representation, for example, where policies are represented in a device-independent manner; and scope, for example, where policies are applicable to more than one device.

This book discusses an application of the policy technology, namely how to get all the devices in a network configured in order to meet some high level goals. The primary use of low level policies for this application is generating the device configuration. As a result, the line between device configuration and low level policies may appear blurry at times, but the reader should keep in mind that the two are different.

Policy Issues with Servers

Providing adequate performance within any environment depends on ensuring that performance is assured on all parts of a system, including the clients, the network, and the servers. Thus, when QoS features are being used within the network, they need to be augmented by similar functions within the servers. In some specific environments, such as the ASP environment, server controls might be more important than network controls.

If the server operating system supports any notion of different levels of service offered to different applications, that service-level information must be encoded into the appropriate configuration for the server platforms. The set of priorities that are needed to manage the performance of the various applications must be specified in some manner in the server configuration.

In cases where server differentiation mechanisms such as support different priority levels are available, the appropriate configurations for the various platforms need to be generated. These configurations must include the appropriate performance priorities (or other suitable information) for the different classes of applications that are supported on a given server or cluster of servers.

Policy Issues with IKE/IPsec

The policy issues associated with IKE involve defining the set of parameters that specify how secure communication using IKE is to be implemented. A typical IKE configuration is specified in terms of the characteristics of the Phase 1 and Phase 2 tunnels that need to be established in order to exchange the keys required for IPsec communication.

The typical IKE configuration consists of specifying three types of records:

- **Phase 1 characteristics.** This defines the characteristics associated with a Phase 1 security association of IKE. These characteristics define how long a key used in Phase 1 would be valid and the type of authentication mechanisms used by the communicating parties to validate each other. Two common techniques that can be used for authentication are the use of a shared common secret and the use of public certificates. With a shared common secret, both parties in the IKE establish a secret key that they use to identify each other. With public certificates, they both trust a certificate-issuing authority that can be used to obtain the public keys of the other party.

- **Phase 1 transform lists.** During the Phase 1 negotiations, the communicating parties discuss a list of encryption and authentication algorithms that they would be willing to accept in communication over a Phase 1 security association. This transform list would be used to secure the exchange of keys for establishing Phase 2 security associations. A transform list would indicate whether encryption or authentication or both should be used for the communication, and which algorithms should be used for this purpose.

- **Phase 1 tunnel descriptions.** This specifies which phase 1 characteristics and phase 1 transform lists should be used for communication between a pair of source and destination machines. The granularity of the source and destination can be further refined by the use of port numbers at the source and destinations.

> **Note**
>
> Here's a quick note on terminology: What I call tunnel descriptions are usually referred to as policies in the IKE/IPsec implementation and RFCs. Because this usage might cause some confusion with the definition of policy I have been using all along, I have opted to call these tunnel descriptions.

The other three types of records are the corresponding Phase 2 characteristics, Phase 2 transform lists, and Phase 2 tunnel descriptions. There are differences in the exact set of characteristics that is specified among the two phases, or for the transform lists that make sense in the two phases of communication.

It is probably apparent to you by now that configuring the IKE correctly is a daunting task. It doesn't help that the configuration must be done not for one firewall, but consistently across multiple firewalls in order to enable some business needs.

Policy Issues with SSL

The typical SSL configuration for the bidding client or bidding server application consists of parameters such as the type of authentication that should be used for the different communication types—such as based on shared secrets or public certificates. Furthermore, the configuration should indicate whether only the server is authenticated or if both the client and the server are authenticated.

Other SSL parameters, such as when the security keys should be renegotiated, also need to be specified as part of the SSL configuration.

Although SSL configuration is simpler than the corresponding IKE configuration, it is essential that the configuration be consistent across the bidding client and bidding server applications so that the establishment of the secure SSL connection succeeds.

The Policy Management Tool

As must be apparent to you at this stage, the policies described in the section "High-Level Policies" and the policies described in the section "Low-Level Policies" of this chapter have very little in common. There exists a large gap between the business needs of an enterprise/ISP/ASP and the technologies that are required to satisfy them. Clearly you need to develop solutions that bridge the gap. One possible way to bridge this gap is by exploiting the IETF policy architecture and the policy definition framework.

Note

The policy definition framework is being done jointly within IETF as well as DMTF. Because it is network-centric, I will refer to it as the IETF architecture. The IETF does the bulk of the architecture, while the DMTF does the bulk of schema definition.

To recap the IETF policy architecture introduced in Chapter 1, it consists of four components: a policy management tool, a policy enforcement point (or the policy consumer), a policy decision point (or the policy target), and a policy server. The management tool populates the policy server, the policy decision point takes policies from the server to determine the configuration and interprets it, and the policy enforcement point enforces that decision.

One of the key components in the policy architecture (and the various scenarios just described) is the policy management tool. The *policy management tool* is the component that translates the specified requirements in terms of the business needs of the deployers into the detailed specifications needed for technology deployment. This section describes how such a policy management tool can be constructed. The rest of this book describes the various components of such a management tool in much more detail.

The purpose of the policy management tool is to take a high-level representation of the business goals or desired functions within the network and translate them into the appropriate configuration of the various devices in the network. The input is called the *high-level policies,* and the output of the tool is the *low-level policies* in the network. Such a tool is composed of the four basic functions shown in Figure 3.6:

- The *graphical user interface* is the means by which an administrator can input the high-level policies within the network. These policies are the ones that need to be enforced in the network, and the configuration of the network must be made conformant to these high-level policies.

- The *resource discovery* component determines the topology of the network and the users and applications that are operational in the network. In order to generate the configuration for the various devices in the network, the capabilities and topology of the network must be known. For any moderately sized networked system, such topology and capabilities must be discovered automatically.

- The *policy transformation logic* component is responsible for ensuring that the high-level policies that are specified by the network administrator are mutually consistent, correct, and feasible with the existing capacity and topology of the network. It also translates the high-level policies into low-level policies that can be distributed to the different devices in the network.

- The *configuration distributor* is responsible for ensuring that the low-level policies are distributed to the various devices in the network. The distribution of the configuration can be done in a variety of ways, such as storing them in a repository from where different devices can retrieve them.

Figure 3.6   Policy Management Tool

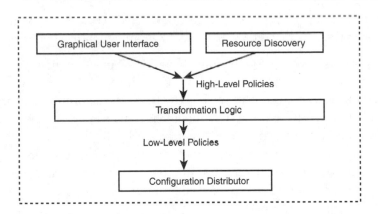

In addition to these components, there needs to be an additional component that is responsible for monitoring the network state and ensuring that the policies are being satisfied by the various devices in the network. For performance SLA, such monitors take the form of the different SLA monitoring tools that are available in the marketplace. For security policies, such monitors take the form of different "watcher" products that are responsible for detecting intrusion and other abnormal behaviors in the network traffic.

The next sections discuss each of the modules in turn.

The Graphical User Interface Module

The graphical user interface module is the component of the policy tool that provides the look and feel of the policy management tool to the end-user. Its purpose is to allow an administrator to enter the high-level policies to the management system. The user interface is largely responsible for making the task of entering policy information simpler. The input from the user is generated into an internal representation of the high-level policies that are to be processed by the policy validation module.

The design of such a user interface must take into account the factors that affect the experience a user would have. In particular, the tool must provide appropriate help screens and useful diagnostics messages when exception conditions are encountered in the tool.

Two common ways of providing the user interface module are via a command-line interface or via a graphical user interface. The command-line interface is preferable when the management tool needs to interface with other automated programs. The graphical user interface is useful to interface with a human administrator. With the increasing emphasis on Web-oriented management, the user interface (in many instances) is implemented as a program that can be accessed via a browser. One way to achieve this goal is to implement the user interface as a Java applet. Other methods include creation of specific Web pages and server-side programs that let a user input the desired high-level policies.

The user interface is a very important component of any practical management tool. Many tool developers consider it the most important component of the management tool. However, for the goal of this book, which is to discuss the algorithms and applications of the policy architecture, the user interface module is just a way of obtaining high-level policies. The focus of this book is on processing high-level policies, so more attention is given to the other modules in the management tool. I will not discuss this module further in this book, but I want to reemphasize that this component is the one that can most dramatically affect a successful adoption of any tool for policy management.

The Resource Discovery Module

The first component of the policy management tool that I will discuss in detail in subsequent chapters (Chapter 5) is the resource discovery module. The purpose of this module is to obtain information about the different types of devices that are active within the network, their capabilities, and their characteristics that might affect policy generation and management.

The resource discovery module is needed in any practical policy management tool. The goal of policy management is to simplify the task of system/network administration. If this management must be done, the tool needs to maintain a current snapshot of the various

PEPs and PDPs that are operational within the network. Because it is not possible for any administrator to correctly enter the topology and configuration of any moderately sized network manually, these characteristics must be discovered by the tool automatically.

Several of the resource discovery capabilities are included in many traditional systems management/network management tools. Such resource discovery capabilities include SNMP-based tools to collect network routing and topology information, as well as many inventory tools that can obtain a summary of all the applications that are installed and active on a server or a desktop. When a policy management tool is included as a component within a larger systems management/network management suite, it can leverage the capabilities of the existing tools in the suite.

I will discuss the issue of resource discovery in more detail in the next chapter.

The Policy Transformation Logic Module

The policy transformation logic module validates the information provided in the high-level policies and transforms them into the configuration of devices in the network. The logic furthermore ensures that the policies specified are mutually consistent and that they cover all aspects of interest to the network administrator.

The validation process must incorporate syntactical checks as well as semantic checks. The semantic validation of high-level policies consists of the following three types of checks:

- **Bounds checks.** This validates that the values taken by any parameter in the policy specification are within specific constraints that are determined by the network administrator. For example, a network administrator should be able to specify that all response times in any defined class of service be less than 1000ms.

- **Relation checks.** This validates that the value taken by any two parameters in the policy specification are within constraints that make sense. For example, two attributes of a class of service are response time and the duration over which the response time must be measured. The latter must be larger than the former, and the network administrator should be able to specify how large the response time should be.

- **Consistency checks.** These checks ensure that each traffic flow is mapped onto exactly one service class, and that each service class is properly defined at all the interfaces. These checks are applied in the manner described next.

After validating that high-level policies are consistent and well-formed, the transformation logic translates them into technology specific low-level policies. These low-level policy definitions may be grouped so that only one set of policy information is generated for many boxes that need identical policy information. In general, boxes that play a similar role in the network (for example, access routers as opposed to core routers in network) are likely to have the same set of policy rules guiding their behavior.

Policy validation logic is discussed in more detail in Chapter 6, "Policy Validation and Translation Algorithms."

The Configuration Distributor Module

As soon as the low-level policies (which drive the configuration of different devices) are generated by the policy management tool, they need to be distributed to the different devices within the network. Several means of distributing devices are possible:

- **Populating a repository.** The management tool can write the device configuration rules into a configured repository in the network. Individual servers and routers pull the policy information from the repository, use the policy information to generate their local box configuration and subsequently configure themselves. The preferred approach in IETF policy working group has been to define a LDAP directory with a standardized schema as such a repository. In this approach, the low-level policies are stored at the repository, and the configuration is generated individually by each of the participating devices.

- **Distributing configuration files.** The management tool can translate the low level policies into the configuration files that would be needed at each device and copy them remotely over to the appropriate router and server. This approach works for all types of devices and does not require any specific software to be running at the device. However, the management tool must understand each type of device and the format of configuration file that can be used with it. The distribution mechanism is available in many systems management products. In this approach, the translation from low-level policies to box configuration is done by the management tool.

- **Command-line interfaces.** Most routers permit remote administration by means of a telnet session and specific command lines. The QoS management tool can use automated scripts to specific routers and control the configuration of the router using commands specific to the router. As in the case of configuration files, the QoS management tool must translate the low level policy definition to the configuration scripts, and must understand the scripts that can be used for different types of routers.

Further details and a comparison of the different distribution approaches are discussed in Chapter 7, "Policy Distribution Mechanisms."

4

Technology Support for Business Needs

In Chapter 3, "The Generic Provisioning Problem," we looked at the business needs and configuration information of different network environments. The business needs of the network environment drive the high-level policies in the environment, and the configuration information drives the low-level policies within the environment. We also looked at the structure of a generic policy management tool which can be used to translate the high-level policies into low-level policies.

Figure 3.1 showed the policy application matrix, which demonstrated the different business needs along the vertical axes and the different technologies along the horizontal axes. Chapter 3 discussed the appropriate policy specification along each of the axes. However, it did not discuss how to deploy the technologies (shown along the horizontal axis) in order to satisfy the business needs (shown along the vertical axis). The details of the deployment are discussed in this chapter.

Support of Business SLAs in the Enterprise Network

Within the enterprise environment, I use an example to show how different technologies can be used to support business SLAs. Consider a small grocery chain. The network consists of several campuses interconnected by a wide-area network. This environment is shown in Figure 4.1. One of the campuses (campus D) is the data center of the enterprise and hosts its application servers. Campuses A and B represent the outlets of the grocery chain that access the data center for its various transactions. Campus C is the administrative office that houses the various administrative and accounting departments. Two main types of applications are deployed in this environment. One application is used to look up the prices of different items as they are scanned for a customer purchasing the item. The other application is used to process credit card transactions. One form an SLA can take in this environment is that of assured response time for a given application. For example, all price lookups must complete within 100ms, and all credit card transactions must be completed within 500ms. Various types of office applications are deployed by the employees at campus C, but no specific SLAs are in place for these applications.

Figure 4.1   Hypothetical Grocery Chain Network

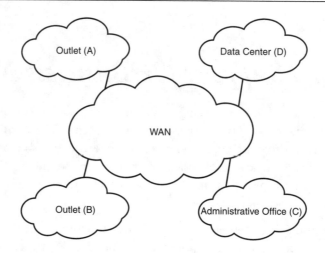

The following sections look at some of the ways such an SLA can be satisfied.

SLA Support Using Capacity Planning

The basic idea behind supporting SLAs using capacity planning is fairly simple: Provide enough link bandwidth and processing capacity that the SLA requirements are satisfied. If an SLA is feasible at all—that is, if it can be met on an unloaded network with unloaded servers—it should be possible to determine the link bandwidth and processing capacity that satisfied the performance objectives under normal operating environments.

The response time of an application in the network is determined by many factors, but the most important ones are the following:

- The processing capacity at the routers used in the network

- The link bandwidth on the wide-area network

- The processing capacity of the server at the data center

The goal of capacity planning is to make sure that none of these three components are overloaded.

In order to ensure that overload does not occur, you need to measure and monitor the usage of the link bandwidth at the different links, as well as the server processing capability. Most routers export information in the format of SNMP MIB (see the overview of SNMP in Chapter 2, "IP Architecture Overview" for details) variables such that the number of packets and bytes transmitted over any link can be estimated. Most servers also provide information and logs that give an estimate of the transactions processed per second and the percentage utilization of the processor. You should also measure the performance of the actual applications to ensure that the SLA limits are being met.

In addition to measuring the current utilization of the various components, you need to estimate their utilization over the course of the next few months. If it is estimated that one of the components might become the bottleneck point with the estimated utilization, that component is replaced with a faster one.

If the load generated by the applications is reasonably stable, and it can be predicted with reasonable accuracy, capacity planning works well to ensure satisfactory operation of the network. In an enterprise environment, where the set of applications running on the network is limited, the traffic load is dependent on the number of installations. This number would be relatively stable. Under these conditions, planning for adequate capacity is usually the best approach.

Applying the concepts to the grocery store example, we need to predict the expected traffic and server load generated by the two key applications, credit card processing and price lookups, as well as the other applications that are expected to share the network or the servers. A network configuration is defined as the speed of the links, routers, and servers that are deployed in the network. If the number of customers expected at the various stores can be predicted accurately, the expected system response for any specific network configuration can be determined. You can then select a configuration where the desired SLA parameters can be satisfied.

However, there are some situations in which capacity planning fails to work properly. If the traffic load on the servers and the networks is very erratic, capacity planning is hard to do. Many capacity planning tools and algorithms depend on the expected mean rate of the traffic. If the variance of the traffic is too high (there are many fluctuations in the traffic load, so at any point in time, the existing load can differ significantly from the mean traffic), the values obtained from capacity planning tools become suspect. For example, in anticipation of a sudden snowstorm, the number of customers in the grocery store might increase dramatically, and the response times might degrade. Similarly, some event on the Web might cause many of the office employees to access the Internet, and the resulting traffic surge might affect the SLAs that are in place.

Similarly, capacity planning does not work well if the network traffic growth rate is very high. When you expect a modest growth rate in the capacity requirements, you can plan so that an installed network would operate properly for a long period of time, such as until the next year. However, if the traffic growth follows the pattern of the Internet traffic, which has been doubling itself every few months, the delays inherent in upgrading a network can make obsolete any capacity growth plans you have developed.

In cases where capacity planning fails to solve the problem, the techniques of rate control, DiffServ, or IntServ can be used to address SLA concerns.

SLA Support Using DiffServ Networks

The basic thought as far as SLA using DiffServ [KILKKI] is as follows:

> You can't ensure specific performance levels for all applications when capacity is scarce; however, a preferred set of applications can have their performance objectives satisfied at the cost of other applications.

The bottleneck in capacity can be reached either in terms of network bandwidth or in terms of the processing capacity at the servers. If the capacity bottleneck is in the network, a DiffServ approach to networking can be enabled to protect the performance of the preferred key applications. If the capacity bottleneck is in the servers, a similar differentiation can be supported in the end-servers. The upcoming sidebar describes some of the techniques that are available for this purpose.

Using the DiffServ approach in the network, all the traffic in the network is divided into multiple classes. Each of these classes is marked with separate code points (see Chapter 2) by an access router. Then, the appropriately marked packets obtain a higher priority in the queuing that occurs at the router, or they get a proportionately larger share of the bandwidth.

The DiffServ architecture consists of core routers that process marked packets and edge routers that mark the packets according to their perceived priority. The core routers need to be told how much bandwidth to allocate to each type of packet marking. The edge routers need to be told how to mark the various packets as they see them in the network.

In the grocery store example, let's assume that the network is the bottleneck and that we need to preserve the performance of the two key applications—namely, price lookups and credit card processing. You can adopt the approach that the DiffServ network supports two classes of traffic on the network. If you prefer DiffServ jargon, we would deploy the class-selector PHBs in the network. One of these traffic classes is the one that is used for the two key applications, and it is given the higher priority queuing behavior in the network. The other one is used for the rest of the applications, and they are transmitted at a lower priority.

Note that the use of DiffServ networks protects the key applications from a surge in the traffic from the other applications. However, the capacity planning and prediction techniques for the key applications still need to be in place if their performance needs, as specified by the SLAs, are to be satisfied.

Operating Systems Differentiation Mechanisms

The ability to assign different priorities to executing processes is available in some form in most operating systems. In most operating systems, the assignment of processes/applications to a priority level is done automatically by the operating system on the basis of processor utilization, and so on. However, some level of user control is also permitted. UNIX systems permit the option to execute some processes at a priority different from the default one by using the nice command. Any user can use nice to lower the priority of his processes. The superuser can use nice to increase the priority of any process. A more sophisticated mechanism to differentiate among applications is found in the IBM mainframes. This feature, called *Work Load Management* (WLM) in OS/390, allows the system administrator to specify business objectives for specific applications. The system administrator can set goals for each application, which can be specified in terms of relative importance and performance goals. An example of a performance goal would be the target response time for completion of an application. Another type of performance goal specifies how often the task must be executed. This goal, which the OS/390 calls velocity, is defined for long-lived processes that need to be run periodically. For any application, the goals might be defined differently over different time periods during which the application is active.

As soon as the administrator has specified the performance goals, the system uses these to divide each of the processes into internal service classes. The service classes are associated with specific performance, and the system tracks the performance of each service class to see if they are meeting their goals. At 10-second intervals, the allocation of system resources (processor, disk I/O) to each of the service classes is updated on the basis of how close the class is to meeting its service goals.

A more detailed description of WLM describing its use in a cluster of OS/390 processors is found in the paper by Aman et al. [AMAN]. WLM is one of the few commercial general-purpose operating systems that offers a complex level of support for meeting a task's requirements. However, many experimental and operating systems provide support for different types of QoS.

continues

The support of different priority levels is almost standard across embedded operating systems. These are lightweight operating systems that are typically used in small processors embedded within larger systems, such as routers, sensor controllers in industrial complexes, or in digital televisions, cars and other consumer equipment. These systems typically have to execute tasks in real-time. Different task priorities are used to ensure that the real-time constraints are met for the different functions that the embedded system is expected to do.

SLA Support Using IntServ Networks

The use of DiffServ in the network only ensures that a set of preferred applications receives better performance than the set of nonpreferred applications. However, if too many preferred applications are active, the relative priority ordering might not be adequate to deliver the required level of performance.

Continuing with our grocery store example, let's assume that a sudden anticipated winter storm forces several customers to stock up on the essentials. As a result, each chain has more checkout counters active than the average number active in the network. If the servers and network were designed for a smaller number of active checkout counters, the different requests from the various checkout terminals would cause the performance to degrade. This degradation would occur even if the grocery store managers ensured that none of the non-key applications were active in the network.

One way around this situation would be to reserve the capacity within the network (as well as the servers) prior to actually initiating any transactions in the network. Before a clerk starts to check out a customer's groceries, the system would make an RSVP exchange to make sure that there is adequate capacity in the network to ensure a satisfactory performance. If the RSVP request succeeds, the transaction will complete in a reasonable amount of time, and the count of satisfied customers will increase.

The tricky thing would be dealing with transactions when the RSVP reservations fail within the network. In these cases, the reservations could be re-tried in the hope that they would eventually succeed. Of course, a customer would have to wait while these attempts are made. An alternative would be to let the transaction proceed without the reservation, where delays are unpredictable. Either of these situations would probably result in an unhappy customer. It is hard to say which one is the better option overall.

If there would be a subset of unhappy customers, is the reservation process really helping anyone? With the reservation process, at least some subset of all transactions is getting carried out with a reasonable overall performance. Without any reservation, chances are high that most of the transactions would experience some performance degradation, and you run the risk of making all customers unhappy.

Extranet Support in the Enterprise Environment

In order to illustrate the support of extranets in enterprise environments, we will look at the example of the soft drink bottling company introduced in the previous chapter. The bottling company needs to procure various types of containers and other materials. It plans to do so by means of a bidding server that runs an application to manage the bids received for any specific component, such as containers. The bidding server will be placed so that it is accessible to the suppliers contracted by the company over the Internet. However, for security purposes, the bidding server must be accessible only to a selected subset of suppliers through the Internet.

The following two sections discuss how such an extranet can be supported and established using the network-level mechanisms of IKE, as well as SSL. You should keep in mind that although we are focusing on network-level mechanisms, any extranet needs to put in place application-level security mechanisms to ensure that suppliers are accessing only data relevant to their needs. For example, a metal can supplier doesn't need access to information regarding bids for distilled water supplies.

Extranet Support Using IKE/IPsec

One of the ways in which an extranet can be supported is by using IKE along with IPsec over the Internet. The manner in which this environment will be used in shown in Figure 4.2. The bottling company allows a portion of its intranet to be accessible to the suppliers via the Internet. This is shown as the Company Extranet LAN, which is connected to the Internet by means of Firewall D. The rest of the company's intranet is protected from access by supplier companies by means of Firewall Y. The intranet may also have direct connectivity to the Internet by going through Firewall D or Firewall Y. The bidding server will be placed on a machine in the extranet, which is protected by Firewalls D and Y.

Figure 4.2   Hypothetical Extranet of a Bottling Company

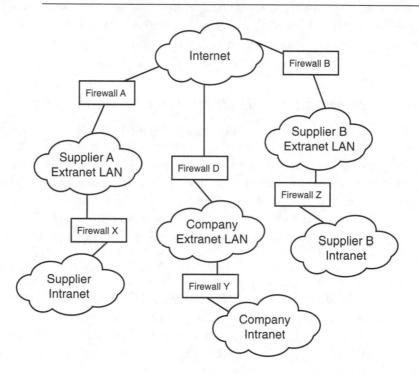

The applications that act as clients to the bidding server will be located in an environment similar to the supplier companies' intranet. The figure shows two such suppliers. Because the suppliers might not trust the bottling companies, they are likely to place the client software on a machine in the extranet, which is protected by two firewalls. For Supplier A, Firewall A protects access to the bidding client software from unauthorized access over the Internet. Similarly, Firewall X protects the supplier's intranet from the bidding client software, which might not be fully trusted by the supplier.

The communication between Supplier A and the bottling company can be protected by means of an IPsec tunnel between Firewalls A and D. Similarly, the firewall between supplier B and the bottling company can be protected by means of an IPsec tunnel between firewalls B and D. Other alternatives are also possible. For example, you could have the IPsec tunnels established between the machines running the bidding client software and Firewall D, or directly between the machine running the bidding client software and the one running the bidding server software. In the latter mode, ESP or AH secure communication can be established using the transport mode of IPsec. In the other configurations, the tunnel mode of IPsec needs to be used.

Extranet Support Using SSL

Instead of using IPsec for securing communication between the bidding client and bidding server, you can opt to use SSL to secure the communication. When using SSL, you have essentially the same set of firewalls that protects the different segments of the supplier and the bottling company's network. However, firewalls A, B, and D need not support IKE or IPsec protocols. These can be normal packet-filtering firewalls, with security and authentication handled by means of SSL running between the bidding client and bidding server applications.

The configuration of the different firewalls when using SSL would be similar to using IPsec in transport mode between the machines running the bidding client and bidding server applications. The only difference would be that the applications would have to be modified to explicitly invoke SSL calls.

SLA Support in the ISP Environment

Supporting SLAs in ISP environments can be done by means of multiple technologies. One of the possible ways to provide SLA support is by operating different physical networks. Another approach is to use a technology such as DiffServ.

SLA Support by Operating Multiple Networks

When different service levels are implemented as different networks, the structure of the operator's network looks like Figure 4.3. Packets belonging to different service levels are directed to different networks. This function is also known as *alternate routing*. With this approach, the core network is effectively split into two core subnetworks.

Figure 4.3   Parallel Physical Subnetworks for SLA Support

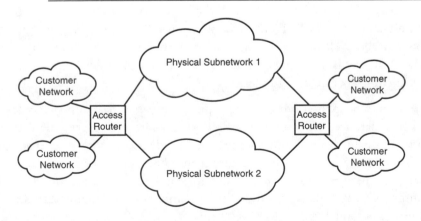

The responsibility of identifying the correct service level to which a packet belongs and routing it to the corresponding core subnetwork belongs to the access router. The access router is typically the place where many customers connect to the ISP network. The access router needs to classify packets into the different service levels on the basis of any combination of IP and TCP/UDP headers. Some fields that can be included in this combination are the source and destination IP addresses and the protocol field in the IP header, and the source and destination port numbers in the transport header.

The choice of the exact fields that are needed to support SLAs depends on the granularity at which SLAs are defined. Consider the case in which different performance requirements are offered at the granularity of a customer organization (in other words, all traffic from a single customer organization is offered the same performance bounds). In this case, the classification can be done simply on the basis of the source IP addresses of the packets. You can alternatively do the classification on the basis of the adapter on which an incoming packet is received. When each customer organization is mapped to a different service level, it is as if each has a separate intranet of its own. They simply happen to share the same access router.

An alternative approach is to assign different service levels to different applications. Each core subnetwork is used to carry a different set of applications. In this case, the classification of packets would be done using a combination of the IP source and destination addresses and the TCP or UDP port numbers used by the applications.

As an example, consider the case of an enterprise that used to operate a *Systems Network Architecture* (SNA) network and that has decided to migrate to an IP-based network. The legacy SNA applications are encapsulated in IP using the *data-link switching* protocol (DLSw). The SLAs for SNA applications typically require a much higher availability. In order to prevent interference among the DLSw traffic and other IP traffic, one of the core networks is used to carry DLSw traffic, and the second core subnetwork is used to carry all other IP traffic. DLSw uses TCP as the transport protocol and typically uses the port numbers 2065 and 2067. The access routers determine the packets that use TCP (the protocol field in the IP header is 6) on ports 2065 or 2067 as source or destination port numbers and direct them to specific core subnetworks.

The identification of applications using only port numbers is best done when applications are run on standard well-known ports or on ports that are used universally within the network. In this case, the port numbers can be used to identify applications. If an application is run on a server at a different port number than the standard one, you have to introduce additional rules specifying the server and the nonstandard port to identify the application. If port numbers are not managed properly, the number of rules required to identify an application can become large.

Running different networks for different service levels has several advantages. Traffic in each service level is insulated from the other traffic. Thus, the idiosyncrasies of one type of traffic do not interfere with the other types of traffic. As an example, voice packets typically happen to be small (less than 100 bytes) and require low jitter in the network. Data packets can potentially be large (a size of 4096 bytes for file transfer is typical). These large packets can cause a significant amount of jitter in the congested nodes. Imagine a voice packet stuck behind a few bulk transfer packets at a queue in the network. Separating the two types of packets into different networks insulates them from each other. This is assuming that the separation point (the access router) is itself not congested and that the interference between the two types of packets at the access router is negligible.

The same arguments hold true for networks that are used to support two different customers' organizations. If a customer requires low delays, its packets can be routed on a subnetwork consisting of faster links. If a customer requires higher availability, you can design a subnetwork that is a more dense mesh of lower-speed links. Other customers can be routed on networks with different characteristics.

The low-level policy issues when running multiple subnetworks relate mostly to the access routers that connect the customer's routers to the different core subnetworks. They have to be configured with the routing rules that direct customers' packets to the right subnetwork. The routers that make up the subnetworks have no significant policy issues to consider.

SLA Support with DiffServ in the ISP Environment

Although running parallel networks simplifies the task of providing different SLAs, it is a relatively expensive solution. It would be much cheaper to combine the different networks into a single network. If the distinction between the multiple physical networks were mostly related to performance, you could use DiffServ to partition the overall network into two logical ones. Each logical network would be specified by a specific *Per-Hop Behavior* (PHB) as defined by the DiffServ specification.

The model of supporting different service levels using DiffServ is shown in Figure 4.4. The figure shows two PHBs supported at each link in the network. Assume that one of these PHBs is a higher-priority forwarding class (with a DS field of 110000) and the other one is the default forwarding class (with a DS field of 000000). The physical network is essentially divided into two logical networks sharing the same physical links. Figure 4.4 shows each link as consisting of two virtual sublinks (one of which is shaded and the other is not). Each of the virtual sublinks corresponds to one of the PHBs used within the network. The bandwidth on each link is allocated among the different virtual PHB-based sublinks in a manner determined by the network operator.

Figure 4.4 SLA Support Using DiffServ

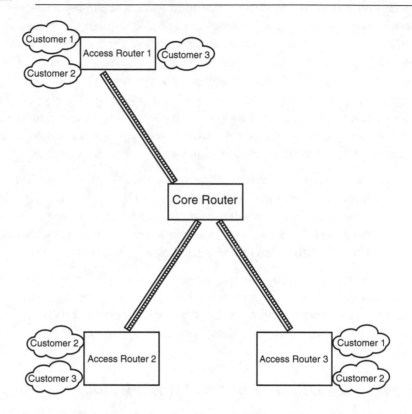

Assume that the allocation of bandwidth along the two priority classes shown is done so that 40 percent of each link's capacity is reserved for the higher-priority class, and the other 60 percent is used for default forwarding. In order to ensure that the DiffServ network meets the desired SLAs, the access router and the core routers must perform specific functions.

The various access routers, as shown in Figure 4.4, must perform the following functions in order to obtain a split into two logical networks:

- Upon receiving a packet, examine the fields in the packet header to determine the packet's service level.

- Determine the rate limits associated with the specific service level, and enforce those limits.

- Determine the correct PHB to be used for the service level, and change the Type of Service field in the IP header to the correct code point for the PHB.

- Keep counters measuring the number of bytes and packets belonging to each service level, and collect any information needed to estimate network performance.

The definition of service levels, how each service level is mapped onto a specific DiffServ header field code point, and the rate limits associated with each service level constitute the low-level policies for the access router supporting the DiffServ function.

Another policy item is the action to be taken on an IP packet when rate limits are exceeded. The packet could be delayed until it conforms with the rate limit, or it could be discarded. If the packet is delayed, it occupies buffers at the access router. The limit on how many buffers can be occupied by packets belonging to a specific service level is also part of the low-level policy for the access router.

The core router needs to implement the queuing behavior that supports the different DiffServ PHBs within the network. Each PHB is associated with a specific scheduling behavior, such as defining the queuing priority level, an absolute limit on bandwidth to be used, or relative ratios in which bandwidth needs to be allocated. The definitions of the priorities, the rate limits, and the action to be taken when the limits are exceeded constitute the low-level policies for the core routers in the network.

VPN Support in the ISP Environment

The cheapest VPN would be obtained if the campus sites simply connected to the Internet and used encrypted tunnels to carry their traffic across the Internet. However, given the wide variety of threats that exist on the open network, as well as the wide performance fluctuations, it is much more likely that the VPN service would be offered on a private network physically separate from the one that the ISP uses for global Internet connectivity. A customer network would have access to both the public Internet and the ISP-private network. Several customers would be multiplexed on to the ISP-private network. This would reduce the overall cost to the ISP of maintaining its network, and the ISP would be able to offer VPN access to the customer at a reduced cost over having his or her own private intranet.

Such a scenario is shown in Figure 4.5. You see an ISP offering VPN services to two customer enterprises on an ISP-private network. The first customer (Customer A) has three sites connected to the network. The second customer (Customer B) has two sites connected to the network. The ISP connects to other peer ISPs at an exchange point, but typically supports the private connections from the customers within its own network. The customer sites are connected to the ISP-private network and through firewalls to the ISP-public network. The firewalls connecting the customers to the Internet typically belong to the customer. At the access routers connecting the customer to the ISP-private network, the ISP has the onus of making sure that the customers are protected from each other. For the sake of brevity, I have shown the access routers and firewalls only at the first campus of both customers. It's implied that a similar structure needs to be in place on each campus.

Figure 4.5   A VPN Deployment Scenario

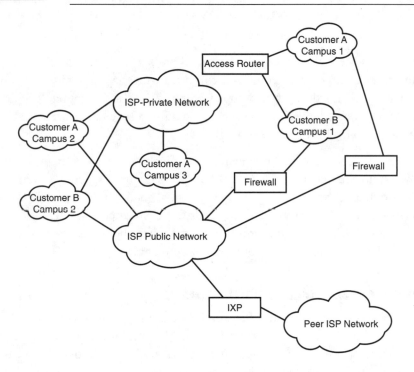

The high-level policies for deployment—in this case, for the ISP—would be to define the correct set of VPNs and to enable access among its customers in the environment shown in Figure 4.5. Such a solution can be obtained by using IKE and IPsec-based encrypted communication.

The low-level security policy for the ISP deploying the VPN service would be the configuration of the access routers, which provides for insulation among the different customers. On the ISP-private network, only the campuses that belong to the same customer are allowed to talk to each other. Therefore, the various access routers in the network must be configured to enforce these criteria.

Our assumption here is that the access routers would implement IKE and IPsec functions to support the VPN service. Therefore, the appropriate low-level policy for each box would be the specification of the IKE configuration, as described previously. These would consist of the specification of the phase one and two characteristics, transform lists, and tunnel descriptions. These need to be obtained so as to support the VPN definitions as required by the supported set of customers.

SLA Support in the ASP Environment

In order to meet the business SLA requirements within an ASP environment, an ASP needs to allocate the different resources that are available within the environment. The two key resources available within a server farm are the network bandwidth and the server processing capacity assigned to a specific customer.

The main aspect of dealing with SLAs for service providers involves the proportion of the network bandwidth that is to be allocated to each of the service levels. In most cases, the bandwidth is the amount of traffic generated by the servers, rather than the traffic coming into the servers. The allocation of access link bandwidth can be done in one of the following ways:

- The access router maintains separate queues for each of the service levels. Most access routers can be configured to support a limited number of queues, and they use the weighted round robin queuing discipline to service the queues. The queuing discipline allows the sharing of access link bandwidth in the specified manner in cases of high load. If a customer is not using its allocated capacity, the remainder is shared among the active customers. The drawback of this approach is that most access routers permit a relatively limited number of queues (four or eight) to be created in this manner. If a service provider is supporting many customers, this approach is likely to be inadequate. The other drawback of rate control at the access router is that the behavior of the TCP connections in the presence of packet drops at the access router results in erratic application performance.

- The access router implements a partial TCP stack and manipulates the TCP header information to control how much traffic flows into the network. The amount of data that TCP sends out into the network is controlled by its congestion control algorithm. At any time, TCP determines the total number of packets in flight in the network by the number of bytes that are acknowledged in each message from the other side. By reducing an acknowledgment of, for example, 1024 bytes into two acknowledgments of 512 bytes each, the transmission rates can be made smoother. Similarly, determining a maximum rate at which these bytes will be acknowledged can reduce the maximum bandwidth used in the network by any application.

- Rates are allowed to different servers, each of which implements packet shaping and rate control at the server. This shaping can be done at the TCP connection level and therefore is more efficient at meeting the desired throughput on a per-connection basis. The advantage of this approach is that unnecessary packet losses (and the resulting TCP cut down of rate) are avoided. Server-based rate control tends to produce more predictable application performance than network-based rate control.

However, the partitioning of bandwidth among different customers means that there might be excess capacity assigned to a customer who is not using it, but no other customer can use that bandwidth. This also requires that the server's TCP/IP stack support packet shaping and rate control. Not all commercial servers provide this support.

Apart from bandwidth, the other resources in the server farm can also be allocated to the various customers. Depending on the hosting environment, these resources could take the form of the space within the hosting complex, the number of servers, the disk space allocated from a common pool, or the number of access links available on the back end. The service provider must put into place policies that dictate how many servers will be allocated to each customer and under what conditions. Similarly, other resources in the server farm may be reallocated among the different customers.

Access Control Support in the ASP Environment

The support for access control in the ASP environment would depend on which firewall solution is used to provide secure access within the server farm. Among the various technologies that you have seen in the network, you can use a combination of the following in a hosting environment:

- **Use of a packet-filtering firewall.** This is commonly be used to protect the applications in the farm from hackers on the Internet.

- **Use of SSL.** This is commonly be used in Web servers (and other applications) to validate that communication with any end-client is happening on a secure channel.

- **Use of IKE.** This is commonly be used to create a VPN from the server farm back to a customer's site for any administrative function, such as code upgrade.

The low-level policy issue in these cases is to simply identify the correct function for all the firewalls in the network and to ensure that they are configured correctly and consistently.

5

Resource Discovery

In Chapter 4, "Technology Support for Business Needs," we looked at the structure of a policy management tool that can be used to simplify the task of specifying high-level business policies in the system.

The basic goal of the policy management tool is to translate high-level business policies into the per-device configuration of the various devices in the system. In order to do so, the management tool must have a notion of the devices that are active in the network, as well as the capabilities and the nature of each of the devices. Information about these devices, which I refer to as resources, must be available to the policy management tool. Without accurate knowledge of the types of devices that need to be configured and the interconnections between them, it is not possible to do a reasonable translation from the high-level policies to the box configuration.

One of the assumptions a policy management tool could make is that the administrator will configure the information about resources. Although this assumption simplifies the design of a policy management tool, it puts too great a burden on any human administrator. Because the primary motivation for a policy management tool is to simplify and make more efficient the tasks of network administration and management, asking a network administrator to input the topology information defeats the purpose. Therefore, the policy management tool itself must discover this information. This chapter looks at some of the techniques that can be used to discover resources.

One of the key components of the policy management tool is the resource discovery module. One of the items that the resource discovery process must obtain is information about the topology of the network. The topology of the network describes how the different network elements, such as routers, servers, and switches, are interconnected. In addition to the topology, the management tool must also determine which *Policy Enforcement Points* (PEPs) are active in the network and what their capabilities are. Similarly, the policy management tool must know which applications are operational in the network. When policies are defined on the basis of individual users, the policy management tool might additionally need to know who the active users in the network are which will provide information needed to associate traffic flows with the users, and define the appropriate policies for those traffic flows.

Depending on the application domain to which policy is being applied, the amount of topology information that is required is different. For some applications, it would suffice to simply know the names of the various machines that constitute a network. For others, you need to obtain the list of machines, as well as the characteristics of the networks and links that connect the different machines.

The following sections discuss the different methods that are available for a policy management tool to discover the various resources and other information needed for policy management. It is also worth noting that the configuration information is not static. The routing tables in the network can change dynamically, as can the set of active users within the network. The policy management tool must take these dynamic changes into account, and re-examine the current set of deployed policies to see if they need to be modified in light of the modified configuration information.

Topology Discovery

The topology of the network is a description of the manner in which the different network devices are connected. The device topology includes a description of the different devices that are in the network, as well as the characteristics of the links that connect those devices.

There are two different types of topologies within an IP network that you need to know in order to manage policies:

- The physical topology, which describes how the different elements are physically connected

- The routing topology, which describes the path that a packet in the network would take between any two points in the network

The physical topology of the network is relatively static and unchanging. Unless the operator upgrades the network, the physical topology does not change. The actions that can change the physical topology include the addition or deletion of one of the links in the network, the addition of a new device (a router, switch, or server) in the network, the upgrading of a link to a higher capacity, and so on. Most of these operations take place over a relatively long period of time, which can be counted in days, if not weeks.

On the other hand, the routing topology of the network depends on the routing protocol deployed within the network. Depending on the characteristics of the routing protocol, the routes taken between any pair of nodes within the network are likely to change relatively more frequently, for example, when a link fails or comes up again. The routing topology of a network is dynamic and changes every hour or so.

The physical topology of a network is not necessarily the same as the routing topology. The primary reason for routing topology to differ from physical topology is that networks are designed to be redundant. Thus, there might be multiple paths that can be taken by a packet between any two devices within the network. However, typically only one of these paths will be selected by the routing algorithms as the preferred one to transmit packets. The other links in the network do not constitute part of the routing topology of the network—at least, not for the purpose of transporting packets between those two end points. (The other links might show up in the routing paths used for transport between other pairs of end points.) Another reason for the physical topology to differ from the routing topology is that the routing topology looks at only the devices in the network that are visible at the IP layer. Thus, an ethernet bridge that connects two LAN segments does not show up as explicitly as part of the routing topology of the network. However, such devices do form part of the physical topology of the network.

The routing topology is the main aspect that you have to worry about when defining policies regarding network performance, QoS, or security. However, the physical topology becomes important in situations where you have to analyze the reliability and fault-tolerance characteristics of the network.

In order to illustrate the fashion in which different topology discovery mechanisms work, consider the network topology shown in Figure 5.1. This figure shows the network of the hypothetical company foo.com, which has a class C IP address assigned to it. This address space allows the company to use 256 addresses in the range of 197.32.54.0 through 197.32.54.255. The network administrator has split the address space into four subnets, each subnet consisting of 64 addresses:

- The first subnetwork consists of addresses from 197.32.54.0 through 197.32.54.63. This is used by two machines: m2.foo.com, which has an IP address of 197.32.54.2, and the management console, which has an IP address of 197.32.54.1.

- The second subnetwork consists of addresses from 197.32.54.64 through 197.32.54.127. Only one machine (dns.foo.com) is present in this subnetwork, which also acts as the domain name server for the entire corporation.

- The third subnetwork consists of addresses from 197.32.54.128 through 197.32.54.195. Two machines (m3 and m4) appear in this subnet.

- The fourth subnet, which consists of addresses from 197.32.54.196 through 197.32.54.255, is used for the intermediate network that connects the other routers.

Figure 5.1   Sample Network for Topology Discovery

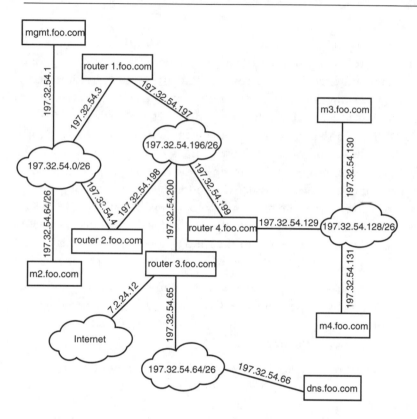

The fourth subnet described above is shown as the central network in Figure 5.1. The IP address that is assigned to each interface of the router is also shown, as well as written above the line that representing the interface. We assume that the topology discovery mechanism (as a component of the policy management tool) is operational on the machine mgmt.foo.com shown in the figure. We assume that router 3 provides connectivity to the Internet for the subnetwork that is shown. We assume that the connectivity is through an ISP that has provided an address (within the ISP address domain) of 7.2.24.12 to the enterprise, and the next-hop ISP router to which they connect is 7.2.24.11.

We assume that the topology discovery component initially is unaware of any node in the system. Subsequent sections will illustrate how the entire network topology will be discovered for the sample network shown in Figure 5.1.

Topology Discovery Using DNS

If the policy discipline simply requires an enumeration of the different types of machines that are available in an enterprise, the *Domain Name Service* (DNS) provides a convenient means for obtaining this information. The DNS (described in Chapter 2, "Background Information") is a mechanism used to translate machine-symbolic names to the corresponding IP addresses. In order to do its translation, it is required that all machines register their names and IP addresses to the DNS that is handling their IP domain.

Most DNS servers support a function known as zone transfer to their clients. DNS was designed to allow for the existence of many servers, any of which can resolve the names of machines to their IP addresses for a single domain. The use of multiple DNS servers provides better performance for the name translations, and it also provides better reliability, even when one of the servers goes down. In order to keep the information among these servers consistent, the zone transfer function was defined. This allowed a secondary name server to query the primary name server for a domain to get a quick dump of all the machines registered within that domain. Of course, a management tool can also make the same query and request the names of all the machines that belong to a specific domain, such as watson.ibm.com. The DNS server would respond with a relatively long message that would contain the names and IP addresses of all the machines that are registered as having a machine name ending with the suffix of watson.ibm.com. The zone transfer scheme is defined in the Internet standards for DNS [DNSRFC] and an optimized version for notifying incremental changes to a zone has also been standardized [DNSZONE].

The information returned by the DNS zone transfer for each machine consists of the domain name of each device registered with the domain and the IP addresses of each of the interfaces that the device has. This information provides a very quick summary of all the devices that are registered with the DNS system.

The information obtained in this fashion does have some limitations. The information obtained by the DNS zone transfer contains only the machines that are registered with the DNS system. Some machines in the network might not be registered with the DNS system. This often happens with machines that tend to use DHCP to obtain dynamic addresses. Because such machines usually tend to be clients rather than servers, many implementations do not register the dynamic addresses with the DNS server. Newer implementations of DHCP clients allow for the registration of the dynamically obtained addresses with the DNS server. In installations where dynamic DNS registrations are supported, the DNS zone transfer mechanism is more successful.

Another aspect of DNS information is that it is relatively static, which implies that it could be out of date. The DNS database consists of a static registration of machines and the IP addresses assigned to them. This information can easily become stale, with many machines no longer being used. Unless the network administrator has been diligent about removing these addresses from the DNS database, the zone transfer is likely to return many machines that are nonexistent. Another limitation of the static registration database is that it provides no information regarding whether the machines being discovered in the network are up or down. Also, the information returned by the DNS zone transfer does not provide any information about connectivity among the different machines.

Because the zone transfer can reveal a significant amount of information about the topology of the network, many network administrators turn off this function for the purposes of denying access from a general client. The network management tool must be configured so that it is allowed to make the zone transfer request to the appropriate servers.

Despite these limitations, the DNS zone transfer provides a useful way of obtaining a listing of a large subset of the machines and addresses in the domain. This information can be refined using the techniques defined in the following sections to obtain a more accurate picture of the network topology.

DNS Zone Transfer Example

Referring to the sample network shown in Figure 5.1, the management console system (mgmt.foo.com) and the topology management software component that is hosted thereon must first contact its DNS server. In order to enable IP communication, each device needs to be preconfigured with the DNS server address (or it acquires this information using a protocol such as DHCP). The management console system then sends a zone transfer request for domain foo.com to the DNS server that it knows to be 197.32.54.66 (also known as dns.foo.com). Assuming that all the machines shown in the figure have registered themselves with the DNS server, the server sends back a response that contains the information shown in Table 5.1 (or an equivalent).

Table 5.1   Information in Zone Transfers

Machine Name	Interfaces
mgmt.foo.com	197.32.54.1
m2.foo.com	197.32.54.2
m3.foo.com	197.32.54.130
m4.foo.com	197.32.54.131
dns.foo.com	197.32.54.66
router1.foo.com	197.32.54.3, 197.32.54.197

Machine Name	Interfaces
router2.foo.com	197.32.54.4, 197.32.54.198
router3.foo.com	197.32.54.65, 197.32.54.200, 7.2.24.12
router4.foo.com	197.32.54.129, 197.32.54.199

The information provided by zone transfer does not include information about the subnets that are available on the other machines. Nor does it return information about how the networks are connected. However, it does provide a complete listing of the machines that are active in the network and that are registered with DNS.

A possibility is that at the time of the zone transfer query, a machine such as m2.foo.com was off for maintenance. However, this does not affect the discovery mechanism. The zone transfer will still provide this information to the topology discovery tool.

Topology Discovery Using SNMP

One way to discover the routing topology as well as the physical topology is to use the information that is available at the different devices in the various SNMP *Management Information Bases* (MIBs) that are commonly defined in the industry. Information defined in the MIBs contains enough data that you could determine a fairly accurate assessment of the physical connectivity of the various devices in the network, as well as the current state of the routing table within the network.

Almost all routers and servers that support the IP protocol support the basic MIBs required by TCP/IP. For each machine, the standard MIBs contain information about the type of machine (such as the machine's manufacturer), the machine's domain name, and the time that the machine has been up. They also specify the number of interfaces that are present on the machine. For each interface, the MIB definition includes information about the IP address and the subnetwork mask for the interface. For discovering the connectivity information, the preceding two values would suffice. However, more information is available for each interface, such as the speed of the interface, the maximum packet size to be transferred on the interface, and a variety of statistics of packets sent and received on the interface. The MIBs also contain information about the routing entries that are available and used at each interface of the router. A routing entry contains information about a set of destination subnets, the IP address of the next-hop router, and the interface to be used to access the next-hop router.

The MIB definitions contain a lot more information than the ones just described. I have focused on the attributes that help you discover the network's topology.

The topology discovery process using SNMP is basically a polling approach that starts at one of the nodes in the network and then reads the IP addresses and subnet entries corresponding to all the interfaces on that node. The routing table entries that are thereby discovered provide the information about all the next-hop routers that are available in the network. This provides connectivity information and the identity of the next-hop router. You then continue the probing in a recursive fashion, with each of the identified next-hop routers identified at each stage of this process.

Note that the SNMP-based polling approach does not discover the identity of machines that do not appear in the routing tables of other machines, which means almost any machine that does not act as a router. The SNMP based approach is not very good at discovering end-stations, and the reason will be apparent when you follow the example in the next section. Using the technique, one can discover the subnet masks to which end-stations belong. Each subnet can contain a number of machines. The topology discovery component might probe these machines to see if they are alive (for example, by sending an ICMP ping message to them). The machines that are found to exist can be probed with SNMP to check their MIB information. However, this polling will be time-consuming and will only be able to detect machines that have an operational SNMP agent.

Another way to augment this discovery component and to discover the machines in the network is to combine the DNS zone transfer and the SNMP probing mechanism. This would provide an indication of the different machines that exist within the network and the connectivity information between them.

One of the significant limitations of the SNMP-based polling approach is that it takes a significant amount of time to poll and discover an enterprise-size network. Also, if some of the machines are not operational for any reason, or if the SNMP agents have not been configured on them, the discovery mechanism will fail. Although SNMP agents are operational by default on most routers, most hosts (PCs, desktops, or servers) do not turn them on by default. Furthermore, the management tool needs to have the right credentials to obtain the desired information from the SNMP agents in the environments where the SNMP agents implement some form of access control. Further details on the exact SNMP messages to issue to obtain the desired set of information can be found in [SNMP].

SNMP Topology Discovery Example

For this example, we assume that the SNMP agents are operational on all the machines shown earlier in Figure 5.1, and that the topology discovery module has been configured with the correct privileges to query any of these agents. We also assume that all the machines are up and responding to SNMP queries when the discovery component is in action.

The topology discovery module starts by looking at its own machine's IP configuration. It queries the local SNMP agent for the following information:

Machine name: mgmt.foo.com

Number of interfaces: 1

Interface 0: IP address is 197.32.54.1; subnet mask is 255.255.255.196

Routing entries:

- Destination is *; next router is 197.32.54.3, interface 0

Note

The preceding information is sent using SNMP syntax and conventions. I am not showing the precise syntax in these examples—only the logical representation of the information that is thus obtained. In the actual SNMP representation, the descriptive names I am using (such as machine name) would be replaced with a long identifier string representing the SNMP object ID for the named attribute.

As a result of querying the local SNMP agent for this information, the topology discovery component has learned about another device in the system—namely, the router 197.32. 54.3. It also knows that the connectivity of the machine mgmt.foo.com to the router 197.32.54.3 is via the interface with the IP address of 197.32.54.3. It then repeats the querying step with router 1, which returns the following information:

Machine name: router1.foo.com

Number of interfaces: 2

Interface 0: IP address is 197.32.54.3; subnet mask is 255.255.255.196

Interface 1: IP address is 197.32.54.197; subnet mask is 255.255.255.196

Routing entries:

- Destination is 197.32.54.64/26; next router is 197.32.54.200, interface 1

- Destination is 197.32.54.128/26; next router is 197.32.54.199, interface 1

- Destination is *; next router is 197.32.54.200, interface 1

Note that no routing table entries exist for the subnets of 197.32.54.0/26 or 197.32.54.196/26. These subnets are directly reachable through one of the interfaces at router 1. Therefore, the router assumes that any machine with an address in these two subnets is directly reachable, and would use MAC layer mechanisms to send the packets directly to the destination.

The last routing entry is indicative of the fact that router 3 (197.32.54.200) is the gateway of the enterprise into the Internet. A destination address specified as 197.32.54.64/26 indicates that up to 26 bits denote the set of addresses in this destination—equivalent to saying that the network mask is 255.255.255.196.

After processing this query, the topology discovery component has discovered two additional machines in the network—those with the interfaces of 107.32.54.200 and 197.32.54.199. It also has knowledge of all the interfaces that are present at router 1, and now it also knows the domain name of router 1 (as opposed to just one of its interfaces). The SNMP tool repeats the process with each of these routers in turn. The routing information for router at 197.32.54.199 would return information of the following format:

Machine name: router4.foo.com

Number of interfaces: 2

Interface 0: IP address is 197.32.54.129; subnet mask is 255.255.255.196

Interface 1: IP address is 197.32.54.199; subnet mask is 255.255.255.196

Routing entries:

- Destination is 197.32.54.0/26; next router is 197.32.54.197, interface 1

- Destination is 197.32.54.0/26; next router is 197.32.54.198, interface 1

- Destination is 197.32.54.64/26; next router is 197.32.54.200, interface 1

- Destination is *, next router is 197.32.54.200, interface 1

Note that there are two routing entries to the subnet of 197.32.54.0/26—one to the interface of 197.32.54.197 and the other to the router at 197.32.54.198. In the routing entry, there would be additional metrics that specify which routing entry would actually be used for packet transfer. The topology discovery tool can also retrieve this metric information.

After this step, the topology discovery component is aware of one more device in the network—namely, 197.32.54.198. It still must probe the device 197.32.54.200, which it discovered earlier. Let's assume that it probes the devices in the order in which it discovers them.

The probing of the device 197.32.54.200 would provide the following information:

Machine name: router3.foo.com

Number of interfaces: 3

Interface 0: IP address is 197.32.54.65; subnet mask is 255.255.255.196

Interface 1: IP address is 197.32.54.200; subnet mask is 255.255.255.196

Interface 2: IP address is 7.2.24.12; subnet mask is 255.255.255.254

Routing entries:

- Destination is 197.32.54.0/26; next router is 197.32.54.198, interface 1

- Destination is 197.32.54.0/26; next router is 197.32.54.197, interface 1

- Destination is 197.32.54.128/26; next router is 197.32.54.199, interface 1

- Destination is *; next router is 7.2.24.12, interface 2

The topology discovery module has discovered a new router, 7.2.24.12, in this step. It now knows the connectivity information for router3.foo.com. The step returns to probing the router at interface 197.32.54.198. This probe returns the following information:

Machine name: router2.foo.com

Number of interfaces: 2

Interface 0: IP address is 197.32.54.4; subnet mask is 255.255.255.196

Interface 1: IP address is 197.32.54.198; subnet mask is 255.255.255.196

Routing entries:

- Destination is 197.32.54.64/26; next router is 197.32.54.200, interface 1

- Destination is 197.32.54.128/26; next router is 197.32.54.199, interface 1

- Destination is *; next router is 197.32.54.200, interface 1

At this stage, no new routers are discovered. The component needs to probe the router at address 7.2.24.12. Because this router is outside of the domain foo.com, two results are possible. The first is that the router responds with the correct information, in which case the topology discovery component can determine that the router is not within the domain foo.com and ignores its response. The second case is that the router does not respond (because the router 7.2.24.11 is not allowed to respond to SNMP queries from the management applications hosted in the foo.com domain). In this case, this router will be deemed unreachable at the point of discovery. No new routers still need to be explored, so the topology discovery component will terminate its discovery process.

At the conclusion of the exploration, the SNMP probing process has discovered all the routers and their connectivity information. It has also discovered the different subnets that are present in the network. However, it does not detect the existence of individual host machines within the network, unless these machines have explicit routes to them.

By modifying this discovery process, such as polling every possible machine address in the subnet, or by combining DNS zone transfer information with the discovered information, the topology discovery module will discover the machines that do not have explicit routes to them.

The information provided by SNMP polling provides connectivity information related to physical interconnections as well as routing interconnections. Keep in mind, though, that the routing topology of the network shown in Figure 5.1 is different from the physical connectivity information. For example, it is possible that router2.foo.com might not be used in any of the existing routes within the network.

The limitation of the SNMP-based discovery mechanism is that it cannot discover hosts and end-stations very well. This is partly because a large number of hosts do not appear in any routing table. However, the most significant problem is that many hosts and desktops do not have an operational SNMP agent.

Topology Discovery Using Routing Information

The discovery of topology information using SNMP is slow and tedious. However, it is possible to obtain the routing information in a much more efficient manner by looking into the IP routing daemons that are already operational within the network.

In order to get this information, the topology discovery component needs to mimic a routing process. It then advertises itself as one of the routing daemons present within the network and connects to the other peer routing daemons. This connectivity is intended to obtain the routing database from the peer daemons, not to change or influence the routing paths in any fashion.

Routing protocols such as OSPF generate enough information among the routing daemons that the entire topology of an enterprise network can be created by each of the participating daemons. This is accomplished by the exchange of information about each link, including the address of the different interfaces, capacity, and other link characteristics.

By participating in these protocols, the topology discovery component can discover the network's topology in a relatively efficient fashion.

Topology Discovery Using Active Probes

The final method presented here for discovery topology is the use of active probing programs such as traceroute. This mechanism generates significantly more load on the network than any of the other mechanisms discussed so far. However, this method works without requiring the SNMP agents to be operational at any of the intervening routers.

The active probe mechanism starts by getting a list of remote points that it wants to process. This list can be obtained by using a DNS zone transfer, or by specification from the user. After the list of remote locations is determined, the paths to those locations are determined using such programs as traceroute.

The traceroute program is available on several platforms. It traces the existing path in the network by following a cycle of expanding paths. The program exploits the *Time To Live* (TTL) field within the IP header. The TTL field is initialized by the sender of the packet. It is decremented every time a router processes an IP packet. When a router sees a packet with a TTL of 0, it sends an ICMP message back to the originating router containing the IP header and 8 bytes of the payload of the unfortunate packet. The ICMP message is sent by the router that discarded the expired packet, and its source IP address contains the identity of that router to which appended the header of the discarded packet.

The traceroute program works by sending probes with increasing TTLs into the network. The packets are addressed to a specified destination and contain a destination port that is randomly selected and unlikely to be of use within the network. The response received identifies the addresses of the routers and the order in which they are encountered along the path to the destination.

The problem with programs such as traceroute is that they generate a significant amount of processing overhead and traffic load on the network. Furthermore, although traceroute can give you a snapshot of the network routes at an instant, collecting the routing information in this way within a large network takes a significant amount of time, during which it is quite likely that the routing information has changed. The advantages are that the program can discover the routes without depending on SNMP being turned on in the network, and traceroute does not require that the prober have any special privileges or permissions within the network.

In practice, the best approach is to use a combination of the various techniques. You should obtain an initial list of machines by using the DNS zone transfer. You should obtain the connectivity between different machines by interacting with the routing protocols. If the routing protocols cannot interact with the management station, or if they do not support adequate routing information, you can use SNMP-based polling as an alternative. This is augmented by SNMP-based polling of the different machines, which returns information about the machine's manufacturer and model number. When the route to a specific destination needs to be re-verified, you can use traceroute to check the current status of the path to the specific destination.

PEP and PDP Discovery

After discovering the number of different hosts and routers in the network, you need to discover the different machines on which applications capable of running the network are actually operational. These machines, which are the *Policy Decision Points* (PDPs) and/or the *Policy Enforcement Points* (PEPs), need to be identified so that the policy management tool can determine how to generate the network policy information for these devices. The policy information needs to be generated only for PEPs or PDPs that are involved in supporting a specific function (for example, shaping of packets) within the network.

The discovery of the different PEPs and PDPs can occur in one of two ways:

- By running a protocol in which the various PEPs/PDPs register themselves with the management server

- By maintaining a database of appropriate PEPs/PDPs at the management server and matching the contents of the registration database against the topology discovered by the management tool

The discovery of PEP/PDP capability must identify the operating system and version number of the PEP. For specific functions, the details of the functions supported by the PEP must also be specified. For example, when policies are generated for DiffServ functions, you must know which scheduling schemes are being supported at a router. Similarly, when policies are generated for firewalls to communicate with each other using IKE/IPsec, you must know which suite of encryption/authentication algorithms are available on each platform.

In addition to the different levels of support available on each device, the policy management tool must also know whether a router is positioned in the role of an access router or a core router (for DiffServ) and which of the various interfaces are connected to a secure network and which to an insecure network. Basically, two types of information need to be discovered about the various components:

- A set of information that does not depend on the role of the device within the network

- A set that changes depending on the role of the device within the network

The former set of capabilities is the set we discussed in this section. The discovery of the roles that different devices play depending on their location is discussed in the following section.

PEP Capability Discovery Using Registration

In order to discover the capabilities of different PEPs that are present in the network, you can assume that the PEPs have a protocol that they register themselves with the policy management tool. This requires that each of the PEPs has an agent that provides this registration function.

An agent on the PEP can provide information about the different types of policy-related configurations that might be needed at a device. This agent can provide information about the operating environment and the version of the different applications that are operational at the device.

An agent running on the device is aware of the operating system and the version that is running on the machine. It can also be configured to contain information about the type of operations it might need to perform. For example, the agent at an access router can determine that it supports the functions of a DiffServ access router or encryptions using the IKE/IPsec capabilities. The agent on the PEP can then inform the policy management tool of its capabilities.

Agents that can take stock of the applications installed at a device and report them to a management tool are included as part of various system management frameworks (such as Tivoli's TME-10 framework or Computer Associates' TNG framework). Such an agent can determine the set of applications that require specific policy-related configuration and report them to the main console of the management framework. On PEPs that run a general-purpose operating system, such as a server or a desktop, such an agent can be installed and configured with relative ease. When a version of the agent is made for a specific operating system and machine information, the information about the device's capabilities can be incorporated into that agent. The agent can then inform any management tool about its capabilities.

PEP Capability Discovery Using Capability Databases

In many cases, the agents that can discover the capabilities of the different devices cannot be made operational on the device themselves. This is true of many devices that act as network access routers. Unlike servers and desktops, which run general-purpose operating systems, these devices run proprietary operating systems on which discovery agents cannot always be easily installed. Because there are no standard protocols for registration of the capabilities of specific devices, the capabilities of such devices cannot be determined by means of a registration process.

One method to determine the capabilities of such devices is to use a capability database that is prestored in the policy management tool. During the topology discovery process using SNMP-based discovery tools, you can determine the manufacturer and model number of the various devices within the network. This information is available as part of the standard MIB definitions.

A policy management tool can maintain a table of the capabilities that are commonly available with the specific models of routers and servers manufactured by different vendors. This database can enumerate the most commonly used vendors and models. It can also be periodically updated to keep track of new models and vendors.

In practice, you might often want to use a combination of the capability database and the registration model. Using this combined approach, use the agent on the PEP to discover the operating system, model, and set of installed applications that are active on the PEP. The exact set of application-specific information, such as the set of supported scheduling mechanisms or the set of encryption/authentication algorithms, can be determined by looking in the capability database using the operating system, model, and application as the keys to index into the capability table.

Role and User Discovery

After discovering the topology of the network, the policy management tool needs to discover the roles that the different devices play within the network. It also needs to discover the set of users who are present within the network, as well as the attributes of each of their users.

Role Discovery

Within a network, similar types of devices might be required to play different roles within the network. The role of the device refers to the set of functions that it is required to perform within the network. The set of roles that a device might be involved in depends on the specific policy discipline that is deployed in the network.

As an example, within the policy discipline of DiffServ networks, a router might have the role of an access router, or it might have the role of a core router. Although each router would typically have a single role, the two similar routers with the same capability might be configured to play different roles within the network.

The definition of the roles can be done at a granularity finer than that of a router. For example, for the purposes of secure communications using IPsec, a role can be defined for each of the interfaces within a firewall. The interfaces can be characterized as the role of internal interfaces that connect to a secure network, or they can be characterized to play the role of external interfaces that connect to an insecure network. Similarly, roles may be defined on aggregates of devices (for example, a collection of routers may be characterized as an insecure network), while another collection of routers may be characterized as forming a secure or trusted network.

The role of a device or a collection of devices cannot be discovered automatically by any type of discovery mechanism. It is dependent on how a network administrator decides to place the different functions required to operate the network. The roles can be assigned individually to the different elements that make up the policy-enabled networking infrastructure.

Because the task of identifying roles for individual devices can be fairly tedious in a large network, a better approach is to permit an administrator to define the rules that determine the roles that are to be associated with specific devices. Consider the networked environment shown in Figure 5.2. It shows a networking provider that uses the network addresses of 13.0.0.0/8 for its own internal use. As a result, all access routers that face the customers will have one interface address in this domain and at least one interface with the customer's address. In such an environment, an administrator can specify the rule that all devices with at least one interface in the subnet 13.0.0.0/8 and one interface outside the subnet 13.0.0.0/8 would play the role of an access router in a DiffServ network, while all routers where all the interfaces belong to the subnet 13.0.0.0/8 would play the role of the core routers.

Figure 5.2   Role Specification Using Rules

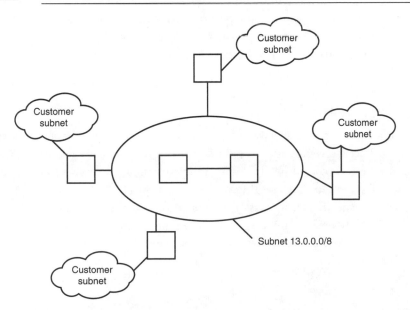

User Discovery

High-level policies related to Quality of Service and security are often easiest to specify in terms of users and employees of an organization, or in terms of the applications they are accessing. The policy within an enterprise might dictate that all regular employees be allowed access to a set of machines within the network. The managers within the enterprise might have access to a larger set of machines, and some specifically named employees might be excluded from accessing a third set of machines.

A listing of all the users within an enterprise can typically be obtained from a directory of employees within an enterprise. Almost every enterprise maintains a directory of its employees, their departments, and the reporting chain that the employees follow. In many cases, such directories support the popular LDAP interface with a well-published schema.

A lookup within the enterprise directory also determines several characteristics associated with a user. These characteristics include a grouping of employees by organization chart, employment types, and various other information. The hierarchy and grouping of the employees can be determined by extending and parsing these directories. Similarly, addresses and locations of the employees can be looked up within the directory, enabling the grouping of employees by their location and sites.

One issue when discovering the set of users is that the user and organization should be discovered only when necessary. Thus, you might want to specify policies only on the basis of specific departments within an enterprise. Clearly, trying to specifically identify all the individual users in an enterprise for the purposes of the application of policy would be counterproductive. However, the departments of users, when specified, can be looked up within the corporate directory, and the existence of the user, department, or role can be verified.

Binding Users to Machines

Although policies are easy to specify in terms of users, they are not easily enforced at the level of a user. Because we are focusing on network-level policies, most of the tools and techniques are geared toward manipulating and processing packets within the network. Any rules for classifying and encrypting packets are most efficiently done when specified in terms of packet header fields, such as IP source and destination address, or the transport protocol (TCP/UDP) port numbers. From an administration perspective, it is much easier to associate policies with users or groups of users than to associate them with the set of IP addresses or even machine names.

For an initial deployment scenario, it is more likely that policies will be specified on department or organization level. In these cases, you need to map department names or organizations to the set of IP addresses they will be using. Because each department or organization has a distinct IP subnet, such a description is fairly easy to provide. In those cases, the task of a policy management tool is simplest. It need not associate individual users with a specific machine or IP address.

However, if policies are specified in terms of users, the users must be mapped to the appropriate set of machines or groups of machines. Unfortunately, the machine information of different users is not readily available in most corporate directories. In this section, we'll discuss some of the techniques that can be used for this purpose.

In the era of multiple terminals that shared the same processor, multiple users were active on a machine at the same time. In the present day, with an increasing emphasis on personal computers and even pervasive handheld devices, most machines tend to be single-user machines. The exceptions are department and mainframe servers that can run many applications. However, these machines typically provide support for applications rather than single-user logon. Thus, the problem of identifying users typically boils down to identifying the user who is active on a specific machine.

Unfortunately, there is no simple way to determine this information in a general manner. Some enterprises maintain a database of users and the machine IP addresses they have been allocated. If this database is current, it can provide the mapping between users and machines. If the database is not updated, it does not provide much useful information.

Within some enterprises, the user logon is authenticated at a single security server. A typical example of such an authentication scheme is Kerberos [KERB]. In such cases, the information available at the security server can be used to determine which user is active at each machine.

There is also a standard TCP/IP service that can be used to determine the identity of users connected to specific ports on a machine. The identity protocol [RFC1413] is a TCP application listening on port 113 of a machine. It receives a text query about open TCP connections at the machine and can return information about who is the active user on that port of the machine. However, security considerations require that the identity protocol only provide information about the TCP connections that are established between the machine to which you are connected and the machine from which the identity query is coming. Because the management console need not be the active location for determining the identity of the connection, the identity protocol might not always work. The identity protocol is not turned on by default in most installations.

Analogous to the identity protocol, a standard identity MIB is also available on most server platforms. When SNMP support is enabled on the server, the identity MIB [RFC1414] provides the information about users listening to active connections on any connected TCP port. Information contained in the MIB is subject to the same caveats as those of the identity protocol—namely, you cannot count on the availability of the SNMP agent on desktops and client machines.

Another option is to have an agent on the managed machine that detects the active users on the machine and reports their identity to the policy management console. Most desktops provide interfaces that allow you to determine the active users on the desktops. An example is the users command that is available on most UNIX machines. Information obtained in this way can be reported to the policy management console to determine the set of users who are active on the machine.

In many cases, the user machines within an enterprise deploy *Dynamic Host Configuration Protocol* (DHCP). With the use of dynamic addresses, the association of each user to the DHCP address it has been assigned to can be obtained from the DHCP server allocation information. This is assuming that there is a way to identify the user from the information provided by the DHCP [DHCP-REF] client. Several implementations of DHCP clients not only obtain the client information, but also register the current machine name to a Dynamic Domain Name Server [DDNS-RFC]. The association of machines to their current address allocation in the network can then be determined from the DNS database using schemes described previously in this chapter.

Application Discovery

Many policy statements refer to how users access specific applications that are running within the network. Therefore, a policy agent must be able to determine the set of applications that are active at a server and determine the network header mappings that would be associated with those applications. Specifically, the policy management tool must be aware of the port numbers and protocol (TCP/UDP) that an application would be using.

For the purpose of identifying applications, they can be classified into two categories:

- Applications in which at least one communicating party uses a fixed port. Most applications fall into this category. Typically, the server program listens on a well-known port number, and the client side uses a randomly selected port number that is told to the server when the client makes initial contact with the server. Examples of such applications include Web servers using HTTP (which typically listen on port 80) and mail servers (which typically listen on port 25).

- Applications in which the control server has a well-known port initially, but new port numbers are allocated for both sides when actual data transfer needs to be done. An example of such an application is the H.323 gateway for carrying Voice over IP. The server listens on a fixed UDP port. When the client connects, it selects a random port number on the server side and communicates with the client using this random port.

An initial guess at the set of applications that are active at a machine can be obtained by looking at the network services database on a machine. It lists all the TCP/UDP servers and the port numbers that are reserved for them at the machine. On most UNIX systems, such a listing can be found in the /etc/services file. It lists the protocol and the port numbers that are used by the corresponding server.

The listing of an application and port number in the services directory does not ensure that the application is running, or even available to run. Also, it does not provide information about which applications are installed and available at the machine. The set of active or possible applications can be discovered by the use of inventory agents or by means of active probing.

Application Discovery Using Inventory Agents

Taking an inventory of installed and active applications is an established area within the general field of systems management. Such inventory agents are available for various operating systems from a large number of network/systems management software vendors.

An inventory management program typically consists of an inventory agent that runs on each of the machines on which the inventory of applications needs to be taken. The inventory agent would go through the configuration of the system. On most operating systems, installed applications create distinctive entries at known areas within the system. For example, on a Windows 95 or NT platform, most applications would create a registry entry. On a UNIX platform, most installed applications would create an entry for the file sets and installed versions that can be obtained from the system information. The information that characterizes the application can be loosely called the *signature* of the application on the platform.

Most of the inventory agents contain a relatively extensive list of common applications and the typical signatures that correspond to those applications. The inventory agent goes through the set of signatures and discovers which of the signatures are found on the machine. The set of discovered applications is then reported back to a main server. In the case of our application, this is the policy management server. Depending on the sophistication and complexity of the inventory agent, you can determine detailed information about the configuration and operation of different applications in the system.

The discovery of the different installed applications only provides information about the set of potential applications that can be made active on the network. This is better than the simple enumeration obtained from the services database, because not all the services might actually be available on the machine. However, this does not provide information about which ports are actually being used by an application. For example, nothing prevents someone from running a Web server on a port other than 80 on any machine. Information about which port numbers are actually being used actively can be determined by probing actively from a central agent. This is described in the next section.

Application Discovery Using Probing

In order to discover the set of applications that is active on a network, you can start by probing all the port numbers that can be used at a machine.

Most of the applications in the network use the TCP and the UDP protocol. All TCP applications begin with the establishment of a TCP connection. A probing agent simply tries to send a connect request to every possible port number on a machine and sees which of these requests are acknowledged. When a server active on a port is identified, the probing agent tries to figure out which application it really is. It determines this by trying out the initial contact message of the known applications and checking whether the server responds with the right answer. After the application is determined, you can try further messages that let you determine more details about the configuration of an application.

This probing process will discover all active instances of an application. Of course, such a probing process is time-consuming. However, such probing techniques are used in security products that analyze network vulnerabilities, and similar techniques can also be used to determine the set of active applications.

If you are specifying policies only for specific applications, it might be sufficient to restrict the polling to occur for a few of the likely ports that the application would be using, rather than attempting to probe all possible combinations. However, from a management perspective, the inventory tools might provide adequate information about the active set of applications so that probing techniques need to be invoked only rarely.

CHAPTER 6

Policy Validation and Translation Algorithms

This chapter takes a closer look at algorithms that are relevant to the policy validation and translation module of a policy management tool. This module is involved with the validation of high-level policies and the translation of high-level policies into low-level policies.

As mentioned in the previous chapters, the main goal of an organization is to ensure meeting its business objectives (for example, performance SLAs), which are defined by the high-level policies. These high level policies need to be translated into the low-level policies which are dependent on the technology (for example, DiffServ) being deployed for meeting those business objectives. In addition to the translation, the specification also needs to be validated to ensure that it satisfies certain criteria, such as being well-formed, is not self-contradictory, and is feasible in a given environment.

During the process of validation and translation, the policy module must perform a variety of validation checks. These validation checks can be of various types. The most basic check is that of validating the syntax of the policy specification. The next level of checking is to ensure that any policy that is specified satisfies any constraints or restrictions that might be required for all policies. Such constraints may arise from the application environments, or a network administrator may impose them. For example, in the area of IP security, there are constraints as to the legal values that an encryption algorithm may take.

The types of checks that can be made on the policy specification depend, to a large extent, on the information model and the language used for policy specification. The next section takes a brief look at the different types of policy specifications that can be used and selects one of them as the basis for the rest of the chapter. The subsequent sections discuss the different schemes that can be used to validate the syntax, detect conflicts among policies, determine if the policies cover all areas of interest, and discuss the translation of policies into a format closer to the configuration of the different devices within the network.

Policy Specification Languages

The high-level policies required for network management can be specified in many different ways. Among the researchers who are involved in specifying policies, multiple approaches for policy specification have been proposed. These approaches range from an interpretation of policies as programs to an interpretation of policies as simple entries in a directory or database.

From a human input standpoint, the best way to specify a high-level policy would be in terms of a natural-language input. You would like to specify the objective of operating a computer network in a simple English sentence such as "All communication between the research site and the engineering site needs tight security." Although these policies are very attractive to specify, the current state of natural-language processing, a special area within the field of artificial intelligence, needs to improve significantly before such policies can be expressed in this manner. For example, it is unclear what the term "tight security" in this phrase implies.

The next approach is to specify policies in a language that can be processed and interpreted by a computer. One way is to interpret a policy as a piece of a program that can be executed by a computer on the occurrence of certain conditions. Examples of this approach include CacheL, a language for specifying caching policies [CACHEL] and LaSCO [LASCO], a language for specifying security policies in the network. Another approach is to specify the policy using a formal specification language. Examples of such an approach include GRAIL [KAOS] and PONDER[PONDER]. The policy example just mentioned would be specified as a program that implements the policy implied in the action. When policies are specified as a computer-interpretable program, it is possible to execute them. However, in general it is difficult to determine whether two computer programs specifying two different policies are mutually contradictory.

A more simplified approach is to interpret the policy as a sequence of rules, in which each rule is in the form of a simple condition-action pair. The rules are evaluated on specific triggers, such as the passage of time or the arrival of a new packet within the network. If a rule's condition is true, the action is executed. A sample specification of the policy in this format would be "If the packet's source or destination IP address belongs to the research or engineering subnet, encrypt the packet." Policies specified in this fashion are easier to analyze than policies specified as full-blown computer programs or by a formal specification language.

Note

Representing policies using "if-then-else" semantics sometimes leads to the misinterpretation that policy representations should be evaluated using an expert system or theorem-proving approach. Although such an approach toward network policies is feasible, I believe that this is not the appropriate approach for the problem. For the most important problems that are of relevance in an application of policies within the network, expert systems-based approaches have several limitations.

An alternative specification of policies is to represent them simply as entries in a table. The table consists of multiple attributes. Some of these attributes constitute the condition part, and others constitute the action part. Different types of tables need to be specified if the condition components or action components of different rules vary. Such a tabular representation is rich enough to express most of the policies that can be specified with a rule-based notation. Furthermore, it is easier to analyze for contradictions and coverage. In the example of communication between the engineering and research branches, such a specification would consist of specifying three types of tables. The first one would define the mapping of the named branches (research/engineering) to IP addresses and subnets, the second one would define the mapping of a security classification (such as tight security to a set of encryption parameters), and the third table would define a mapping from the source/destination branches to that of a security classification (tight).

The IETF [POLICYWG] has chosen a rule-based policy representation in its specification. However, due to the need to store this representation in an LDAP directory or database, this representation essentially follows the tabular specification just described. From my experience in the field of networking, such a tabular specification of policies is rich enough to capture all the practical scenarios you can construct. Therefore, I will focus on the tabular representation and the rule-based notation in the rest of this chapter.

Figure 6.1 shows the various specification languages that can be used in the context of policies and compares them in terms of ease of usage and complexity of analysis.

Figure 6.1   Policy Specification Languages

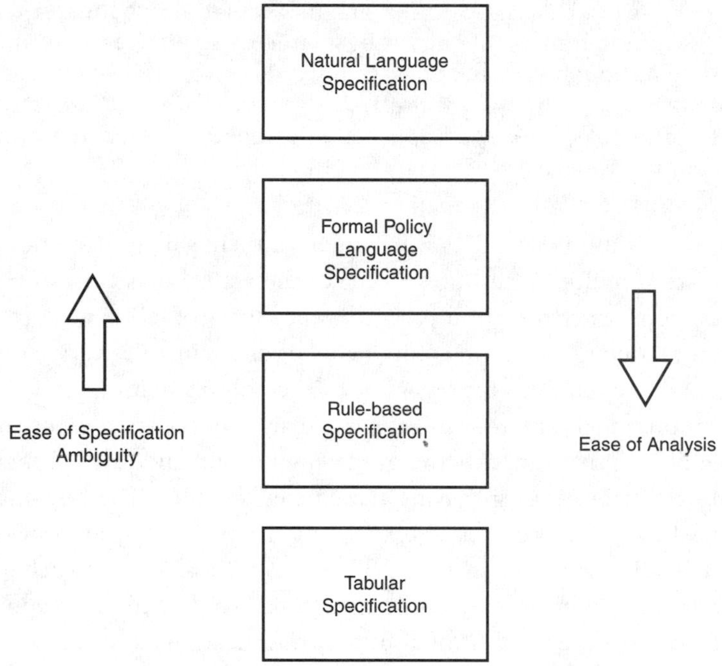

A Policy Case Example

In order to illustrate the different validation algorithms that are examined in this chapter, I will use a simple example that commonly arises in the enterprise environment. Assume that this is an enterprise that wants to support application-level SLAs for its customers. These SLAs are specified in terms of the application response time that occurs when a specific client accesses an application. The high-level policies that will be specified by a user will map each usage scenario, a client accessing an application on a server, to a service class. The service class has specific performance objectives associated with it.

A simple set of six tables can be used to represent these policies, as shown in Figure 6.2. A table of users provides the mapping of users to the different subnets and IP addresses. A table of applications provides information about the port numbers that different applications will use. A table of routers and a table of servers provide information about the different policy enforcement points that exist in the network, and whose configuration information needs to be generated by the validation module. The fifth table provides information about the different service levels that are defined within the network. The entries in the tables of users, applications, servers, routers and service classes are tied together with entries in the table of policies, which maps the different application flows to a class of service.

Figure 6.2   The Set of Tables that Represent Enterprise SLAs

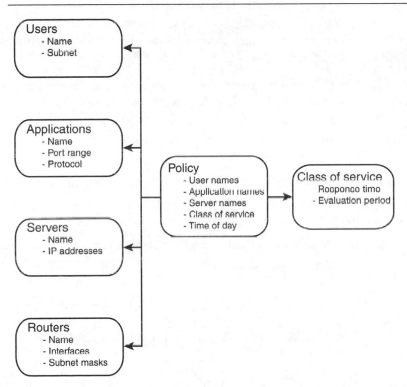

In order to simplify the discussion of policies, I will list only the most basic set of classes and a very basic set of attributes. In a more realistic implementation of the policy specification, many other attributes can be specified in order to provide a more comprehensive solution. A more realistic implementation is also likely to provide more classes, such as a way to hierarchically group applications or users into more easily addressable entities.

Let's briefly examine the attributes shown in Figure 6.2. The description for each user includes a short name for the user and the IP address or subnet from which the user can connect to the network. The description for each application consists of a name, the protocol that the application uses (usually TCP or UDP), and the range of ports that the application can use. The description for a server and a router contains their names and the IP addresses and subnet masks for all their interfaces. The servers are the end points of communication—machines where applications execute. The routers are intermediary. The service class contains a response time for the flow and an interval over which the response time needs to be satisfied. In a more realistic implementation, the response time will be qualified (such as a response time to load a page of fixed size or to execute a transaction of a fixed nature). Instead of specifying absolute bounds on response time, a practical implementation would probably specify a percentile goal, in which no more than a certain percentage (such as 95%) of application flow transactions will exceed the desired response time delay. However, the simple deterministic bound will suffice for the purpose of algorithm description in this book.

The policy class contains the name of a user, an application, and a server on which an application is executing, and it maps that to a service class. Even though it is implemented as a table, it can be interpreted as a rule in which the condition part of the rule consists of the user, application, and server names, while the action part of the rule consists of the class of service that it is assigned to.

Let's consider an instance in which the high-level policies expressed in this tabular representation can be utilized. Figure 6.3 shows a hypothetical enterprise with four branch campuses that are connected by a core network.

Figure 6.3   An Enterprise Environment for Sample SLAs

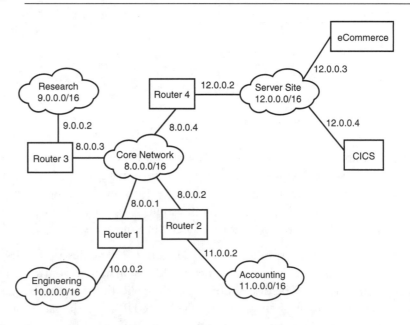

The figure shows the subnet addresses that are assigned to each of the branch campuses, as well as the interface addresses of two key servers and the access routers that connect the different campuses to the core network. There are two key servers. One houses a Web server (eCommerce), and the other hosts a transactional database system (CICS) server. One branch campus hosts the servers, while the other three branch campuses belong to the engineering, research, and accounting departments. Five applications are operational on the network: a Web server, a mail server, a video server, Data Link Switching, and Enterprise Extender. The last two items are two common ways of carrying legacy IBM SNA applications over an IP network. These five applications (with some details shown in Table 6.2) are categorized into three levels: business-critical, office support, and utility applications. Data Link Switching and Enterprise Extender are classified as business-critical, the Web server is classified as an office support application, and the mail server and video server are classified as utility applications.

The policies that are put into place are as follows:

- Business-critical applications on the eCommerce server take the highest precedence.

- Engineering access to office support applications on the eCommerce server is a preferred communication.

- Any access to the CICS server is a preferred communication.

- Staff utility applications get best-effort service.

- By default, all applications get best-effort service.

These policies and their associated definitions result in the table of policies shown in Tables 6.1 through 6.6. I will use this example throughout the chapter to illustrate the functioning of the policy management algorithms.

Table 6.1   Users

Username	Subnet
Accounting	10.0.0.0/24
Engineering	11.0.0.0/24
Research	9.2.0.0/16

Table 6.2   Applications

Name	Port Range	Protocol
DLSW	265	tcp
Enterprise Extender	300	udp
MailServer	11	tcp
VideoCharger	4000-6000	udp

Table 6.3   Application Groups

Name	Members
Business Critical	DLSW; Enterprise Extender
Office Support	MailServer
StaffUtility	MailServer;VideoCharger

Table 6.4   Servers

Name	Interfaces/Subnet Prefix
eCommServer	12.0.0.3/16
CICSServe	12.0.0.4/16

Table 6.5   Routers

Name	Interfaces/Subnet Prefix
router 1	8.0.0.1/16; 10.0.0.2/24
router 2	8.0.0.2/16; 11.0.0.2/24
router 3	8.0.0.3/16;9.0.0.2/16
router 4	8.0.0.4/16; 12.0.0.2/16

Table 6.6   Policies

Clients	Applications	Servers	Class of Service
Any	Business Critical	eCommServer	Precendence
Engineering	Office Support	eCommServer	Preferred
Any	Any	CICS	ServerPreferred
Any	Staff Utility	Any	Default
Any	Any	Any	Default

Policy Constraint Validation

After the policies are specified as a set of rules, or as entries in a set of tables, they must be validated to ensure that they satisfy the syntactic and semantic constraints that are imposed on them by the usage scenario and the mechanisms used to describe the policies. These constraints can be of various types. They are discussed briefly in this section.

Syntax Validation

The first type of validation is to ensure that the syntax for policy specification is valid. Syntactic validation depends on the language that is used by a policy management tool to describe policies. The policies are input to the validation module in a descriptive format. This format is different among different management tools. Most often, it takes the form of a configuration file with a specific syntax that must be followed. The conventions used to represent the language must be validated to make sure that the policy representation is well-formed.

With the recent popularity of tagged languages such as those permitted by the XML standards (details of XML can be found at http://w3.org/xml), a tagged syntax can also be used to represent the high-level policies. The XML representation is normally required to follow the syntax dictated by a *data type definition* (DTD). Thus, the initial step in validating any set of policies specified in an XML syntax is to check that it conforms to the DTD's specifications. An XML based representation that captures the high-level policies illustrated in Table 6.1 through Table 6.6 is shown in Listings 6.1 through 6.6. Some explanation behind the XML representation can be found in the sidebar "XML Representation of Policies."

Listing 6.1	XML Equivalent of Table 6.1

```
<UserList>
 <User>
   <Name>Accounting</Name>
   <Subnet>
     <Network>10.0.0.0</Network>
     <PrefixLength>24</PrefixLength>
   </Subnet>
 </User>
 <User>
   <Name>Engineering</Name>
   <Subnet>
     <Network>11.0.0.0</Network>
     <PrefixLength>24</PrefixLength>
```

continues

Listing 6.1   Continued

```
      </Subnet>
   </User>
   <User>
     <Name>Research</Name>
     <Subnet>
       <Network>9.2.0.0</Network>
       <PrefixLength>16</PrefixLength>
     </Subnet>
   </User>
</UserList>
```

Listing 6.2   XML Equivalent of Table 6.2

```
  <ApplicationList>
   <Application>
     <Name>MailServer</Name>
     <PortRange>
       <Port>11</Port>
       <Protocol>tcp</Protocol>
     </PortRange>
   </Application>
   <Application>
     <Name>DLSW</Name>
     <PortRange>
       <Port>265</Port>
       <Protocol>tcp</Protocol>
     </PortRange>
   </Application>
   <Application>
     <Name>Enterprise Extender</Name>
     <PortRange>
       <Port>300</Port>
       <Protocol>udp</Protocol>
     </PortRange>
   </Application>
   <Application>
     <Name>VideoCharger</Name>
     <PortRange>
       <StartPort>4000</StartPort>
       <EndPort>6000</EndPort>
       <Protocol>tcp</Protocol>
```

```
      </PortRange>
    </Application>
  </ApplicationList>
```

Listing 6.3   XML Equivalent of Table 6.3

```
  <ApplicationGroupList>
   <ApplicationGroup>
     <Name>Business Critical</Name>
     <Members>
       <NameReference Type="Application">DLSW</NameReference>
       <NameReference Type="Application">Enterprise Extender</NameReference>
     </Members>
   </ApplicationGroup>
   <ApplicationGroup>
     <Name>Office Support</Name>
     <Members>
       <NameReference Type="Application">MailServer</NameReference>
     </Members>
   </ApplicationGroup>
   <ApplicationGroup>
     <Name>Staff Utility</Name>
     <Members>
       <NameReference Type="Application">MailServer</NameReference>
       <NameReference Type="Application">VideoCharger</NameReference>
     </Members>
   </ApplicationGroup>
  </ApplicationGroupList>
```

Listing 6.4   XML Equivalent of Table 6.4

```
  <ServerList>
   <Server>
     <Name>eCommServer</Name>
     <InterfaceList>
       <Interface>
         <IPAddress>12.0.0.3</IPAddress>
         <SubnetPrefix>16</SubnetPrefix>
       </Interface>
     </InterfaceList>
```

continues

Listing 6.4   Continued

```
    </Server>
    <Server>
      <Name>CICSServer</Name>
      <InterfaceList>
        <Interface>
          <IPAddress>12.0.0.4</IPAddress>
          <SubnetPrefix>16</SubnetPrefix>
        </Interface>
      </InterfaceList>
    </Server>
  </ServerList>
```

Listing 6.5   XML Equivalent of Table 6.5

```
  <RouterList>
    <Router>
      <Name>router1</Name>
      <InterfaceList>
        <Interface>
          <IPAddress>10.0.0.2</IPAddress>
          <PrefixLength>24</PrefixLength>
        </Interface>
        <Interface>
          <IPAddress>8.0.0.1</IPAddress>
          <PrefixLength>16</PrefixLength>
        </Interface>
      </InterfaceList>
    </Router>
    <Router>
      <Name>router2</Name>
      <InterfaceList>
        <Interface>
          <IPAddress>11.0.0.2</IPAddress>
          <PrefixLength>24</PrefixLength>
        </Interface>
        <Interface>
          <IPAddress>8.0.0.2</IPAddress>
          <PrefixLength>16</PrefixLength>
        </Interface>
      </InterfaceList>
    </Router>
```

```
<Router>
  <Name>router3</Name>
  <InterfaceList>
    <Interface>
      <IPAddress>9.2.0.2</IPAddress>
      <PrefixLength>16</PrefixLength>
    </Interface>
    <Interface>
      <IPAddress>8.0.0.3</IPAddress>
      <PrefixLength>16</PrefixLength>
    </Interface>
  </InterfaceList>
</Router>
<Router>
  <Name>router4</Name>
  <InterfaceList>
    <Interface>
      <IPAddress>12.0.0.2</IPAddress>
      <PrefixLength>16</PrefixLength>
    </Interface>
    <Interface>
      <IPAddress>8.0.0.4</IPAddress>
      <PrefixLength>16</PrefixLength>
    </Interface>
  </InterfaceList>
</Router>
</RouterList>
```

| Listing 6.6 | XML Equivalent of Table 6.6 |

```
<PolicyList>
  <Policy>
    <ClientSite>Any</ClientSite>
    <ServerApplication>
      <NameReference Type="ApplicationGroup">Business Critical</NameReference>
    </ServerApplication>
    <ServerReference>
      <NameReference Type="Server">eCommServer</NameReference>
    </ServerReference>
    <CoSReference>Precedence</CoSReference>
  </Policy>
  <Policy>
```

continues

Listing 6.6   Continued

```
    <ClientSite>
        <NameReference Type="UserGroup">Engineering</NameReference>
    </ClientSite>
    <ServerApplication>
      <NameReference Type="ApplicationGroup">Office Support</NameReference>
    </ServerApplication>
    <ServerReference>
      <NameReference Type="Server">eCommServer</NameReference>
    </ServerReference>
    <CoSReference>Preferred</CoSReference>
  </Policy>
  <Policy>
    <ClientSite>Any</ClientSite>
    <ServerApplication>Any</ServerApplication>
    <ServerReference> <NameReference Type="Server">CICSServer</NameReference>
►</ServerReference>
    <CoSReference>Preferred</CoSReference>
  </Policy>
  <Policy>
    <ClientSite>Any</ClientSite>
    <ServerApplication>
      <NameReference Type="ApplicationGroup">Staff Utility</NameReference>
    </ServerApplication>
    <ServerReference>Any</ServerReference>
    <CoSReference>Default</CoSReference>
    <Priority>1</Priority>
  </Policy>
  <Policy>
    <ClientSite>Any</ClientSite>
    <ServerApplication>Any</ServerApplication>
    <ServerReference>Any</ServerReference>
    <CoSReference>Default</CoSReference>
    <Priority>0</Priority>
  </Policy>
 </PolicyList>
```

XML Representation of Policies

XML is a tagged syntax that allows the marking of different types of information. Any type of information can be expressed in the XML format, and exchanged among different entities that agree upon the set of tags being used. This agreement often takes the form of a DTD, or document type definition which is a set of rules specifying which tags are allowed and under what circumstances.

An XML document typically has a header identifying the DTD (if any) that it conforms to, and items such as the character-set used for writing the document. It then has two tags that enclose the information contained in the document, the first one (starting tag) marks the beginning of the document, and the second one (closing tag) end-tag marks its end. Tags are always enclosed in angular braces, and a closing tag begins with a slash. An SLA description would be of the format <SLA>...</SLA> where <SLA> is the starting tag, </SLA> is the closing tag, and the ... portion contains the information that makes up the SLA description.

The simplest type of tagged information contains a text string between the beginning and closing tag; for example, a name may be defined as <Name>Accouting</Name>. Other types of tagged information can contain nested tags. As an example, an IP address can be represented as

```
<Subnet>
        <Network>9.2.0.0</Network>
        <PrefixLength>16</PrefixLength>
</Subnet>
```

The nested tags can be repeated. As an example, the UserList tag in Listing 6.1 contains multiple repetitions of the nested tag User. Tags can also contain attributes, for instance, the text <NameReference type="User"> marks the beginning of a tag called NameReference which has an attribute called "type" and whose value is "User".

The DTD defines the format of each tag; for example, it defines that a UserList tag can contain multiple nested User tags, but that it cannot contain any other types of nested tags, or that the Subnet tag consists of a Network tag and a PrefixLength tag, with the latter two tags containing string data. It would also specify which attributes are permitted for each tag.

The DTD that is used for examples in this chapter is a rather simple use of XML that does not use any advanced features. A DTD is represented using a syntax whose description would require more space than is appropriate for this book. However, the reader can follow the information contained in a fairly simple manner. Each table is marked with tag containing several nested entries, and each nested entry is used to

continues

represent one row in the table. Where necessary, references to the names contained in other portions of the XML representation are provided. I am assuming that the entire XML fragments shown in various excerpts are kept in a single document so that the names can be resolved appropriately.

The mapping from the table entries to the XML representation is relatively straightforward for the high-level policies that are illustrated in Tables 6.1 through 6.6. Similar mappings can be easily constructed for defining mappings from high-level to low-level policies (Tables 6.8 through 6.10), as well as for the low-level policies illustrated in Tables 6.11 and 6.12.

Attribute Validation

After validating that the syntactic requirement in high-level policy specifications is satisfied, the validation module must check that the value specified for each of the attributes is valid. The validity requirements for each entry depend on the type of value it represents.

In Tables 6.1 through 6.6, several of the fields are IP addresses/subnets and must conform to the requirements of being 4-byte addresses with a subnet prefix of less than 32 bits. Examples of attributes which must satisfy this contraint include the subnet field in the table of users (Table 6.1), the interfaces field in the table of servers (Table 6.4) and the interfaces field in the table of routers (Table 6.5). However, syntactic checks are not the only constraints that need to be satisfied by an attribute. Some of the attributes must be restricted to specific ranges. For example, the percentile attribute in the class of service should take values between 0 and 100. Depending on the meaning of the different attributes, the value taken by each attribute must specify these constraints. These constraints must be verified by the policy validation logic.

Interattribute Validation

Which values are legal for one attribute might depend on the value taken by another attribute by the same entry in a table. The simplest example of such a relationship is between the domain name and the IP address of interfaces for a server and a router. These interface addresses must be the ones that are returned by a DNS lookup of the domain name of the server or the router. Similarly, the interval over which the performance metrics of a service class is measured must be larger than the response time that is desired of transactions in that class of service.

The policy validation module must check that all interattribute relations that are required in the policy specification are satisfied. Depending on the policy discipline, these relationships vary, but the code and logic to validate them is usually straightforward.

A very common type of interattribute relations is reference, in which the value that a specific attribute may take must be a reference to another attribute elsewhere in the table. The class of service that is specified in the policy must be the name of a class defined in the table of service classes. Similarly, user and server references in any policy must be defined in the appropriate tables. Such cross-references must be checked as part of the interattribute validation.

It is usually a good idea to restrict the values that such references can take to one of a set of multiple values when a GUI is used to input the high-level policies. Be sure to carefully consider the selection method. Because you expect the number of service classes in a network to be fairly small (typically less than 10), a drop-down menu might suffice. The number of users or servers in a typical network can run into the hundreds, so a drop-down menu would not work in that case. An editable text input area that provides look-ahead and lets someone choose from a set of possibilities might be a better choice in that case.

Policy Conflict Detection and Resolution

One of the key validation steps is to verify that the policies do not contradict each other. Given a set of policies, one or more policies may be applicable when a packet arrives at a router. If the actions specified by all the applicable policies can be taken, then there is no contradiction in the applicable policies. On the other hand, if the actions of two applicable policies cannot be taken simultaneously (for instance, one policy sets DiffServ field to be 0, other policy sets DiffServ field to be 1), there is a contradiction. A set of policies is *consistent* if it can be shown that no contradictory policies will ever be found. Regardless of the type of packet arriving at the router, the applicable policies should not have contradicting actions.

The definition of policy conflict depends on the approach used to specify policies. If a rule-based approach that represents the if-condition-then-action format is used without any constraints on what constitutes the condition or the action, the policy conflict detection can be shown to be *NP-complete*. See the following sidebar for details. However, if appropriate constraints are placed on what constitutes the policy definition, the conflict resolution can be done in a much more efficient manner.

Running Time for Algorithms

Any algorithm such as the ones described for consistency checking in this section takes some time to execute. In general, the more efficient an algorithm is, the less time it takes. The runtime efficiency of a program that implements an algorithm depends on many factors independent of the algorithm, such as the speed of the processor on which the program is run. In order to focus on an algorithm's efficiency, the running time of algorithms is often described using its order, generally represented in the "Big O" notation. Here the running time is expressed as a function of the size of the input given to the function.

For example, you might find an algorithm to sort integers described as $O(n^2)$, where n is the number of integers it is sorting. (In other words, this is an algorithm of the order n-squared.) What this means is that the time taken to sort n numbers is less than Cn^2, where C is some fixed but unknown constant. The constant will be smaller for a faster machine than for a slower machine. Also, this property is true asymptotically. In other words, it holds true for a large value of n.

In general, an efficient algorithm has a running time complexity of $O(f)$, where f is a polynomial function of n. A *polynomial function* is one that is expressed as n raised to some power. Such functions always grow at a lesser rate than exponential functions, in which a fixed number is raised to the power of n.

A set of problems are known for which the best running solutions are nonpolynomial. At the same time, no one has been able to show that a polynomial solution does not exist. However, it has been shown that if you can solve any of these problems in polynomial time, all the problems can be solved in polynomial time. This set of problems is known as *NP-complete problems*. When you encounter an NP-complete problem, the most practical approach is to avoid trying to get an exact solution for the problem, and to look for an approximate solution (usually called a *heuristic*).

Conflict Definition

A *policy rule* can be specified as a set of rules with the if-condition-then-action semantics. The consistency criteria is that if two rules can both apply under some conditions, the actions to be performed must be uniquely identified and be doable simultaneously.

As an example of conflicts among different policies, consider a simple case of policies that are defined according to the tables shown in Figure 6.2. Two classes of service are defined—Gold and Silver. An application called WebServer is defined to operate on the protocol of TCP and the port number of 80. A set of users called HighPowerUsers is also defined that has IP addresses in the subnet 9.2.34/24. Two policies are defined as follows:

P1: Any access to WebServer gets Silver service.

P2: Any use of the network by HighPowerUsers gets Gold service.

Both of these rules are perfectly okay by themselves, but there's a problem when the two are taken together. In the case of a HighPowerUser who is trying to access WebServer, it is unclear whether the Gold service or the Silver service should be applied.

When policies are actually being enforced and executed by the packet forwarding paths in the network, such a conflict can cause erratic and unpredictable behavior. Therefore, the policy management tool must take steps to detect any conflicts that might be present among a set of policy rules, and furthermore provide mechanisms to resolve the conflicts among these rules. The different mechanisms that can be used to resolve policy conflicts are discussed later. The next section focuses on how to detect such conflicts.

Conflict Detection Using Expert Systems

Because policy definition looks very similar to the rule definitions used in rule-rewriting engines and theorem-proving systems, you might think that they would be a suitable medium for detecting policy conflicts. Unfortunately, as you will see in this section, conflict detection might not be the easiest thing to do for many expert systems.

A set of policies can be expressed as consisting of many rules in a normalized fashion called the *conjunctive normal form*. The set of policies consists of the logical anding of all the rules specified in the set, and each rule consists of a logical oring of one or more Boolean predicates. If within this set there are two contradicting rules, such as a rule and its logical negation, the set of policies has a logical contradiction. The logical contradiction may be present in the existing set of rules or between a derived set of rules that contains additional rules that are logically derived from the initial set of rules. Expert systems are typically developed to detect the logical contradictions in an initial set of policies. They include many efficient techniques for expanding the set of rules that can be logically derived from that initial set. The later sidebar "Symbolic Logic" provides more details on this topic.

Unfortunately, a set of policies can have conflicts without having a logical contradiction. In the earlier example of HighPowerUsers accessing Web servers, the rules P1 and P2 do not logically contradict each other. To see this, consider a notation in which Web is a logical expression that is true for a flow whenever the flow is used to access a Web server and HiPo is a logical expression that is true whenever a flow is being used by a HighPowerUser. The rules P1 and P2 can be written in their normalized logical expression equivalents like this:

L1: ~Web V Silver

L2: ~HiPo V Gold

These two rules do not logically conflict with each other, but you need to add the domain-specific rules that are true for the present system—namely, that a flow could not be both Gold and Silver. This must be done by means of a rule:

L3: ~Silver V ~Gold

The set of the three policies just specified is adequate to capture the scenario that causes a conflict among the policies. However, there is no logical contradiction among these three policies. A logical contradiction would imply that you wouldn't be able to find a set of values for the variables (Web, Silver, Gold, HiPo) that will satisfy all the rules. However, the values of (Web = true, Silver = true, Gold = false, HiPo = false) or the values of (Web = false, Silver = false, Gold = true, HiPo = true) can be seen to satisfy the rules very well.

The conflict arises only when a flow has the characteristics of Web = true and HiPo = true. However, you can't introduce those rules as additional ones in the policy set (unless you assume that all flows are HighPowerUsers accessing WebServers). When the policies were defined, there was no logical contradiction among the rules. However, when the policies need to be applied, some of the predicates take well-known values, and a logical contradiction can be detected.

There are three ways you can envision working around this problem while still using rule-based expert systems:

- One approach is to consider all the possible characteristics of a flow (all combinations of users and applications) and try out the number of policy sets that are generated in this fashion. Unfortunately, this approach will result in an exponential runtime algorithm.

- The other approach is to invoke the rule-based engine when the flow is to be acted on, rather than when the policy management tool is invoked to translate high-level policies to low-level policies.

At the time of policy application, the rule-based system will definitely be able to determine the logical conflicts. However, this requires that rule-based inference be done on the arrival of every packet or (in some systems) on the arrival of every new connection. Although tremendous progress has been made in increasing processor speeds, as well as expert systems algorithms in recent years, we are still far from the day where the performance of rule-based inference would be fast enough to be deployed in this fashion.

- The third method that can be used within the policy management tool is to move to a more complex form of symbolic logic that is rich enough to capture the problem statement. However, such enhancements add substantially to the overhead involved in analyzing the policy rules. Therefore, you must look elsewhere for algorithms that can identify conflicts among different policies.

Symbolic Logic

The simplest form of symbolic logic aims to study the satisfaction of logical expressions. Logical expressions are built up from predicates, which are variables that can have a value of either true or false. For example, you can use a predicate such as Web to denote the case that a flow is to or from a Web server. To build up logical expressions, you can combine the predicates using a variety of operators. The most common operators are the logical and ($\wedge$), the logical or , negation , and implies ($\rightarrow$). Logical anding is also known as *conjunction,* and logical oring is known as *disjunction*.

A logical expression takes a value of true or false, depending on the predicates within the expression. If predicate A is true, negation ~A is false, and vice versa. For predicated A and B, the expression (A $\wedge$ B) is true if both A and B are true, and (A V B) is true if at least one of A and B is true. The logical expression of A $\rightarrow$ B is true whenever A is true B is also true. You can verify that logically A $\rightarrow$ B is equivalent to ~A V B. The statement if A then B is the same as A $\rightarrow$ B. Logical expressions that always take the value of true (such as A V ~A) are called *tautologies*. If a logical expression can never take the value of true, it is a logical contradiction. The most common example of a contradiction is A $\wedge$ ~A.

The two logical expressions (A $\wedge$B) and ~(~A V ~B) can be shown to be equivalent. Similarly, (A V B) can be shown to be equivalent to ~(~A $\wedge$ ~B). These two equivalencies are known as *De Morgan's laws*. They lead to an important property of all logical expressions: Any arbitrary logical expression can be expressed in two fashions, which are called *normative forms*. In the *Conjunctive Normal Form* (CNF), any logical expression can be expressed as a conjunction (logical anding) of subexpressions, where each subexpression consists of nothing but logical oring of simple predicates or the negation of simple predicates. In the *Disjunctive Normal Form* (DNF), an expression is a logical oring (disjunction) of several subexpressions, where each subexpression consists of

continues

nothing but logical oring of simple predicates or the negation of simple predicates.

For example, a set of rules that states that 'any access to the WebServer gets Silver service'; 'any use of the network by HighPowerUsers gets Gold service'; and 'you can't get both Gold and Silver service at the same time' would normally be expressed like this:

$$(Web \rightarrow Silver) \wedge (HiPo \Rightarrow Gold) \wedge \sim (Gold \wedge Silver)$$

This can be expressed in CNF notation as the following:

$$(\sim Web \vee Silver) \wedge (\sim HiPo \vee Gold) \wedge (\sim Gold \vee \sim Silver).$$

The same set of rules can be expressed in DNF notation like this:

$$(\sim Web \wedge \sim HiPo \wedge \sim Silver) \vee (\sim Web \wedge Gold \wedge \sim Silver) \vee$$
$$(\sim Web \wedge \sim HiPo \wedge \sim Gold) \vee (Silver \wedge \sim HiPo \wedge \sim Gold)$$

The CNF form is normally used for theorem proving and deriving new rules. Each of the ored terms in the CNF form of the logical expression can be considered an individual rule. The basic technique used for deriving new rules is to combine two rules with a common predicate—one using the predicate and the other using the negation of the predicate. Thus, the rule (A ∨ B) can be combined with the rule (~A ∨ C) to come up with a new rule (B ∨ C) .

When a theorem needs to be proven in an inference engine, the general procedure is to add the logical negation of the theorem to the set of rules. Then, the system tries to infer new rules and validate if a logical contradiction is reached. A logical contradiction is reached if two rules are derived (or are present initially)—one stating predicate A and the other its logical negation (~A).

Unfortunately, the running time for deciding whether a theorem is provable is not bounded.

Conflict Detection Using Topological Spaces

An alternative to detecting conflicts among the different rules is to look upon each policy rule as consisting of multiple independent terms and one or more derived terms. A policy rule consists of the generic form if-condition-then-action. This restriction implies that the terms that define the condition be distinct from the terms that define the action portion of the rule. This is a slightly more restrictive definition of a rule than a general logical expression. However, in most networking policy applications, this requirement does not pose any significant restrictions. Business SLA policies, as well as security policies, are often defined in terms of classes of service (dealing with performance or security). Each class of service combines several actions that can be taken together.

Suppose n terms make up the condition part of a policy expressed in the format, if condition then action.

Each of the independent terms can be looked upon as independent axis in a hyperdimensional space. Each rule defines a region in the hyperdimensional space. Each such region can be associated with a dependent term (such as the service class) that is identified by the rule. If any point in space has multiple dependent terms that conflict with each other, you have a potential conflict.

For example, consider the case of policy definitions that have two independent terms. Each of the policy definitions would carve out a two-dimensional space, as shown in Figure 6.4. The policies A and B have no overlap in the spaces they carve out, and they have no conflicts. The policies C and D overlap and might have a potential conflict if the dependent terms in the policy definition can't be done together.

Figure 6.4   Policy Conflict Detection

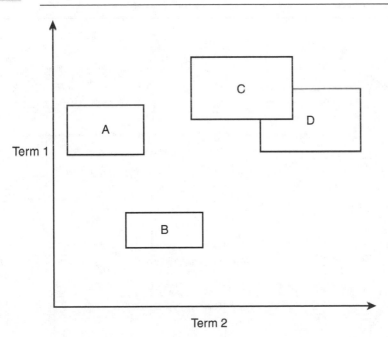

For a more specific example, consider the simple case of two-dimensional policy as illustrated by the following:

P1: Any access to the WebServer gets Silver service.

P2: Any use of the network by HighPowerUsers gets Gold service.

The two independent axes in this case are the applications (identified by their port numbers) and the users, identified by their IP address. These two rules define regions in a two-dimensional space, as shown in Figure 6.5. The first rule, P1, is illustrated by a horizontal line showing the region characterized by the WebServer running on port 80. The vertical shaded band illustrates the HighPowerUsers who have a client IP address in the subnet 9.2.34/24 (in the range 9.2.34.0 through 9.2.34.255). The horizontal line indicates the Silver class of service. The intersection of the horizontal line with the vertical shaded band is the area that has an overlap and contains a conflict with two different classes of service.

Figure 6.5   Policy Conflict Resolution Example

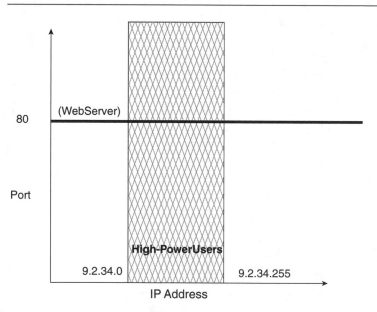

More realistic cases of policy definition would tend to have more independent terms and corresponding dimensions defining the policies. For the sample policies using the policy classes defined in Figure 6.2 and applicable to the network shown in Figure 6.3, we have three independent terms, each defining an axis in the policy definition—namely, users, applications, and servers. The four policies (plus a fifth default one) defined in this network are as follows:

1. Business-critical applications on the eCommerce server take the highest precedence.

2. Engineering access to office support applications on the eCommerce server is a preferred communication.

3. Any access to the CICS server is a preferred communication.

4. Staff utility applications get best-effort service.

5. By default, all applications get best effort service.

We will use the users' IP addresses as the first axis, the application port numbers as the second axis, and the server IP addresses as the third axis. Using these three axes, we get the following spaces defined by the individual policy rules:

1. Any client IP address; application port numbers of 265 and 300; server address 12.0.0.3

2. Client IP address of 11.0.0.0/24; application port number of 11, server address 12.0.0.3

3. Any client IP address; any application port; server address 12.0.0.4

4. Any client IP address; application ports 11 and 4000 through 6000; any server address

5. Any client IP address; any application port; any server address

The last one is the default rule that maps all applications to best-effort.

The default rule overlaps with all the other rules. Rules 2 and 3 overlap, as do rules 2 and 4. Note that the overlap of rules 2 and 3 does not result in any conflict because they both map to the same class of service—namely, preferred communication. Rules 2 and 3 do result in a conflict, which needs to be resolved.

Different algorithms determine if a conflict exists among a set of policies. The simplest algorithm is to compare each pair of policies to determine if there is an overlap and, if so, that there are no conflicts among them. If there are n policies to be compared against k dimensions with c classes of services, this algorithm will have an average (as well as worst-case) running time of $O(kn^2)$.

You can use some tricks to improve the running time of the simple comparison algorithm. One approach is to leverage the fact that you would typically have many more policy rules than service classes defined in an environment. The number of security classes, or the service-level classes defined in any environment, is not likely to be more than 10. The policy rules that map different applications to the same service class will not conflict with each other, even if they overlap with each other in the hyperdimensional space. This algorithm will have a running time of $O((n/c)^2)$ and is likely to run much faster than the previous version.

One of the key features regarding overlap of two regions in the topological spaces is that the overlap between the two regions must occur along all the independent axes. Thus, if you can eliminate policies that do not overlap by examining one of the axes, you can cut down on the number of comparisons you have to make.

One way to reduce the number of policies to be compared is to sort the policy rules along one of the dimensions using one of two methods. You could increase the order of the beginning of the region defined by the policy along one of the dimensions, or you could increase the order of the end of the region defined by the policy. You can then start with the policies in the order in which they begin and compare each only against the other policies whose ending points are before its ending point. You only need to check against other dimensions for policies that are found to be overlapping in one dimension. The sorting of policies along each dimension will take a time of $O(nlog)$, and this algorithm will have an average running time of $O(knlog)$. However, its worst-case running time (given some particularly badly formed input) can still be $O(kn^2)$.

By combining these techniques, you can substantially reduce the running time for a fairly large set of practical policies.

Policy Conflict Resolution

As soon as a conflict has been detected, it must be resolved somehow. There are many ways to resolve a conflict that arises among the policies.

Although it would be nice to have a method that can result in an automated conflict resolution, it is not possible to deduce the intention of the person administering the policy rules in an automated fashion. One heuristic that many systems use is to choose the policy set that is more specific (in that it has more terms specified) as the one that takes precedence over the policies where less-specific terms are defined. Although this approach works well in many cases, it can't resolve the conflict when the same number of terms are defined. An example in which the specificity of policy rule can't be used is given by this set of three rules:

R1: If the application is WebServer and the client is accounting, use service class Preferred.

R2: If the client is accounting and the server is eCommerce, use service class Precedence.

R3: If the application is WebServer and the server is eCommerce, use service class BestEffort.

All three of these rules use two terms to define the policy and are equally specific. However, any two of these rules conflict with each other, because it is unclear which rule should be applied for Accounting access to the WebServer application running on eCommerce. An automated way to resolve conflicts among these three policies is difficult to determine.

The most common way to resolve the conflict is to allow the administrator to choose which policy is intended to be used in the case where policies overlap. The user can express his policy preference by assigning each policy a priority or precedence level. When two policies conflict, the one with the higher precedence is the one to be applied.

Looking back at the hyper-dimensional space algorithm for policy conflict detection, assigning precedence eliminates conflict by introducing an additional independent axis. Policies with different precedence levels do not overlap along this new axis, so the conflict is avoided.

Policy Coverage Analysis

The coverage problem among policies arises most often in the case of security policies. The problem is to determine if there are any cases in which a policy rule is not being put into place. For example, suppose that the security policy is defined by mapping a set of application flows into security classes. The default security class is to have no security. You want to know which applications will be mapped into the default class, and therefore will have no security.

You might question the policy of having no security be the default. However, because of the performance penalties associated with encryption and authentication protocol, having the default policy of open communication might be a reasonable choice in many environments.

Yet another example of coverage determination occurs in situations in which you want to determine if there is insecure access to any specific subset of application flows. For example, assume that a set of security policies is defined within the network. An administrator might want to determine if there are any users who can access a given application in the clear.

Like the conflict problem, the coverage problem cannot readily be solved by converting it into a set of logical expressions using simple predicate logic. Using more complex types of logical expressions can do it. The hyper-dimensional space representation can be used to provide a more efficient solution.

In terms of the hyper-dimensional space representation introduced in the preceding section, the coverage problem can be specified as follows:

> Given a hyper-dimensional space with limits along each of the independent dimensions, determine if the regions described by a given set of policies cover the entire hyper-dimensional space.

This specification can be seen as an exact representation of the problem that required you to determine the set of application flows that got the default class of service. However, the same representation can also be used to represent the problem when you need to determine which users have default access to a specific application. In this case, you are simply solving the coverage problem for a smaller hyper-dimensional space—one in which one direction has been specified to take a fixed value.

In order to solve the coverage problem, you start with a list of hyper-dimensional spaces initially consisting of only one hyper-dimensional space that describes the original hyper-dimensional space with the full limits. Then you remove the region described by a specific policy from all the hyper-dimensional spaces contained in the list. After all the policies have been used to eliminate the regions from the list of hyper-dimensional spaces, you examine the remaining list. If the list of hyper-dimensional spaces is empty, the set of policies covers the entire original hyper-dimensional space. If any hyper-dimensional spaces are left in the list, they describe the portions of the hyper-dimensional space that are not covered by a set of default policies.

As an example of the application of this algorithm, consider the following (familiar) set of policy definitions:

- Business-critical applications on the eCommerce server take the highest precedence.

- Engineering access to office support applications on the eCommerce server is a preferred communication.

- Any access to the CICS server is a preferred communication.

- Staff utility applications get best-effort service.

- By default, all applications get best-effort service.

Now you need to figure out which applications on the eCommerce server receive the best-effort service. In order to solve this problem, you specifically select the policies that apply to the eCommerce server. This would be policies 1, 2, 4, and 5. You also eliminate policies that define the default best-effort service—namely, policies 4 and 5. Thus, you only have to analyze the coverage left after the application of policies 1 and 2. You also have to look at only two dimensions—the applications and the client IP addresses. You will also confine yourself to the set of applications and the set of IP addresses that are explicitly mentioned in Figure 6.3.

You start with an original hyper-dimensional space, as shown by the bold lines and shaded spaces in Figure 6.6. You then remove the portions of the hyper-dimensional space that are affected by policy 1. The result of eliminating the hyper-dimensional space represented by policy 1 is shown in Figure 6.6. In the next step, you eliminate the portions of the hyper-dimensional space affected by policy 2, resulting in the hyper-dimensional space shown in Figure 6.6. This is the set of application flows that will receive the default best-effort service. The set of application flows that results is Research and Accounting's access to the mail server, and any client accessing the Web server or the video server application. This set receives the default best-effort service.

If there are k dimensions of the policy hyper-dimensional space and n policies, this algorithm will have a complexity of $O(kn^2)$.

Figure 6.6   Policy Coverage Analysis Example

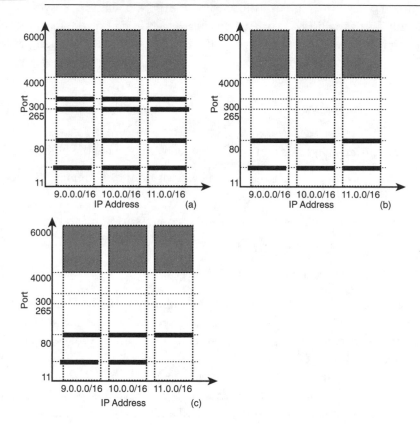

Discipline-Specific Policy Validation

The coverage and conflict algorithms are independent of the specific discipline to which a policy is being applied. However, there is a set of tests that can only be applied in a discipline-specific fashion. One of these checks is to validate that the high-level policies are indeed feasible within the network. For SLAs and performance-related policies, it boils down to verifying whether the specific performance targets can be achieved within the network. For security policies, it boils down to validating that a pair of firewalls that are required to communicate support a set of encryption algorithms and parameters that allows communication to occur between them.

QoS Feasibility Analysis

The goal of QoS feasibility analysis is to determine if a desired set of high-level policies can be achieved within a given network. Because the high-level policies in more environments reflect the SLAs that are in effect within the network, the objective of the feasibility analysis is to determine whether a given set of SLA objectives can be achieved within the network.

Because the predominant component within the SLAs deals with the performance metrics, you want to determine whether a specific set of performance metrics can be achieved within the network. In order to achieve this goal, you will model the network as a graph and will consider the queuing behavior at each node in the graph. The queuing behavior at different routers can then be combined to determine the end-to-end delays and loss rates in the network.

The performance feasibility analysis involves the following steps:

1. Determine a queuing model for each component in the network.

2. Determine the routes that packets will take within the network.

3. Estimate the amount of traffic that will be used on all the flows in the network.

4. Analyze the queuing network thus obtained to determine the appropriate end-to-end delays that will be obtained within the network.

Each of these steps can be done in a variety of ways. They are discussed in the next few sections.

Determining a Queuing Model

Many low-end and access routers are single-processor routers. These routers have one dedicated processor that obtains packets from the different input interfaces and stores them in the processor's memory. The processor parses the header, determines which outgoing interface to place the packets on, and gives them to the link hardware for transmission. The link hardware buffers the packets until the outgoing link is available for packet transmission, and then it transmits the packet on the link.

There are two places where queuing occurs in such routers:

- One for the processing of the packets by the router's processor

- One for the transmission of the packets on the outgoing link

In most cases, one of these two statements would hold true:

- The processor is fast relative to the link hardware and the link transmission rate so that queues at the processor are not significant.

- The link hardware and link transmission rate are fast relative to the router processor so that the queues at the output links are not significant.

In the second case, the only queues of significant size occur at the processor, and the entire model can be collapsed into a single queue representing the processor. In the first case, the queue at the router can be eliminated, and the model would consist of several queues representing the outgoing link. Thus, each router (and server) within a network can be represented as one or more queues within the network.

The other common type of router architecture consists of deep adapters. In a *deep adapter,* an embedded processor is dedicated to each of the link interfaces. There may be an additional processor to handle control flows and configuration of the entire router. Packets are received at an adapter, and a forwarding decision is made. The packets then contend for access to a switch fabric to reach the outbound adapter, from where they are transmitted out on the link. In many cases, the packets are stored in a common memory shared by all the adapter processors, and only packet headers or a small amount of header information is transmitted on the shared bus (or other switching fabric). This header information is sufficient to determine the output adapter for the packet, and the output adapter then fetches the entire packet from the shared memory for transmission on the link. In other cases, the shared bus is used to transmit the full packet to the output adapter, and no shared memory is needed. The former architecture (shared memory) makes sense when the speed of the shared bus is relatively low compared to the output link speeds. The latter (no shared memory) is more appropriate when the shared bus can operate at speeds greater than that of output links.

These routers can be represented as a pair of queues modeling the input and output queuing at each of the adapters, and one additional queue modeling the behavior of the access to the switch fabric. However, it has usually been observed that the bulk of queuing in these systems occurs at the processing associated with the output queues, so they can often be modeled by one output queue for each of the adapters.

Given a topology of the network, the routing used within the network, and the specific routers and servers under consideration, you can create the queuing model that represents the behavior of the network. From this information, you can use queuing theory (see texts such as [KLEIN1] [KLEIN2] [WOLFF]) to predict the performance of the network, provided that the traffic load within the network is known.

The interconnection among all the queues is determined by the physical interconnection among the different routers. The output from a queue (or queues) representing a router is connected to the input of other routers that are physically connected to it. As a result, you have a network of queues modeling the original IP network.

Determining the Routes in the Network

Within each network, there are multiple ways for a packet to get from one node to another. Packets are typically routed in IP networks according to a shortest-path algorithm (such as OSPF, described in Chapter 2, "Background Information"). Within these shortest-path algorithms, each of the links in the network is assigned a weight that reflects how expensive the link is for the purpose of determining network routes. The weight can be determined by combining a number of factors, including the link's monthly cost, capacity, and length.

Links with lower weights are preferred over links with greater weights. It is quite common for the weight to be set at 1 so that the resulting routing pattern in the network picks the shortest hop path between any two nodes.

Note
You can determine the shortest path among all pairs of nodes using several algorithms, the simplest one being Floyd's Algorithm. The description of this algorithm, as well as many others that achieve the same purpose, can be found in most texts on graph theory.

Sometimes, there are multiple shortest paths of equal length between two access nodes in the network. During the operation of the network, any of the possible paths may be used by the network routing algorithms. If you are looking for bounds on delays, one way to approach this situation is to consider one configuration of the shortest paths at a time, and compute delays for the queues in the selected configuration. The worst-case configuration can then be selected from all the possible shortest-path configurations. If there are several alternatives, this approach might become computationally expensive. A more practical option in those cases would be to look at the paths that a real routing algorithm such as OSPF would use, and consider only those shortest paths in the network.

Collecting the online routing information may be done by using some of the techniques described in Chapter 5, "Resource Discovery." Effective ways of obtaining the routing information in the network include reading the routing table entries using SNMP, participating in the routing protocol, or actively tracing routes using programs such as traceroute.

Traffic and Service Time Estimation

In order to determine a queue's performance characteristics, you need to determine both the input traffic rate and the service rate at the queue. These values need to be determined for all the queues that represent the entire network.

One way to determine the traffic in the network is by measuring the traffic on an existing network. An estimate of the traffic (in terms of packet counts) is maintained as part of normal IP processing at each of the routers. This information is readily available via SNMP MIBs. However, the information measured via SNMP is dependent on the current traffic conditions in the network, not on the high-level policies specified in the network.

In order to convert the high-level policies into traffic estimates, you need to know how many instances of each application will be active at a server, how many connections per second will be used for each instance of the application, and how many packets or bytes will be generated for each connection. Such a characterization of the application can be done by instrumenting the application characteristics. In an operational network, these values can also be determined by observing the characteristics of an application.

The application characteristics can be combined with the routing information to determine the load in packets per second (or bytes per second) at each of the routers in the network.

In a similar fashion, you need to determine the capacity of the servers and routers. The capacity of the server would be how many application transactions it can handle at a satisfactory level of performance. Similar capacities of routers and servers in terms of how many packets per second they can handle also need to be determined. Such a determination is often done by means of benchmarking tests that are done on the servers.

Performance Estimation

After the traffic rate and service rate at the queues have been determined, you can use a variety of techniques to determine the delay and loss rates that would be experienced by packets at the server or router.

The determination of the delay (or loss) characteristics depends on the assumptions you make about the traffic arrival patterns and the service rates of the packets and connections coming into the queue. The easiest process to analyze is the one from the M/M/1 queue, in which both arrival patterns are service rates are assumed to be Poisson. However, the assumption of Poisson arrivals and service rates is not very realistic.

More complex queuing models provide more realistic estimates of the delays in the network. In IP networks, the time to process the predominant type of packets (IP packets with a simple header that has no options) is relatively constant. Thus, a queue with a deterministic service time will be a reasonable approximation of packet processing time when modeling a router. For queues that model a link, the service time depends on the packet sizes. The distribution of packet sizes divided by the transmission rate provides a reasonable estimate for the service time.

For distribution of service times, you can use a more complex model that represents packet distribution more realistically. An alternative approach is to use a simple model and then overestimate the delays or losses it predicts. For example, you can use an M/M/1 model but multiply all delays and loss factors by a fudge factor (for example, double all the delays) to account for the assumptions in the model that are unrealistic.

After you estimate the delays at a single router, you can combine the delays along the different paths and the propagation delays along the links to obtain the end-to-end delays for the different applications. You can analyze this end-to-end delay to determine if the performance targets for the applications can be satisfied.

Keep in mind that each of the steps of the analysis process relies on a number of assumptions that might or might not hold true in practice. Thus, the performance feasibility assurance test must be treated as an estimate as to whether the performance levels within the network will be satisfied. It should not be treated as an absolute check or a guarantee that the performance will actually be met within the network.

Security Feasibility Analysis

Compared to the feasibility analysis of QoS, the security feasibility analysis is relatively simple. The feasibility analysis checks that communication is possible among the different firewalls and routers. In this case, the feasibility check consists mainly of making sure that the requisite communication can be supported among all the firewalls or other security gateways that are present at the different sites and that they are involved in the secure communication required by the high-level policies.

Consider the example of a high-level security policy that requires the establishment of a Virtual Private Network between three sites, protected by firewalls A, B, and C. The high-level security policy further specifies that all communication on this VPN must be encrypted. In order to enable this communication, each of these three machines needs to talk to the other. Each of the three firewalls supports a set of encryption/authentication algorithms. In order to communicate, each pair of firewalls must have a common set of algorithms that they can use to communicate with each other. Furthermore, the common set of algorithms must have at least one set that still meets the requirements imposed by the high-level policy requirement. The security feasibility analysis simply validates that this requirement is satisfied.

Another aspect of security policies is to map higher-level constructs such as VPNs, extranets, or remote access in terms of secure communication tunnels. A secure communication tunnel is a communication pipe on which packets (or other data) are encrypted or authenticated. The security associations created by IP-sec or the secure connections created by SSL or TLS are examples of such secure communication tunnels. These secure communication tunnels form an overlay network among the different firewalls involved in a set of high-level security policies.

As mentioned in previous sections, the high-level security policy is likely to specify a business need such as a VPN, extranet, or remote access. A VPN provides secure communication among the set of firewalls. In the case of a VPN that involves n firewalls, the overlay network consists of the secure communication tunnels that are established between each pair of the n firewalls. An extranet provides secure access from some external business partners to a set of servers within the enterprise. For this case, the overlay network consists of a secure communication tunnel from each of the external suppliers/sources to each of the servers that are involved in the business relationship. For remote access, the overlay network consists of a secure communication tunnel from each active user to a firewall within the enterprise that is being accessed.

The set of overlay links that are required to support specific business needs form an intermediary step toward the generation of device-specific low-level policies. This process is described in the next section.

Policy Translation: Conversion from High-Level to Low-Level

The final step in bridging the gap between the business needs and the technology being deployed is to translate the needs into a representation that corresponds to the configuration of each device that is needed to support that business need. This is the step of translating the policies from high-level to low-level.

As soon as all the checks outlined in this chapter have been executed and completed successfully, the translation process is relatively simple. Of course, the translation process depends on the technology that is being used to support the specific business needs. The technology in turn drives the low-level policy specification.

I'll demonstrate the steps involved in the translation process by means of an example, which requires you to support enterprise SLAs using the technology of Differentiated Services. For the case of the enterprise SLA, we will assume that the environment is as shown in Figure 6.3, in which using the model shown in Figure 6.2 specifies the SLA policies.

In order to perform the low-level translation, you need a representation of the low-level policy that would be required at each policy enforcement point (or policy target) within the network. If you assume that the technology being used to support the SLAs is DiffServ, you can use a low-level policy, as shown in Figure 6.7. For each device within the network, you need to define two types of tables—one defining a set of classification policies, and the other defining the different network levels supported at the device. The tables that would be constructed would depend on the role the device is playing in the network; for example the policies at an access router in DiffServ would be different from the policies at a core router within the network. A classification policy contains the five tuples that describe an IP packet flow (source and destination address, source and destination port numbers, and the protocol) and a mapping to the network level. The network level definition contains DiffServ-specific details, such as the appropriate marking of the ToS byte within the IP header, and the rates that are appropriate for each of the network levels. Within the network, a group of devices or interfaces may have the same set of policies that are relevant to them. Only one set of policies needs to be generated for this entire group of devices. It is very likely that devices or interfaces that perform similar functions in the network will have an identical set of policies associated with them. As an example, several access interfaces in an ISP's DiffServ domain that connect to the same customer may have identical classification and marking policies.

Figure 6.7   A Sample Low-Level Policy Representation for DiffServ

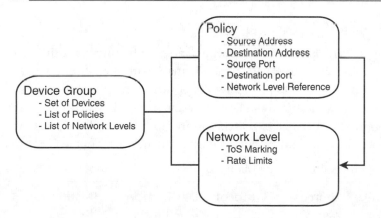

The translation step consists of mapping the representation specified in terms of Figure 6.2 to the representation in terms of Figure 6.7. Let's start with the set of policies listed in Tables 6.1 through 6.6. This is our familiar example with the following five high-level policies:

• Business-critical applications on the eCommerce server take the highest precedence.

- Engineering access to office support applications on the eCommerce server is a preferred communication.

- Any access to the CICS server is a preferred communication.

- Staff utility applications get best-effort service.

- By default, all applications get best-effort service.

As discussed, this set of rules has some conflicts. Assume that the conflicts have been resolved by assigning priority levels to the rules, with a higher-priority rule overriding a lower-priority rule in the case of a conflict. If rule 5 (the default rule) is assigned the lowest priority, and rule 3 is assigned the highest priority among the rules, the conflicts arising among these rules can be resolved. Of course, this is only one of the many ways to assign priorities that can resolve the potential conflicts.

The translation process consists of four steps: name mapping, in which the high level constructs like names of users or applications, or groups of users and applications are mapped to header fields like IP addresses and port numbers; CoS mapping, in which the definition of high level classes of service is changed into technology-specific parameters like DiffServ; PHBs relevancy determination, where the relevancy of a policy to a device or a set of devices is examined; and grouping, wherein devices which have identical sets of applicable policies are grouped together into a common structure.

Name Mapping

In order to convert them to lower-level policies, the first step is fairly mechanical. This consists of replacing the user names and identities with the IP addresses and port numbers of the corresponding elements. The results of such a transformation are shown in Table 6.7. In this table, wildcards are indicated by an asterisk. Furthermore, communication in both directions, from clients to servers and from servers to clients, is shown in the table as the list of policies that must be enforced at all the network routers and servers.

Table 6.7 Results of Name Mapping

Source IP Address	Source Port	Protocol	Destination IP Address	Destination Port	Class of Service
12.0.0.3	265	6	*	*	Precedence
*	*	6	12.0.0.3	265	Precedence
12.0.0.3	300	17	*	*	Precedence
*	*	17	12.0.0.3	300	Precedence
12.0.0.3	11	6	11.0.0.2/24	*	Preferred
11.0.0.2/24	*	6	12.0.0.3	11	Preferred
12.0.0.4	*	*	*	*	Preferred

Source IP Address	Source Port	Protocol	Destination IP Address	Destination Port	Class of Service
*	*	*	12.0.0.4	*	Preferred
*	11	6	*	*	Default
*	*	6	*	11	Default
*	4000-6000	17	*	*	Default
*	*	17	*	4000-6000	Default
*	*	*	*	*	Default

CoS Mapping

The next step in the translation process is to determine the mapping from the class of service specified in the higher-level policies to the network levels specified in the lower-level policies. The class of service contains parameters such as delays assigned to different application flows, and the network level contains DiffServ-specific details such as ToS encoding and the maximum rates assigned to the traffic falling within that network level.

In an ideal solution, the set of network levels and the rate allocated to each network level would be determined automatically. It is indeed possible to extend a performance prediction tool such as the one described in the section "QoS Feasibility Analysis" to try to find a set of network levels that satisfy the performance specified in the high-level policies. However, such a tool would have to be based on many assumptions regarding traffic flows and the details of the queuing model. Furthermore, the exact determination of the network level rates depends on the current traffic conditions in the network, which cannot be captured adequately by an offline provisioning and configuration tool. I don't believe that an approach for automatic determination for mapping classes of service to network levels is appropriate for a provisioning tool.

Instead, you can depend on a simpler method, such as assuming that an expert user has preconfigured the mappings from the classes of service to the different network levels. Such a mapping would specify how a class of service can be mapped into the appropriate network level for use within the tool. The expert user would be able to determine the correct rates to be allocated to the different devices on the basis of expected traffic usage within the network. The mapping rules should also specify the network level that should be used for packets in cases of overflow, such as when a packet can't be mapped into the network level it normally would be mapped into. This situation arises when the traffic rate allocated to a specific network level is exceeded at a device so that no more packets can be allowed in that network level.

An example of a mapping table that can be used for the example we are considering is shown in Tables 6.8 through 6.10. Table 6.8 enumerates the characteristics of the different service classes that are defined and used by the high-level policies. Each service class is identified by the amount of latency that packets belonging to that service class should experience in the network. The latency is associated with a percentile, and a duration over which the percentile limits must be met. Thus, Table 6.8 states that 99% of packets belonging to the precedence class experience a network latency of less than 100ms when measured over any duration exceeding 1 hour. Similarly, packets belonging to the precedence class experience a latency of less than 300ms when measured over any duration exceeding 1 day, and 99% best effort packets receive a latency of 500ms or less when measured over a period of one month. Table 6.9 maps the classes of service to the different service levels. The mapping identifies the network level to which a class of service is mapped to, the maximum rate at which packets should be mapped into this network level, and the network level to which packets that do not satisfy the rate constraint are mapped to. The mapping can also specify the set of interfaces where this mapping definition is valid. Table 6.10 defines the network levels that are supported within the different routers. Each network level is identified by the value that packets should carry in the DiffServ field, and by the interfaces on which the network level is supported. Note that the mapping table provides for an interfaces field (although this example uses wildcards). The assignment of rates to a class depends on the location of a device within the network, rather than being a constant throughout the network. Therefore, different rates may be assigned to different network levels at different interfaces.

Table 6.8 Class of Service Table

Class of Service	Delay	Percentile	Duration
Precedence	100ms	91	1 hour
Preferred	300ms	99	1 day
Default	500ms	100	1 month

Table 6.9 Mapping Table

Class of Service	Network Level	Rate Limit	Overflow	Interfaces
Precedence	Expedited Forwarding	10Mbps	Best Effort	*
Preferred	Expedited Forwarding	12Mbps	Best Effort	*
Default	Best Effort	50Mbps	Drop	*

Table 6.10	Network Levels Table	
Network Level	DiffServ Field	Interfaces
Expedited Forwarding	101110	*
Best Effort	000000	*

A better solution would be to have an online adaptation system that would automatically determine the appropriate rates to be assigned to each service level on the basis of the current network state. Such systems are discussed in Chapter 10, "Advanced Topics." However, the correct adaptation algorithms to be used within such systems are still the subject of active research.

Relevancy Determination

The third step in the translation process is to determine the set of devices that are affected by each of the policies just defined. Each policy specifies a client, an address, an application, and a class of service. Follow these guidelines:

- A policy affects a server if one of the server interfaces is either the source or the destination to which the policy applies. For example, one of the server interfaces can be used as either the client or the server fields of the policy definition table.

- A policy affects a router if it lies along the path between the client and the server fields within the policy.

The set of routers affected by a policy can be determined from the routing topology deployed in the network.

Grouping

The fourth and final step in the translation process is to identify the group of devices that share the same set of policy definitions. In general, devices that perform similar types of functions within the network are likely to have the same set of policy definition. Within the IETF policy framework working group [POLICYWG], devices that have the same set of policies are said to have the same role within the network. Thus, the grouping process can be seen as determining the role of different devices within the network.

With a policy management tool, it is possible for an administrator to explicitly specify roles to different devices. However, the assignment of these roles to various devices so that all devices with the same role would have the same policy may not be straight-forward. In the example illustrated by Figure 6.3, one natural assignment of roles would be to assign all the different routers in the role of an edge-router, and assign eCommServer and CICS server in the role of a server. However, the assignment by an administrator is not guaranteed to satisfy the definitions of the IETF, which requires that all machines in the same role have the same set of policies.

A better option would be for the policy management tool to determine the roles automatically by grouping together the different devices that have the same set of applicable policies. All devices (or interfaces) belonging to the same group must have identical policies. When this criteria is applied to the example we are considering, we see that there are two groups of devices that can have common policies. The first group consists of the server eCommServer, and the second group consists of the CICS server and the different routers within the network. These two groups can then be assigned two different roles (in the IETF meaning of the word) within the network.

The resulting set of policies are shown in Tables 6.11 and 6.12. Table 6.11 shows the set of policies that are applicable to eCommServer in the system, and Table 6.12 is applicable to all the other devices in the system. I use the abbreviations EF for Expedited Forwarding and BE for Best Effort.

Table 6.11   Low Level Policies for eCommServer

Source IP Address	Source Port	Protocol	Dest IP Address	Dest Port	Priority	Network Level	Overflow Network Level
12.0.0.3	256	6	*	*	1	EF	BE
*	*	6	12.0.0.3	265	1	EF	BE
12.0.0.3	300	6	*	*	1	EF	BE
*	*	6	12.0.0.3	300	1	EF	BE
12.0.0.3	11	6	11.0.0.0 /24	*	1	EF	BE
11.0.0.0 /24	*	6	12.0.0.3	11	1	EF	BE
12.0.0.4	*	*	*	*	2	EF	BE
*	*	*	12.0.0.4	*	2	EF	BE
*	4000-6000	17	*	*	0	BE	Drop
*	*	17	*	4000-6000	0	BE	Drop

Table 6.12   Low-Level Policies for Routers and CICS Server

Source IP Address	Source Port	Protocol	Dest IP Address	Dest Port	Priority	Network Level	Overflow Network Level
12.0.0.3	256	6	*	*	1	EF	BE
*	*	6	12.0.0.3	265	1	EF	BE
12.0.0.3	300	6	*	*	1	EF	BE
*	*	6	12.0.0.3	300	1	EF	BE
12.0.0.4	*	*	*	*	2	EF	BE
*	*	*	12.0.0.4	*	2	EF	BE
*	4000-6000	17	*	*	0	BE	Drop
*	*	17	*	4000-6000	0	BE	Drop

These low-level policies can subsequently be used to configure the device, as described in the next chapter.

Policy Distribution Mechanisms

As mentioned in Chapter 1, "Policy-Enabled Networking Architecture," the goal of policy-based management is to simplify network operations and provisioning. This simplification is obtained by providing higher-level abstractions to the network administrators. These higher-level abstractions can then be translated by a management tool to an abstract representation of the policy/configuration required for each of the devices deployed in the network using the techniques described in Chapter 6, "Policy Validation and Translation Algorithms." The configuration/policy information thus generated is still located at the machine where the management tool is operational. From this central location, the configuration/policy information needs to be distributed to different devices in the network, and these devices need to be configured in accordance with the low-level policies. This function is performed by the distribution component of the policy architecture.

The main problem being resolved by the distribution component is that of sending configuration information from a central location to many other devices in the network. This chapter looks at the various common approaches that can be used to distribute policies within the network and compares their relative merits and demerits. A simple set of policies is used to illustrate the distribution process using each of the different approaches. These policies are described in the next section. Another section is devoted to each of the different distribution schemes. Finally, the "Summary" section compares the merits of all the distribution schemes and discusses scenarios in which two or more of these schemes can work together to solve the distribution problem.

An Example of Policy Distribution

In order to demonstrate the features of the different distribution schemes, let's assume that a device called eCommServer must be configured with the following three policies:

- All outgoing packets that originate with a local port of 265 and that use transport protocol 6 are to be marked as EF packets with a DiffServ field value of 101110.

- All outgoing packets that originate with a local port of 11 and that use transport protocol 6 are to be marked as EF packets with a DiffServ field value of 101110.

- The default is to mark all packets as BE packets with a DiffServ field value of 000000.

You should recognize these rules as a subset of the low-level policies relevant to the eCommServer from the example used in the previous chapter. We will use two of the rules from the previous section and will focus on only DiffServ field marking of outbound packets in order to provide a very simple example. The distribution of the remaining rules in that example would become obvious from the discussion of this subset.

An administrator familiar with the operating system used for eCommServer will find it relatively easy to configure the server to support the three policies. Let's assume that the eCommServer is an AIX server (AIX is IBM's version of the UNIX operating system) with an operating system. There are two ways to configure the system to obtain the target set by the above policies:

- Using a configuration file

- Using command-line scripts

Using a Configuration File

The first way to configure the system is by writing a configuration file for QoS policy enforcement on the system. The configuration file is read by a policy agent program running on the system, which ensures that the networking stack is configured in accordance with the input specified in the configuration file. The configuration file consists of different types of records. Each record has a name and several attributes. Here is the format of each record:

```
<RecordType> RecordName { attributes }
```

The attributes consist of a list of attribute names and values.

The AIX configuration allows for two types of records, a `ServicePolicyRule` entry and a `ServiceCategory` entry. Tables 7.1 and 7.2 show a subset of the attributes defined for each of the two types of entries. The `ServiceCategory` records define the attributes of a

DiffServ (or IntServ) traffic class that may be supported at the server. The parameters of such a class include definitions such as the outgoing ToS marking to be used for the class, the maximum bandwidth to be used for a class, and so on. The `ServicePolicyRule` specifies which flows are mapped onto each of the service classes.

Table 7.1   IBM Server QoS Schema: Attributes for `ServicePolicyRule`

Attribute	Description
PolicyName	The policy's name.
SelectorTag	A unique string to search for policies relevant to a device.
TcpImageName	On mainframes with multiple networking stacks, identifies the IP stack to which the policy is relevant.
DaysOfWeekMask	Specifies which days (Monday through Friday) the policy rule is valid.
TimeOfDayRange	Specifies what time(s) of the day the policy rule is valid.
PolicyScope	IntServ or DiffServ.
ServiceReference	Contains the name of a service category.
ProtocolNumber	The protocol number in the IP header (usually TCP or UDP).
SourceAddressRange	The source address of packets to which the policy applies.
DestinationAddressRange	The destination address of packets to which the policy applies.
SourcePortRange	The source port number in the TCP/UDP header for applying policies.
DestinationPortRange	Destination port numbers in the TCP/UDP header for applying policies.

Table 7.2   IBM Server QoS Schema: Attributes for `ServiceCategory`

Attribute	Description
ServiceName	The name of the `ServiceCategory`.
SelectorTag	A unique string to search for policies relevant to a device.
TcpImageName	On mainframes with multiple networking stacks, identifies the IP stack to which the policy is relevant.
DaysOfWeekMask	Specifies which days (Monday through Friday) the policy rule is valid.

continues

Table 7.2	Continued

Attribute	Description
TimeOfDayRange	Specifies what times of the day the policy rule is valid.
MaxRate	The maximum rate for flows in this class.
OutgoingToS	The ToS field value in outbound packets.
Priority	The queuing priority at local interfaces.

The entries in Table 7.1 and 7.2 are present in the IBM QoS schema for servers, which is discussed later in this chapter. However, all the attributes except PolicyName, ServiceName, SelectorTag, and TcpImageName are also present in the records specified in the configuration files.

Listing 7.1 shows a sample configuration file that can be used to configure an AIX machine in accordance with the policies just described.

Listing 7.1	Sample Configuration File for AIX

```
ServiceCategories    EF {
        PolicyScope    DataTraffic
        OutgoingTOS    10111000
}

ServiceCategories    BE {
        PolicyScope    DataTraffic
        OutgoingTOS    000000000
}

ServicePolicyRules rule1 {
        Direction Outgoing
        ProtocolNumber 6
        SourcePortRange 265
        ServiceReference EF
}

ServicePolicyRules rule2 {
        Direction Outgoing
        ProtocolNumber 6
        SourcePortRange 11
        ServiceReference EF
}
```

```
ServicePolicyRules default {
        Direction Outgoing
        ServiceReference BE
}
```

The configuration file defines two service categories (named EF and BE, respectively), says that the scope of the categories is used to mark data packets, and specifies the ToS field (which covers the 6 bits of the DiffServ field and 2 extra bits set to 0) for each category. The rules can be seen to readily correspond to the policies just described. When a rule does not specify a field, it assumed to apply irrespective of the field's value. Therefore, the default rule would apply to all outgoing packets. When such a configuration file is copied to a well-known location, such as /etc/pagent.conf, the system automatically configures itself in accordance with the specified rules.

Using a Command-Line Script

The second way to configure an AIX machine is for an operator to type a set of commands that can perform actions equivalent to those specified by the configuration file. AIX provides commands that can create, modify, or delete a `ServiceCategory` or `ServicePolicyRule`. The attributes of each type of entry are provided by means of several command-line options. Without going into the details of the different command lines that are available, Listing 7.2 shows a shell script that uses these command lines. You can see the correspondence between the configuration file and the command line.

| Listing 7.2 | A Script for Configuring AIX Servers |

```
#/bin/sh
add_service -s EF   -t  10111000
add_service -s BE -t 0000000
add_policy -s EF    -r rule1 -n 6 -P 265-265
add_policy -s EF    -r rule1 -n 6 -P 11-11
add_policy -s BE -r default
```

The default behavior of the different commands is to apply to the outbound direction, so that parameter is not explicitly shown.

Note

An actual production script to configure the server would check whether a named service or rule were already present and would modify the rule if it were found. It would also check for error conditions that resulted from the script invocation. Listing 7.2 shows the minimum set of commands needed to illustrate the example, rather than the actual script you would use in a production environment.

As we go through the different schemes for policy distribution, you will see how the different schemes can achieve the configuration of the AIX machine from a specification of the three sample policies.

Policy Distribution Using Management Frameworks

The need to manage different devices from a central location has been felt by the network operator community for a while. Some existing solutions have been designed specifically to address this concern. These solutions are usually proprietary and are referred to as management frameworks by their developers. Examples of such management frameworks are the TME-10 framework [TME10], which is used by Tivoli Systems for its management product offerings, and the TNG framework from Computer Associates [TNG].

> **Note**
>
> The management frameworks we examine in this section were developed for systems and network management in enterprise environments. We will not cover the management frameworks developed for telephone networks, because they are very different in nature.

An Overview of Management Frameworks

Although the exact details of frameworks vary from vendor to vendor, they share many common features. Each framework is typically deployed in an environment with a management console and several agents. One agent is located on each of the devices that are being managed. The agents are responsible for enforcing the directives that come from the management console, and they can send reports, alarms, or alerts to the console.

The management framework usually includes middleware that provides a common set of services to the agents and servers. One example of such middleware includes a portability layer, which attempts to hide variations among the different platforms, communication primitives between the manager and the agents, directory services to locate other types of devices or agents in the network, and so on.

On top of the common framework, additional modules can be provided to enable the management of a specific function. For example, in order to provide an inventory function, an inventory module is added to the each of the agents. The inventory module on the agent searches for all applications installed on the local machine. Similarly, an inventory manager would be added to the management console. The inventory manager controls the invocation of the inventory module at the agent side and also collects and consolidates the information from the different database agents. Depending on the vendor implementations, some of the management frameworks provide a minimal set of modules as an initial installation and allow the downloading and installation of additional modules dynamically. The set of modules making up the minimal set is vendor-dependent.

Most management frameworks, such as TME-10 and TNG, use a distributed communication middleware based on CORBA, an open standard for developing object-oriented distributed systems. The structure of a typical management framework is shown in Figure 7.1. The base management framework provides common services, such as the ability for users to communicate with the management applications, the ability to install new applications on managed nodes, and the ability to communicate among the different managed nodes and the management console machine. Such communication is often built on top of CORBA. The framework provides interfaces by which agents can be plugged into the framework to provide specific functions. Figure 7.1 shows two such agents. One is responsible for performance statistics collection, and the other is responsible for taking inventory of all applications installed on the system. These agents have corresponding management counterparts at the management console machine. An administrator can invoke these functions and manipulate them from the console station. Figure 7.1 shows a single manager controlling several agents, but many management frameworks also allow a hierarchy of submanagers that control different machines indirectly. Such a hierarchy can substantially increase the number of managed devices.

The Policy Distribution Process

In order to allow policy distribution by using a management framework like the one shown in Figure 7.1, you need to develop two modules for the management framework:

- A policy console module that will be provided as an extension module on top of the management framework at the console machine

- A policy agent module that will be provided as an extension module on top of the management framework on each of the devices being managed

The policy console module would include all the functions described in Chapter 5, "Resource Discovery" and Chapter 6. The distribution component in the module simply pushes any configuration out to the agents using the distribution functions provided in the management framework.

Figure 7.1   A Typical Management Framework Structure

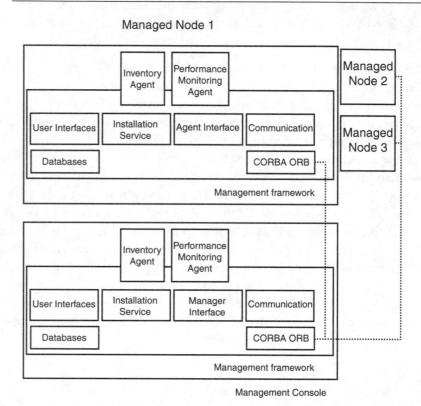

The distribution process in this case is taken care of by the management framework. The management framework usually includes a publish-subscribe functionality. This functionality lets any extension modules on agents or the console communicate in a relatively easy fashion. Each of the agents involved in policy handling on the devices simply registers with the publish-subscribe system using a name (such as its machine name) and a common group name (such as the policy group). It can then simply request to the framework layer that a message be sent (published) to a specific group. It can also subscribe to the messages, indicating to the framework that it wants to receive any messages sent to the group.

In addition to publishing and subscribing to messages sent to a group, a publish-subscribe system can provide other types of criteria to put or get the information. For example, a publish-subscribe system may allow for *typed* messages. In this case, each message is tagged with a type attribute. Every time a module wants to send a message, it specifies the message's type or types. The subscriber can specify that it wants to receive all messages with a specific type.

When such functionality is present in the management framework, it is relatively easy to solve the problem of policy distribution. If publish-subscribe systems based on groups are permitted within the framework, the management console and the agents can simply join a group with a well-known name (such as a group named "policy-distribution"). The policy console module can simply send messages to this group. The policy agent modules receive messages from that group, and they can send back any reports related to policy configuration to the policy console module.

One way the policy console module can operate is to translate the abstract policy/configuration information into the actual configuration of the devices and then send the configuration using the management framework. An alternative approach is for the policy console module to send the abstract policy/configuration itself to the agents. The agents then translate the abstract configuration to the exact local configuration and ensure that the devices are configured properly.

A Sample Distribution

In order to distribute the policies described in the earlier example section, the management framework approach can operate in one of the following four ways:

- The policy console module generates the low-level policies. The policy agent module converts the low-level policies into the configuration file that corresponds to those policies. In other words, it generates the configuration file shown in Listing 7.1. The console sends the configuration file to the policy agent module running on eComm-Server, which then installs the configuration file in the appropriate location (such as /etc/pagent.conf) to cause the policies to become effective within the AIX kernel.

- The policy console module generates the low-level policies. These policies are represented in a format understood by the console and the agents, such as an XML representation of the low-level policies. The console sends the XML representation to the policy agent module running on eCommServer. The policy agent module converts the XML representation to the configuration file shown in Listing 7.1, and it installs the configuration file in the appropriate location (such as /etc/pagent.conf) to cause the policies to become effective within the AIX kernel.

- The policy console module generates the low-level policies and converts them to the shell script shown in Listing 7.2. The policy console module then sends the script to the policy agent module, which executes the script and informs the policy console module of its success or failure in executing the scripts.

- The policy console module sends the low-level policies in its proprietary format (such as the XML representation) to the policy agent modules, which then covert them to the shell script shown in Listing 7.2 and execute them.

In the second and fourth approaches, the policy console module only has to worry about generating the low-level XML files, and the agents on the individual machines convert it to the machine-specific configuration. In the first and third approaches, the policy console module does the translation into the format understood by each of the machines. Usually, it is preferable to use the latter approach if the agent extensions are written in a manner that is independent of the underlying platform.

Advantages and Disadvantages of Using the Management Framework for Policy Distribution

If a management framework is deployed in an environment, it provides the easiest path to distribute policies. You can even argue that building the entire policy management tool on top of the management framework is the right approach. Many of the functions that are needed for the proper operation of a policy management tool—such as discovery of network topology and devices and discovery of applications—are provided as standard modules in existing management frameworks. Thus, building on top of an existing framework provides added functionality using very little development effort.

There are some drawbacks associated with using a management framework. Management frameworks are typically designed for general-purpose operating systems. Although most management frameworks support systems such as mainframes, UNIX-based servers (Solaris, HP, AIX), and PCs (different versions of Windows), support for management frameworks within routers is not that prevalent. A related fact is that many management frameworks require a large number of resources on the devices they manage. Because many management frameworks are based on CORBA, they use a large number of connections using a dynamic number of ports between the manager and the devices. This makes it difficult for them to be deployed outside an enterprise environment. Although some implementations of CORBA go across the firewall in a secure fashion, usually by tunnel-ing these flows across a few connections on a fixed number of ports, their adoption has not been as widespread. Part of the reason might be that most management frameworks are developed for an enterprise environment in which there are no firewalls between the management console and the managed devices.

Policy Distribution Using Scripts

Most routers provide a way for a human administrator to configure them over a console. The configuration process usually consists of invoking the right set of commands that will set the appropriate parameters and knobs at the device. The commands that are issued by a human operator can also be generated by a programmed script invoked by a computer. A policy management tool could generate such scripts to configure the various devices within a network.

In order to generate the right set of scripts, the policy management tool needs to know the different types of devices that are present within the network. From the description of the type of device and the abstract configuration, the management tool can determine the appropriate set of commands to be created for each type of router. The management tool can then connect to the device and invoke the right set of commands to configure the router appropriately.

The biggest advantage of this approach toward policy distribution is that it does not require the installation of any software on the routers. This approach can be used with any type of router. However, it does require that the management tool understand the peculiarities of all the different types of routers that are deployed in the network.

A similar approach can be used with servers and PCs to configure their support for QoS or security. A command-line script can be invoked by logging into any machine that provides a remote logon facility. Almost all servers support remote logon facilities, which can be exploited for this purpose. However, on PCs, such support is not always available.

Let's consider how a scripts-based approach would work for the set of sample policies described earlier in this chapter. The management tool generates the script commands that are shown in Listing 7.2. It then telnets into the eCommServer and executes the command script shown in Listing 7.2. One common way to execute command scripts in an automated manner is provided by interaction languages, such as *expect* [EXPECTREF], which lets a machine mimic the actions of a human administrator at a local or remote console. An expect script would execute the command script shown in Listing 7.2 by logging on to the eCommServer machine, waiting for the command prompt to appear and then invoking one line from the script. When the command execution is completed, and the expect script sees the command prompt appear again, it invokes the next line. It repeats this cycle until all the commands shown in Listing 7.2 are executed.

Policy Distribution Using LDAP

The problem with using scripts for policy distribution is that a management tool must be aware of the different types of scripts that are applicable to each of the different types of devices in the network. For example, in order to distribute the policies for DiffServ within a network that includes routers manufactured by Cisco, Nortel, and Lucent, the management tool must be aware of the configuration scripts that will be supported by these three different manufacturers. In many cases, the configuration commands differ for different models belonging to the same manufacturer, and the policy management tool must be aware of these differences.

It would be wonderful if there were a standard way to state the DiffServ policies that would apply to a device. In that case, the management tool can simply specify the policies using this standard format. Each of the devices, or the policy servers acting on their behalf, would download the policies from the standard format and convert them to the appropriate configuration that would be necessary for the enforcement of the policies.

One way to provide such a scheme is to use a central site to store the low-level policy/configuration information. The management tool populates the repository, and agents running on different devices retrieve their policy/configuration information from the repository.

One type of repository that you can use for this purpose is a directory server accessed by the LDAP protocol. The use of such a repository provides several operational advantages within a network. LDAP clients are available on most platforms and do not require the development of any new protocols to be developed. Similarly, most LDAP servers can be easily configured to hold different types of records, including records that can specify policy information. Furthermore, most organizations need to maintain a directory of employees and thus have a staff capable of administering and operating directories. The ubiquity of LDAP clients and servers and the ease of policy deployment using an LDAP directory server are some of the factors driving initiatives, such as directory-enabled networks [DENWEB], and are why the Policy Framework Working Group [POLICYWG] has opted to use LDAP as a primary means of specifying policies. The standard format to store policies using LDAP would be the definition of the schema that is used to represent policies in the directory.

The Policy Distribution Process

In order to distribute the policies using LDAP [LDAPREF], the management tool converts the abstract policy into entries that can be populated into an LDAP directory. After the LDAP entries are written into the directory, any LDAP clients running on each of the devices, or on policy servers that manage the configuration of groups of devices, can access the directory to read the entries and determine the appropriate policy to implement locally.

In order to distribute policies using LDAP, there must be agreement among the management tool and the agents (in this case, LDAP clients) on two aspects of directory usage:

- A common format must be used to specify policies stored in the directory.

- A common convention must be used for each device to determine how to obtain policies that are relevant to itself.

The common format that the directory uses is determined by defining a schema that both the management tool and the clients on the devices access. A *schema* defines the types of objects that can be created within the directory and the ways in which relationships between objects are represented. The schema definition to be created depends on the discipline for which the low-level policies are being defined.

As an example, consider a simple LDAP schema that is implemented by IBM servers to support QoS policy configuration. The UML object model [UMLREF] corresponding to this schema is shown in Figure 7.2 and consists of only two classes, a ServicePolicyRule class and a ServiceCategory class. Tables 7.1 and 7.2 earlier in this chapter show a subset of the attributes defined in each of the classes. The ServiceCategory class defines the attributes of a DiffServ (or IntServ) traffic class that may be supported within a device. The parameters of such a class include definitions such as the outgoing ToS marking to be used for the class and the maximum bandwidth to be used for a class. The ServicePolicyRule specifies which flows are mapped onto each of the service classes. The dates and times when these mappings are valid are also included as part of the ServicePolicyRules. One of the attributes in the ServicePolicyRules, the ServiceReference attribute, points to the appropriate ServiceCategory, and it implements the association between the two classes shown in Figure 7.2.

Figure 7.2   Object Model for IBM QoS Schema

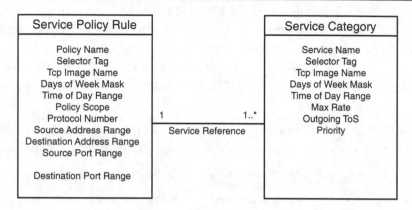

Consider the set of sample policies discussed earlier. Two ServiceClasses are defined—one called EF and the other called BE. You want to map the application running on ports 265 and 11 to EF and the other applications to BE. The management tool creates five directory entries corresponding to these specifications—three of type ServicePolicyRule and two of type ServiceCategory. The two entries of type ServiceCategory correspond to EF and BE. One of the entries of type ServicePolicyRule maps the application on port 265 to EF, another entry of the same type maps the application running on port 11 to EF, and a third entry maps all applications to default. However, the one point that has not been addressed is where these entries should be located in the LDAP directory.

As described in Chapter 2, "IP Architecture Overview," entries in the LDAP directory are placed in a tree hierarchy. Each entry is accessed using a distinguished name. Each of the four entries that are stored in the directory needs to have a *distinguished name* (DN) assigned. The management tool creates the entries with the right DN, and the agents running on the different machines retrieve them from that location. There must be a common understanding between the agents and the management tool as to where the entries will be placed in the directory. This understanding reflects the scheme used by the agents to retrieve policies relevant to them.

In the IBM server implementation, it is assumed that the policies can be placed anywhere in the directory. However, the management tool creates special attributes in each entry that allow the agents to determine which policies are relevant to them. The two attributes used for this purpose are SelectorTag and TcpImageName. The convention is to use a machine's IP address in the SelectorTag attribute to determine which policies are relevant to the specific machine. The TcpImageName (which is relevant only to the mainframe implementation, which supports multiple TCP/IP stacks on the same machine) adds a further search criteria to determine which policies apply to a specific functional stack.

The convention used in the IBM server implementation requires that the search for policy be made in the entire directory. In order to make the search more restrictive, you can specify a top-level entry in the directory that acts as the root of a tree that contains all the policies defined in the network.

Let's examine the sample entries that will be created for the sample policies using the IBM Server schema. I will show the set of entries using the "ldif" textual format, which is a common way to represent LDAP directory information [LDIFREF]. Using the ldif format, entries are separated by a blank line. For each entry, the attributes and values are listed on a line, with a colon separating the name of the attribute and the value. The location of an entry in the directory hierarchy is shown by its distinguished name (the attribute with the name dn). Assuming that the policies are based on a tree with the DN of `loc=policy, o=ibm, c=us`, one possible set of ldif entries is shown in Listing 7.3. This set of LDAP entries is created by the management tool and is retrieved by the eCommServer, assuming that it knows the root location to search from—namely, `loc-policy, o=ibm, c=us`.

Listing 7.3   Sample ldif Entries for the IBM QoS Schema

```
dn: cn=categ1, loc=policy, o=ibm, c=us
objectClass: ServiceCategory
SelectorTag: eCommServer
ServiceName: EF
PolicyScope: DataTraffic
OutgoingTos: 10111000

dn: cn=categ2, loc=policy, o=ibm, c=us
objectClass: ServiceCategory
SelectorTag: eCommServer
ServiceName: BE
PolicyScope: DataTraffic
OutgoingTos: 00000000

dn: cn=rule1, loc=policy, o=ibm, c=us
objectClass: ServicePolicyRule
SelectorTag: eCommServer
PolicyName: rule1
Direction: Outgoing
ProtocolNumber: 6
SourcePortRange: 265
ServiceReference: EF
```

continues

Listing 7.3	Continued

```
dn: cn=rule2, loc=policy, o=ibm, c=us
objectClass: ServicePolicyRule
SelectorTag: eCommServer
PolicyName: rule2
Direction: Outgoing
ProtocolNumber: 6
SourcePortRange: 11
ServiceReference: EF

dn: cn=default, loc=policy, o=ibm, c=us
objectClass: ServicePolicyRule
SelectorTag: eCommServer
PolicyName: default
Direction: Outgoing
ServiceReference: BE
```

The set of directory entries shown in Listing 7.3 needs to be augmented with the entries that represent the root of the policy tree (the entry corresponding to the DN of loc= policy, o=IBM, c=us). As soon as the root entry is present, the other entries shown in Listing 7.3 can be readily added to the directory server.

In order to search for the set of policies that are applicable to it, the agent on eComm-Server needs to know its SelectorTag and the location of the root of the policy tree. Using the SelectorTag of eCommServer, it searches the policy subtree for all entries of type ServiceCategory or ServicePolicyRule, where the SelectorTag attribute is eCommServer. The result is the set of five entries shown in Listing 7.3, which can be readily used to configure the server to obtain a result identical to the configuration defined in Listing 7.1.

There are other ways to determine which policies apply to specific servers. These methods do not require searching through a subset of the LDAP directory. One such way is to create a specific entry for each of the devices in the network and provide a pointer from that location to all the policies relevant to that device. The advantage of this approach is that it is a more efficient way to look up policies. The disadvantage is that each device needs to know how to locate and identify the original location entry.

Using one of these conventions (or a different one), an agent on each machine can obtain the set of policies relevant to it. It can then periodically check to see if the policies have been updated in the directory server by a management tool and incorporate those changed policies into the local operation of the machine. The agent or LDAP client (which could be on the managed device or on a separate policy server managing multiple devices) must convert the directory entries into specific commands or configurations for the local machine's kernel and networking stack.

IETF/DMTF Policy Schemas

The LDAP schema shown in Figure 7.2 has the limitation that it is supported only within the set of IBM servers. Therefore, a management tool can control IBM servers within a deployment by writing out the entries in accordance with that format. However, it is quite likely that a real network would include not only servers from IBM, but also from various other vendors such as Sun, HP, and Microsoft. Some of these servers do not support the retrieval of policies from an LDAP directory. Others do, but they utilize a schema different from the one shown in Figure 7.2. Because the servers do not share a common schema, the management tool needs to understand the various schemas supported by each platform. On the other hand, if there was a standard schema that all the server (and router) platforms supported, the job of managing and configuring them would be substantially reduced.

The standard schemas and information model being developed within the Policy Framework Working Group within the IETF and the corresponding working groups within the DMTF are trying to define such a standard schema. Their work will hopefully lead to the development of an industry-wide standard schema that will provide for interoperability among the various platforms. Although the standards had not been finalized at the time this book was published, I hope that a stable schema will be ready soon.

In order to have complete interoperability, three things need to be standardized:

- A standard protocol must be used by the devices and the management tool to retrieve and extract policies.

- A standard format must be used to specify policies.

- A standard convention must be used for each device to determine how to obtain policies that are relevant to that device.

With a directory-based approach, LDAP is the standard protocol used. The policy framework model provides a standard way to store information in the directory.

The work within the standards bodies is being done with much attention to the generality of the solution. Unfortunately, this results in a somewhat more complex solution. The approach adopted has been to define a core information model first. The core information model is an abstract description of the type of classes that would be needed to describe any type of policy. This description would be valid regardless of the type of policy repository being used (you could use an LDAP directory or even a relational database) or the specific type of policies being defined (you could apply the model to the policies for DiffServ or IPsec). There are two ways to refine this abstract core information model and make it more specific. One is to map them to specific types of repositories, such as an LDAP repository. The other is to map them to specific disciplines, such as QoS. These two refinements are independent of each other. When both of these refinements are made, the result is a concrete description of policies that apply to a specific environment.

The core information model being developed within the standards bodies is based on the DMTF *Common Information Model* (CIM) [DMTFCIM]. The information model defines six central classes, as shown in Figure 7.3. Lines between the classes show the associations between them. The `CIM_system` class contains the definition of a system to which policy definitions apply. The `Policy` class itself consists of a Condition part and an Action part, with the semantics of "if Condition, then Action." One of the Condition parts of the model is the `TimeOfDayCondition`, which defines the times when the policy is valid. A `PolicyGroup` groups several policies. An example of such a group is the group of all the policies that apply to a particular administrative domain, such as all the policies associated with the East Coast Sales Organization.

Figure 7.3   IETF/DMTF Policy Core Information Model

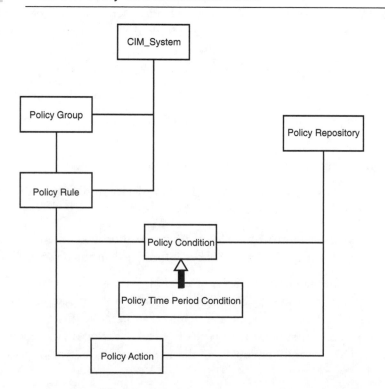

The information model has a class called `PolicyRepository`. `PolicyRepository` provides a way to store conditions and actions that need to be reused across multiple devices. Thus, these commonly used conditions and actions need not be defined separately every time they need to be used. Note that this is an information model class definition. It is distinct from the policy repository as an architectural or framework concept, as discussed in Chapter 1. In order to use this information model, you first need to map it into a concrete policy representation, such as an LDAP schema. The tentative LDAP schema that is being worked on in the IETF, as a mapping of the policy core information model, consists of six general classes:

- `policy` (an abstract class)

- `policyGroup`

- `policyRule`

- `policyConditionAuxClass`

- `policyTimePeriodConditionAuxClass`

- `policyActionAuxClass`

Two auxiliary classes let a specific manufacturer introduce its own classes—`vendorPolicyConditionAuxClass` and `vendorPolicyActionAuxClass`. A few additional classes have been introduced for optimizations that improve the efficiency of directory access.

Note

Classes in an LDAP schema can be structural or auxiliary. An object defined in an LDAP directory must be an instance of a structural class. To any such object, you can attach attributes that belong to an auxiliary class. In other words, auxiliary classes act as modifiers that can be associated with structural classes. An abstract class is one that can't really be instantiated in the directory. It is used so that you can define more precise classes that can then be instantiated in the directory.

In order to apply this schema to a discipline such as QoS, you need to further refine the core LDAP schema to make a DiffServ specific schema. This implies defining classes that define the specific conditions and actions that are relevant to DiffServ. After such a schema is defined, it can be used instead of the proprietary IBM schema shown in Figure 7.2 for interoperability.

More information and details on the information model and schemas can be found in the book by Strassner [STRASSNER]. For the latest iteration of the schema development activity within the IETF, the Web site for the Policy Framework Working Group [POLICYWG] would be the appropriate starting point.

The IETF/DMTF approach to policy specification is much more complex than the simple schema presented in Figure 7.2. Although the complexity is a drawback, it does provide a richness and extensibility that is not that straightforward in the IBM schema. More importantly, because it is a standard schema, it is likely to provide for interoperability.

Advantages and Disadvantages of Using LDAP for Policy Distribution

The use of an LDAP directory and a predetermined schema for policy distribution has many attractions. The management tool must support writing to only one type of schema, and an administrator can easily look at the directory entries to determine the network's current configuration. Furthermore, the fact that it is the preferred approach within the standards bodies is a strong argument for using it with the various products.

At the same time, you must be aware of some of the limitations of LDAP as a policy distribution mechanism. LDAP directories are designed mostly to optimize access and lookups, not to perform rapid updates. Thus, policies that need to be changed frequently are inappropriate for storing in the LDAP distribution. Also, LDAP does not support a very good mechanism for notifying agents when something has changed in the directory. As a result, the agents have to keep on polling the directory to track any changes that might have occurred, or be notified of such changes by a different mechanism so that they know when to get new policy information. LDAP servers do support a simple form of asynchronous notification. They allow a client to register a search with them and notify the client when the results of the search change. However, the support and performance of this mechanism are relatively poor.

Another key challenge with the LDAP-based distribution scheme is its adoption by the different platforms. In an ideal world, all different products would support the same schema with the same semantics. However, in practice, many products tend to interpret different attributes in a slightly different manner, or they support some variances from the standard schema. Although the standards are evolving, a different schema is likely to emerge for each different product, and their interoperation won't be very clean. Of course, this same challenge exists with other approaches, including SNMP, as noted later.

Policy Distribution Using SNMP

Because the distribution of policies to the devices and configuring them is part of the management aspects of the devices, you can use existing management protocols to achieve this goal. In the case of routers and networking policies, the preferred protocol to use is SNMP. SNMP was described briefly in Chapter 2.

SNMP is firmly established in the networking community, and every new protocol and technology that comes up invariably defines a MIB that allows the configuration and instrumentation for that technology. MIBs that will allow the configuration of DiffServ capable routers are being worked on in the standards bodies. The same holds true for IP security protocols.

Given the existence or eventual existence of the MIBs, you can exploit them to transfer policy/configuration information to the devices. In order to do so, a policy management tool must convert the low-level policies into the appropriate MIB values that will conform to the specific configuration. It then invokes the SNMP set command to configure the device appropriately.

Two approaches can be taken when using SNMP to distribute policies. One approach is to configure the policies using the MIBs defined for the specific policy discipline. For example, you would use the MIB definition for DiffServ to distribute DiffServ policies (see the next section for details on this approach). Using the discipline-specific MIB configuration does not provide for a general scheme to distribute policies and configure devices using SNMP.

A second approach is being investigated by the "Configuration Management with SNMP" working group within IETF [SNMPCONF]. This working group is exploring MIB definitions that will allow for a generic policy-based configuration. The generic policy is customized for each discipline by a discipline-specific policy MIB. The advantage of this approach is that some common policy filters can be shared across disciplines. For example, if you're using the same type of filters for IPsec and DiffServ, you can coordinate them through the common policy MIB. However, the policy MIB defined in this manner for a discipline is different from the MIB defined for the discipline. In other words, the DiffServ policy MIB defined by the SNMPCONF working group [SNMPCONF] is different from the DiffServ MIB defined by the DiffServ working group [DSWG]. Both these MIBs overlap in scope, and the SNMP agents on various platforms must ensure that operations performed using the two different types of MIB definitions are reflected in both of them. Although the definitions of both types of MIBs for DiffServ (and other disciplines) are still evolving, the two working groups involved in them are coordinating their definitions with each other.

A Sample Distribution

As with the other scheme, I will illustrate how the SNMP approach can be used to distribute the example low-level policies described earlier. We would use the DiffServ MIB to illustrate the policy distribution scheme using SNMP. At the time this book was written, the MIB was still undergoing standardization. Therefore, some of the details in the following steps might change. However, the major steps involved in the distribution process should largely remain the same.

The current version of the DiffServ MIB can be found on the home page of the DiffServ working group [DSWG]. At the time this book was written, the DiffServ MIB definition was associated with each direction of each interface of a DiffServ -capable router/server. For an eCommServer with one interface, two instances of the MIB would be defined—one for the packets coming into the server, and the other for the packets leaving the interface. Of course, you are primarily interested in the MIB associated with the outbound packets on the interface of eCommServer.

The DiffServ MIB contains three types of entries:

- A group of tables that define different types of entries

- A set of objects that help you manipulate the tables

- A set of compliance attributes

The compliance attributes describe whether a device is providing the MIB in read-only mode (for monitoring only) or is allowing values in the MIB to be modified. In order for distribution via SNMP to happen, the values in the MIB must be writable.

The set of tables that are defined in the MIB contain the following:

- `DiffServSixTupleClfrTable`: This contains a set of entries that define up to six fields in the IP header. The six fields include IP source/destination addresses, IP source/destination ports, transport protocol, and the DiffServ field.

- `diffServActionTable`: This contains a set of entries that define how packets are to be treated. This entry is used only to reference one of the more specific actions described in the next three tables.

- `diffServDscpMarkActTable`: This defines a set of DS field values that can be referenced by an entry in `diffServActionTable`.

- `diffServCountActTable`: This defines an action whereby packets and byte counts are maintained.

- `diffServAlgDropTable`: This defines a set of actions whereby packets are dropped. The conditions for dropping packets are also specified as part of the entries in this table.

- `diffServMeterTable`: This contains a set of entries that are used to keep counts of packets/bytes and to check if they have exceeded any thresholds. Each entry in the meter table also points to up to two entries in `diffServActionTable`. One of these is the action that is to be taken if an incoming packet has not exceeded the threshold specified in the meter table entry. The other is the action to be taken if the packet has exceeded the threshold. Instead of an entry in the action table, the entries may point to another entry in the meter table that can provide another set of thresholds.

- `diffServClassifierTable`: This contains a set of entries that define classification rules. These entries typically reference entries in `diffServSixTupleClfrTable` and `diffServActionTable` or `diffServMeterTable`. If a packet matches the criteria defined by the entry in `diffServSixTupleClfrTable`, the action specified by any entry referenced in `diffServActionTable` is taken. If entries in `diffServMeterTable` are referenced, the action taken depends on meeting specific thresholds in the meter entries.

The general way to add entries to these tables is by using a `nextFree` variable (one per table) that is kept under the objects group within the MIB. When an SNMP manager needs to create a new entry in a table, he reads the `nextFree` variable corresponding to that table and then creates a new entry at the corresponding index in the table. If the operation succeeds, the agent increments the `nextFree` variable so that the next entry can be created.

With this brief overview behind us, let's examine how the MIB tables must look in order to meet the low-level policies in the example we are considering:

- `diffServDscpMarkActTable` must have two entries. The first one has a value containing 000000 for BE, and the second one has a value containing 101110 for EF.

- `diffServActionTable` must have two entries. The first one points to the first entry in `diffServDscpMarkActTable`, and the second one points to the second entry in `diffServDscpMarkActTable`.

- `diffServSixTupleClfrTable` must have three entries. The first entry defines a source port of 265 and a protocol of 6. The second entry defines a source port of 11 and a protocol of 6. The third entry doesn't have any definitions. Items without definitions are treated as wildcards and match any packet by the definition of the MIB.

- `diffServClassifierTable` needs three entries. The first one points to the first entry in `diffServSixTupleClfrTable` and the second entry in `diffServActionTable`. The second one points to the second entry in `diffServSixTupleClfrTable` and the second entry in `diffServActionTable`. The third one points to the third entry in `diffServSixTupleClfrTable` and the first entry in `diffServActionTable`.

- Other table entries need not be defined.

Figure 7.4 illustrates the references among the different tables. The management tool must ensure that these tables are set up properly.

Figure 7.4   SNMP MIB Table Values for Sample Policies

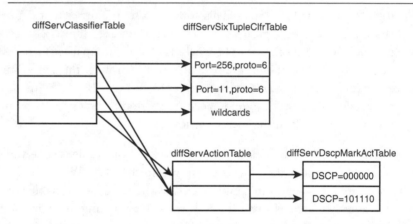

Let's look at the steps that the management tool needs to perform in order to initialize these entries. In order to create each row of the tables, the SNMP manager needs to have a message exchange with the agent in order to determine the `nextFree` variable and then have another set of exchanges to create the corresponding rows in the table. Each variable must be set in an independent set-request. The number of exchanges required to create SNMP tables corresponding to the relatively simple set of policies in the example can easily be seen to be in excess of 20 SNMP exchanges. Thus, policy provisioning using SNMP is likely to be relatively slow compared to obtaining the corresponding configuration using LDAP.

The SNMP agent that receives the MIB definitions from the manager must ensure that the local server and routers are configured to honor the commands coming in from the MIB. In the case of the AIX server considered in our example, the agent must ensure that the SNMP requests result in the same eventual configuration as the configuration files and scripts shown in Listings 7.1 and 7.2. It can do so by mapping SNMP MIB requests into the corresponding commands shown in Figure 7.2. However, a more efficient approach would be to configure the network stack directly using the SNMP MIB definitions as input.

Advantages and Disadvantages of Using SNMP for Policy Distribution

The main advantage of using an SNMP-based approach for policy distribution is that it is likely to work across all the routers in a standard manner. Of course, for every new technology that comes along, there would be a period before a standard MIB for it evolves. Eventually, when the MIB is developed and standardized, you can use it to configure and monitor any of the devices.

The SNMP protocol permits operations from a managing site, as well as asynchronous trap notifications from a device. However, its security characteristics are relatively weak, so you might not want to run SNMP across a firewall. This restricts the use of SNMP-based policy distribution in many applications of security policies, such as support of VPNs or extranets.

Another aspect of SNMP that is often criticized is its inefficiency in that each MIB data element must be written using separate requests. The bulk-transfer operations in higher versions of SNMP do address this issue somewhat. However, SNMP-based MIB configuration would still be relatively tedious and time-consuming. The question is whether the inefficiencies are really significant for configuration and policy distribution. The answer depends on how often you expect to change the policies. If the policies change rarely, such as every few hours, the inefficiencies of SNMP do not pose a problem for enterprise-scale networks (up to 1,000 routers). If the policies change very rapidly, SNMP-based configuration might not be appropriate. In the bulk of policy applications that we have considered in this book, policies are likely to change only rarely.

Another problem associated with SNMP is that it is not supported at the same level for desktops and servers that it is for routers. Furthermore, MIBs have been extended in proprietary ways by individual vendors, and the explanations of those proprietary extensions are not always available to those who write management applications.

Policy Distribution Using Common Open Policy Service

In place of SNMP, you can use a protocol such as *Common Open Policy Service* (COPS) to distribute policies to the different devices. COPS is a protocol that was originally developed for use within the context of a signaling protocol such as RSVP, but extensions to the protocol have been proposed that can also be used to provision policies for DiffServ or IP security.

An Overview of COPS

The original specification of COPS was intended for use within the context of admission control with signaling protocols such as RSVP. In a signaling protocol, a host intending to establish a communication channel with some level of performance assurance sends messages to various routers along the path of the communication channel in order to reserve resources it might need to meet a desired level of performance. When a router receives such a signaling message, it needs to decide whether to accept the connection request. Some of the conditions used for accepting connections can be easily determined by the router. For example, it can determine whether it has enough resources to meet the performance level desired by the incoming request. However, a network administrator might want to establish somewhat more complex conditions for accepting connections that are based on information such as the identity of the signaling entity, the validity of a purchase account established by a client with the network operator, and so on. Instead of having each of the routers make this determination, you might want to have this determination made by an external policy server.

The standard COPS protocol operates by maintaining a TCP connection between the router and the policy server. The router connects to the policy server by issuing a client-open message that describes its capabilities and the type of policy decisions it can enforce. The policy server responds with a client-accept message that contains parameters for maintaining their connection. When the router or the policy server wants to terminate the connection, they exchange a client-close message. While the connection is open, periodic keep-alive messages are exchanged in order to ensure that the router and the policy server are maintaining consistent state with each other.

When a router needs to consult the policy server regarding any decision, it sends a request message to the policy server. The policy server responds with a decision message advising what action the router should take. The router reports the result of enforcing these decisions to the policy server using a report-state message. The router and policy servers can use a couple of other messages designed for them to synchronize any state information regarding the active connections at the routers and the policy decisions that are applicable to them. In addition to the decision messages generated as a result of the request message, a policy server can also send unsolicited decision messages to the router.

Each of the messages exchanged within the COPS protocol consists of various types of COPS objects. These objects are data structures that include items such as details of a request, handles identifying clients making a request, the policy decisions, or other types of information needed within the different messages.

The standard COPS protocol was not designed to distribute policies from a central site to multiple routers. However, there are modifications proposed to the protocol that let a policy server send configuration and provisioning information to the other routers for disciplines such as DiffServ and IPsec. The types of messages that are exchanged remain the same as in the original COPS protocol. However, a new set of objects are defined that can carry the provisioning information related to DiffServ or IPsec back to the routers.

The set of objects that carry the policy information back to the routers constitute a *Policy Information Base* (PIB). A PIB is a collection of policy rules that are to be implemented and supported at a router. The PIB is formatted in a tree structure, with specific rules appearing at the leaves of the PIB structure. Each of the rules is named using an identifier, and they can be grouped into a hierarchy to combine different rules of a similar nature into a single entity. For example, all rules that apply to DiffServ may be combined under one node of the tree, and all the rules that apply to IP security may be combined under another node.

The PIB is specified using the same convention and notations as SNMP MIBs. Their purpose is almost identical to that of a MIB. The idea behind the use of PIBs for COPS is the same as those of MIBs within SNMP—namely, a general way to specify policy information. For each new discipline for which provisioning is needed, you can simply define a new PIB while reusing the existing set of protocols and tools. You can find more details on the current specification of the COPS protocol and PIB definitions at the home page of the RAP working group in IETF [RAPWG].

The Policy Distribution Process

Policy distribution using COPS happens between a COPS client (the device, or PEP) and a COPS server (the PDP) using a set of message exchanges. The COPS client (the device) should be able to locate the COPS server that is responsible for providing provisioning information to it. The identity of the COPS server can be configured into the device, or it can use a discovery protocol (such as Service Location Protocol [SLPREF]) to identify the COPS server.

The device then establishes contact with the COPS server. After an initial handshake, the device provides information about its interfaces, the different types of classification rules it can support, and the different types of queues it has at the various interfaces. The different types of classification rules that a COPS client can support include service differentiation using IP headers, or service differentiation using different priority schemes available at the link layer (such as priority bits available in Gigabit Ethernet standards). In the case of the eCommServer example we are reviewing, the COPS client simply informs the COPS server that classification on the basis of IP headers is supported and that the device can mark the DS fields of outbound packets. The device also provides the definition of the "role" it is playing in the network. The "role" is used to select policies that are relevant for the device. It is assumed that each device will have its role configured by some mechanism.

After the COPS server has obtained information about the capability of the devices, it sends policy provisioning information to the COPS client. The policy information in the sample case would be structured to indicate that it corresponds to the DiffServ provisioning. It would further contain the details of the DiffServ policies. The DiffServ policies are structured according to the DiffServ PIB definition. The PIB definition is an evolving standard whose latest iteration can be found at the DiffServ working group home page [DSWG].

At the time this book was published, the PIB definition for DiffServ consisted of four tables:

- `policyFilterTable`. Each entry in this table is a classification entry that contains filters such as 5-tuples (IP source/destination addresses, source/destination port numbers, protocol) or the 6-tuple (5-tuple plus the DiffServ field) that can be used to classify packets.

- `qosActionTable`. Each entry in this table provides an action that can be performed by the device, such as marking the DiffServ field with a specific value, shaping packets, or dropping packets.

- `qosMeterTable`. Each entry in this table provides thresholds on the maximum bandwidth that a flow can use. A meter can be one of three types: one without any thresholds, one with a committed rate limit, and one with a committed rate limit and a peak rate limit. If thresholding is turned off, all packets in a flow are considered to have high conformance with the meter. If the committed rate is specified, packets could be in high conformance or medium conformance, depending on whether the actual rate usage is above or below the committed rate. If both the peak and committed rates are specified, three levels of conforms (low, medium, and high) are defined, depending on whether the actual rate compares with the thresholds. For each level of conformance, you can have entries in the `qosActionTable` that will be performed on packets, depending on their conformance level.

- `qosTargetTable`. Contains entries that tie together entries in the `policyFilterTable` with entries in the `qosMeterTable`. Each entry also specifies the "role" of devices for which it is applicable.

For the low-level policies in the example, we need to define three entries in `policyFilterTable`, each operating at the IP level. One has a source port number of 256 and a protocol of 6, the second has a source port number of 11 and a protocol of 6, and the third matches all IP packets. `qosActionTable` will have two entries—one marking the packets with the DS Field value corresponding to EF (101110), and the other marking the packets with the DS Field value corresponding to BE (000000). Two entries in `qosMeterTable` will be defined. Neither will have any thresholds, and each entry will point to one of the different entries in `qosActionTable`. `qosTargetTable` will have three entries that tie together the entries in `qosMeterTable` and the entries in `policyFilterTable`. The resulting relation between the tables is shown in Figure 7.5.

Figure 7.5   COPS PIB Table Values for Sample Policies

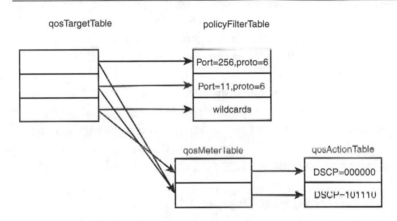

Compare the MIB table structure of Figure 7.4 with the PIB table structure shown in Figure 7.5. As is apparent from the two figures, the semantic information and the relationships among different tables in the PIB model are very similar to that in the MIB model. The difference among the two is in the syntax used to represent the various entries, and the protocol used to download the tables to the devices. In the case of COPS, all the PIB tables are written in a single operation to the device over a TCP connection. In the case of SNMP, the MIB tables are written one element at a time over UDP.

Advantages and Disadvantages of Using COPS-Based Distribution

The advantage of using COPS for policy distribution is that the protocol was designed with the intent and purpose of outsourcing policy decisions. Therefore, it can be used for sending unsolicited provisioning information as well as sending information on request from a router. It can also distribute policies much more efficiently than SNMP. However, it is doubtful whether this gain in efficiency is of significant importance in real networks, where policy information is not likely to change significantly.

Because COPS is a relatively new protocol, its support and deployment are not likely to be as widespread as that of SNMP.

Policy Distribution Using Web Servers

An alternative to policy distribution using the standard specification based on LDAP, COPS, or SNMP is to develop a simple policy distribution scheme using Web servers and cgi-bin scripts. In some sense, this approach can be seen as a poor man's network management framework.

The advantage of the approaches based on LDAP, COPS, or SNMP was that they provided a single way to store and define policies for the various devices, using a schema, PIB, or MIB definition. However, three stages of translation are involved with any of these schemes. The management tool must convert its local representation of device-level policies into the schema/PIB/MIB representation. Then an agent on each of the devices must convert this schema/PIB/MIB representation into a format that is suitable for consumption by the kernel of the networking device. This transformation is mainly just a syntactical translation and adds no new functions. However, it could be the most complex part of the entire policy distribution process. A different agent is needed for each new policy discipline, because the agent needs to understand and translate the standard schema/PIB/MIB specification. The goal of the Web server-based approach is to develop a generic agent that can work with any new discipline.

The Policy Distribution Process

Policy distribution in the Web server-based approach is provided by a Web server that provides URL-based access to five server-side programs (cgi-bin scripts). These cgi-bin scripts provide for the following six functions:

- **registration.** Lets any device register itself with the server.
- **unregister.** Lets devices unregister from the server.
- **get-policy.** Allows a device to obtain the configuration files and scripts to enforce its local policies.
- **set-policy.** Used by the policy manager to install policies at the server.
- **get-registered.** Allows a manager to get the list of devices that are registered with the server.
- **status-update.** Allows a device to report on the outcome of installing policies obtained using the get-policy script.

Each device has an agent that registers with the Web server by invoking the registration script. In the registration information, the agent provides information about a port number on which it may receive notifications about configuration updates, as well as details about the device, such as its operating system, version information, and so on. The agent can then request the get-policy script to determine the appropriate configuration file or scripts it needs. The policy manager tool needs to obtain a list of all registered devices and needs to generate the appropriate configuration files for all of them. When it changes the configuration file for a device, the put-policy script sends a notification to the agent running on the specific Web server, asking it to come back and check for updates to the policy.

The system based on Web servers was developed as a prototype within IBM Research. It provides a flexible way to distribute policies both inside and outside a firewall. By having the agents use a fixed port to receive the notifications, and by using SSL to encrypt communication between the agents and the Web servers, this approach can be used to provide secure distribution of configuration information using well-established Internet technologies.

To see how the sample policies will be distributed using the Web server example, look at the operation of the management console and the agents on the eCommServer machine. The agent registers its operating system and characteristics with the Web server, and it also registers a port on which it can listen for a configuration update. When the management tool learns about the characteristics of the agent on eCommServer, it translates the low-level policies into a configuration file, as shown in Listing 7.1. It then sends the configuration file to the Web server. The Web server notifies the agent that an updated configuration file is available. The agent then retrieves the updated configuration file, configures the local server, and provides an update of the status to the Web server. Instead of a configuration file, a script like the one shown in Listing 7.2 can also be used to configure the device using the same process.

Advantages and Disadvantages of Using Web Server-Based Distribution

The distribution of policies using Web servers has the advantage of being very scalable and able to traverse firewalls. It is appropriate for distributing security policies. Because it leverages established technologies of SSL and Web servers, it can ride on the back of performance and scalability enhancements that are taking place in those two domains. Web servers can support thousands of requests per second in current environments, and their security characteristics have found widespread acceptance in the Internet community.

Another advantage of this approach is that you can use a simple agent to determine the policies for any specific discipline. In some sense, the agent present on the devices is nothing but a remote installer for the scripts and programs that are created at the policy management tool. Such a simple application can be put on any of the platforms relatively easily. Also, it avoids the translation into intermediate formats required by the LDAP/COPS/SNMP schemas.

The disadvantages of this approach are that it is nonstandard and that the policy management tool must be aware of the different configuration scripts and capabilities of the different devices. Thus, a bigger burden is placed on the management tool, while a very simple agent is placed on each device. Another disadvantage is that this solution can't work on closed boxes such as routers. For such platforms, you need to develop a proxy running on a desktop or server that can invoke the appropriate scripts for the routers by telneting into them as described earlier in this chapter.

Summary

This chapter looked at various ways in which policies and configuration information can be distributed from the management tool to the different devices in the network. Although each approach was presented in isolation, a practical network is likely to deploy a combination of all these approaches, depending on the nature of policy-capable devices within the network. Even within the IETF policy architecture, the work follows a model that policies are stored in the directory and *Policy Decision Points* (PDPs) retrieve the policy using LDAP. Communication between the PDPs and the *Policy Enforcement Points* (PEPs) uses COPS or SNMP. If a router supports a COPS client, you can use COPS to distribute the policies to it. If it supports the SNMP MIBs described earlier, you can use SNMP to provide the appropriate policies and configuration information. If a router does not support COPS or SNMP MIBs, it is likely that a proxy using command-line scripts will be used to configure the router. In many cases, it is likely that a PEP and PDP are present on the same device. In this case, you can avoid SNMP or COPS and use some lightweight internal mechanism for communication between the PDP and the PEP.

Each of the different approaches presented has its strengths and weaknesses. Table 7.3 compares the different distribution schemes. The basis of comparison assumes that a management console running the policy management tool and several devices running a software agent are configured using the specific distribution scheme. Multiple criteria are used to compare the various schemes, as shown in Table 7.3.

Table 7.3	Comparison of Different Distribution Schemes					
Criteria	Management Scripts Frameworks		LDAP	COPS	SNMP	Web Server
Console complexity	High	High	Low	Low	Low	High
Agent complexity	Low	None	Medium	Medium	Medium	Low
Error control	High	Poor	OK	High	High	High
Delay	Low	Low	Medium	Low	Low	Low
Central repository	Maybe	No	Yes	No	No	Yes
Standards	Proprietary	Proprietary	Standard	Standard	Standard	Non-standard
Maturity	Varies	High	High	Low	High	High

The first two criteria comparing the different distribution schemes are the relative complexity of the software that needs to run on the management console and the one on the agent side. In a management framework approach, or the Web server-centric approach described in this chapter, the bulk of complexity is on the management console side. The agents on the devices are relatively lightweight and general-purpose. With the use of scripts, no agent is present on the device. With LDAP, COPS, or SNMP, the management console outputs policy information in only a single format and is less complex, but the onus of converting policies into configuration files is shifted to the agent side, which therefore is shown as having medium complexity.

The next criterion is the ability of the distribution scheme to detect any exception conditions that can occur in the configuration process, and the logging/reporting of those error conditions back to the management console. This requires the agent to detect error conditions that can arise in the device's operations and configuration and to have a feedback mechanism to the management console. Management frameworks and Web server-based approaches offer the best feedback path to log any operational errors back to the management console. Scripts provide some ability to detect the error conditions that arise when the policies are being installed, but they do not provide a way to capture errors that occur when policies are applied to the packet-forwarding path. LDAP provides no feedback path, and it is not expected that agents will write any operational logs to the directory server. However, devices can update entries in a directory server to indicate some types of errors that occur, and it is possible to develop notification schemes. SNMP provides the standard trap mechanism to detect errors, and COPS allows a client to contact the COPS server to notify it of any exception conditions.

The next criterion deals with the delay that is incurred when existing policies are changed, and the agent on the device configures the device in accordance with the changed policies. In most management frameworks, the change occurs relatively quickly. Because the console is primarily responsible for getting the device configured using scripts, the change is quick in almost all approaches except a pure LDAP-based approach. Because asynchronous notification is not ubiquitously available in LDAP servers, agents on the clients need to periodically poll the repository to detect changes in the policies. A larger delay might be incurred in the configuration of the devices. Of course, you can augment the agents on the devices with a signaling scheme (such as a message to a fixed port) to trigger the retrieval of the policies.

Another criterion examines whether there is a central location where policies are stored, and where you can develop tools to monitor the configuration of the entire network. This centralized information might be available in management frameworks, depending on their implementation. The same is true of an LDAP-based approach and a Web server-based approach. With a script-based approach, the central repository need not exist. Similarly, an SNMP-based approach or COPS-based distribution scheme typically doesn't need to use a central repository. However, as mentioned earlier, these can be coupled with an LDAP backend, which can act as the central repository of policies.

Another criterion with which to compare the different approaches is whether they are proprietary, or subject to current standardization efforts. Management frameworks, scripts, and even a Web server-based scheme are proprietary nonstandard schemes. LDAP- and COPS-based schemes are becoming standardized within IETF, and SNMP is an established standard. However, with SNMP, many proprietary MIB extensions are available on many different platforms.

The final criterion compares the maturity and stability of the underlying protocols used for policy distribution. The management frameworks can be mature or evolving, depending on the vendor supplying them. TME and TNG are fairly mature frameworks. The use of scripts for configuration has been around for at least a decade. LDAP and SNMP are well-established protocols, as is the underlying HTTP-based communication for Web server-based distribution. COPS is a relative newcomer, so its maturity is designated as low in Table 7.3.

If you must decide which policy architecture for distribution is appropriate within a network, you must consider whether you want a proprietary or standards-based solution. If you opt for a standards-based solution, decide whether you want a central repository of all policies. If so, you probably should use an LDAP-based approach. Otherwise, if your devices are likely to have COPS clients enabled, choose a COPS-based approach. If your devices are likely to have SNMP agents enabled, choose an SNMP-based approach. Of course, you can also use a mixture of the various techniques, as described in the first part of this section.

Policy Enforcement Point Algorithms

Thus far in this book, we have looked at the algorithms and mechanisms that can be used at the policy management console and how they are distributed to the various devices. This short chapter looks at the algorithms and mechanisms that need to be implemented at the devices themselves in order to enforce compliance with those policies.

This chapter begins with a description of an abstract model of the device that actually enforces the policies specified by the management console. This is followed by a description of the set of algorithms that is appropriate when the policies need to be applied to the traffic flows passing through the device. Then we'll look at the various algorithms that can be used by a device to ensure that the policies it has received from the repository or the management tool are well formed and valid. These local validity checks are needed to guard against any possible corruption during the distribution process.

Policy Enforcement Point Components

In order to present the discussion of the *Policy Enforcement Point* (PEP), a simple model of a device is assumed, in which the operations are broken into two areas that I call the *data path* and the *control path*. The data path refers to all the operations that are performed at a device on packets, connections, or other units of traffic flowing through the device. The control path refers to operations and algorithms that need to be executed in order to obtain the configuration information or other information needed for the operation of the data path.

The control path in most applications predominantly consists of an agent running on the device that will be involved in the distribution of policies to the device, as discussed in the preceding chapter. After the policies are received (or retrieved) at the device, the agent must configure the data path to ensure that its operations comply with the desired set of policies.

The structure of the agent depends on the mechanism that is used for policy distribution. If policies are distributed using LDAP, the agent needs to incorporate an LDAP client. In this case, the agent is performing both the functions of a *Policy Decision Point* (PDP) and a PEP, as defined by the IETF Policy architecture (see Chapter 1, "Policy Enabled Networking Architecture," for an overview of architecture). When the agent is only implementing the functionality of a PEP as defined within the IETF architecture, policy distribution can occur via SNMP or COPS. If policies are distributed using SNMP, the agent needs to incorporate the functionality needed for the SNMP protocol. If policies are distributed using SNMP, the agent must incorporate a COPS client. When proprietary management frameworks are used for distribution of policies, the agent takes on the form of extension modules to those management frameworks.

One of the operations that the agent must perform at the device is to ensure that the policies being enforced by the data-path are valid and consistent. When a large number of policies might be in effect at the device, the agent must ensure that the most appropriate set of policies is cached locally and is being used by the data path. Furthermore, the agent needs to translate the policy representation on the wire into a local representation. The policy representation on the wire is in terms of the MIBs/PIBs or LDAP schema entries. The agent can choose to maintain the same representation locally. However, in most cases, conversion to a local representation format leads to better performance along the data path. The agent is responsible for ensuring consistency between the wire format and the local policy representation.

The details of the operations to be performed in the data path are very dependent on the policy discipline you are exploring. These operations are the ones that are invoked on the actual traffic flows. They may be triggered on the arrival of a packet or a new connection. For the most common applications of policies, in the case of network QoS or IPsec, the operations are performed on a per-packet arrival. However, there are many instances in which similar operations can be applied on the arrival of a connection. For example, DiffServ policies are often applied at a router on a packet-by-packet basis. However, at the end points of a connection, you might opt to do such classification on the first packet of the connection (such as on the arrival of the packet containing the SYN flag within the TCP header), and reuse the classification information for all packets on the flow. Similarly, a Web proxy might opt to provide such a classification every time a new URL is requested by a client. This classification occurs many times during a single TCP connection for Web proxies and servers that implement the HTTP 1.1 protocol.

For a router implementing the DiffServ function you can assume a simple logical set of operations to be performed for the processing when a packet is received at the router. When the packet is first received by the router, it applies a classification function on the packet to determine how to handle the packet. The classification is typically done by looking at up to six fields in the network and transport headers. These fields include the source and destination IP addresses, the source and destination transport port numbers, the transport protocol, and the incoming ToS byte. In some cases where DiffServ functions are implemented across ISPs, it is expected that the classification will be done simply by looking at the incoming ToS byte. After the classification process is complete, the router will choose to perform various actions such as validating that the bandwidth restrictions placed on this class of packets are enforced. The router can re-mark the DiffServ Field (part of the original IP ToS byte) and collect statistics based on packet arrival.

For a router implementing the *Integrated Services* (IntServ) function, you can assume that the packets are processed in a manner similar to that of DiffServ. However, the classification of packets is done on the basis of up to five fields in the network and transport header (all the fields mentioned in the DiffServ case except the ToS byte). These fields identify the flow to which a packet belongs. Within IntServ, rate limits are associated with each flow (as compared to predefined PHBs in DiffServ), and these limits are established using a signaling protocol.

For a firewall implementing the IPsec function, one needs to check on the basis of the five fields whether or not the packets need to be encrypted/authenticated prior to their transfer. If a policy stating the type of transformation to be made to the packet is found, the corresponding transformations are applied to the packet.

In all these cases, the router/firewall has to perform a classification function on the basis of multiple fields within the network and transport fields. One of the key issues facing policy enforcement in routers is to implement efficient algorithms to perform packet classification.

Therefore, one focus of the algorithms that we will examine for a PEP is the efficient classification algorithms. The other set of algorithms we will consider are the ones needed to validate the relevant set of policies within the PEP.

Classification Algorithms

Here is the basic classification problem faced by the router:

> Given a set of policies and an incoming message (such as a specific packet header), determine which policy applies to the packet in question.

We assume that the policies at the PEP have all the conflicts resolved among themselves and that priorities have been established such that there is exactly one policy which applies to any packet. We further assume that the agent will convert the policies that are received in the standard format (based on MIBs or PIBs) into more efficient data structures for rapid classification and searching for policies. Along with the classification algorithms, we also present schemes by which such efficient data structures can be constructed.

Simple Linear Search

The classification algorithm that is applied in most current implementations of a policy system is a simple linear search. In this case, the policies are simply stored in an array in which the policies with higher-priority ordering are stored first in the list. The priority ordering can be specified by an administrator (or created by the policy management tool). Quite often, implementations also order the policies with the same priority ordering so that policies that are more specific occur earlier than policies that are less specific. A more specific policy is one in which more fields are specified. Generally, the last policy to be applied is the default policy.

As an example, consider the six policies defined in Table 8.1. Each row in the table defines a policy where the destination IP address and the source port form part of the condition expression of the policy. Thus, rule P1 is "if a packet has destination IP address of 9.0.0.0/8 and a source port number between 200-440, treat it as a class one packet." We are only using two of the fields that can be used for policy definition in order to present a simple example. These rules map different packets into one of four classes, and each rule has a priority field which determines the relative importance of that policy. When multiple policies are applicable, the one with the highest priority must be applied first. Each class corresponds to a different type of behavior in the network depending on the policy discipline; for instance, for DiffServ these might indicate different types of markings for the DiffServ field. In order to apply the linear search, the policies shown in Table 8.1 are searched in the sequence {P5, P2, P4, P1, P3, P6}. The order is obtained by simply enumerating the policies in the order of highest priority first.

Table 8.1   Example for Linear Search

Policy Name	Dest	IP Address	Source Port	Priority Class
P1	9.0.0.0/8	200-400	1	One
P2	9.2.0.0/16	265	2	Two
P3	*	4000-6000	1	Three
P4	10.0.0.0/8	*	2	One
P5	10.4.0.0/16	3000-4000	3	Two
P6	*	*	0	Four

In order to determine which policy rule is applicable to an incoming packet, the ordered list of policies is examined. The first policy that matches the contents of the header fields within the conditional expression of the policy rule is applied to the packet.

As an example, consider a packet with the destination IP address of 10.2.0.4 and a source port number of 343. The packet does not match P5 (IP address does not match), but does match P4. Therefore, the rule P4 is applied to this packet. For another packet with destination IP address of 9.2.4.56 and a port number of 265, rule P2 is the first one in the list to match and apply. For a packet headed to 8.2.22.46 with a source port of 265, rule P6 matches and applies.

The advantage of the linear search is that it is fairly straightforward to implement. In situations in which the number of policy rules is small, such a scheme performs reasonably well. However, when the number of policy rules are large, the time to determine an applicable policy can become fairly large. The running-time complexity of the simple linear search is O, where n is the number of applicable policy rules.

If packet headers follow a random distribution pattern, you would expect to scan about half of the list before a match is found. If the packet headers do not follow a random pattern, and some types of packets are more likely to occur than others, the list can be reordered so that the chances of having a hit early on are maximized. The list of policies can be reordered because not all policies are applicable to all the packets.

If we examine the linear list of policies in Table 8.1, we see that policies P1 and P2 can never apply to the same packet because they contain a disjoint range of port numbers in their condition part. Two policies can apply to the same packet only if they overlap in all the fields that make up the condition part of the policy. In the example shown, only rules that have a common set of destination IP addresses and port numbers overlap with each other and can both be applicable to the same set of packets. There are three groups of policies that overlap:

- Group 1—Policies {P5, P4, P3, P6} that are shown in the order of decreasing priority.

- Group 2—Policies {P1, P6} shown in the same order.

- Group 3—Policies {P2, P6} shown in the order of decreasing priority.

The key observation is that the policies that belong to different groups can be placed anywhere in relation to each other without affecting the outcome of the linear list search. Thus, instead of ordering the list for searching policies as {P5, P2, P4 ,P1, P3, P6}, positions of P2 and P5 can exist and the list is maintained as {P2, P5, P4, P1, P3, P6} without any impact on policy decisions.

In mathematical terms, the set of policies have a partial order relationship. Given any two policies in the set, we could say that P1 takes precedence over P2 (or vice-versa) if they belong in the same group, and say that the two do not have any ordering relationships with each other if they belong in different groups. A partial order relationship can be shown as an inverted tree where the policy takes precedence over the policies below it on the same branch. The partial order relationship among the policies in Table 8.1 is shown in Figure 8.1.

Figure 8.1   Partial Order Relationship for Policies in Table 8.1

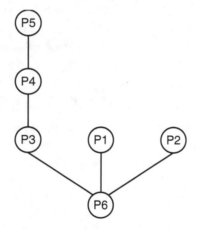

This result allows you to restructure the lists to minimize the number of list items examined for matching a policy. For example, a PEP might decide to reorder the list of policies every time interval T (such as, for packet processing, assume that T is 100 ms). The PEP can keep track of the percentage of packets that match each of the policies, use the past history to develop an estimate of the expected percentage of the policy hits for the next interval, and use the estimated percentages to reorder the list for the next interval. The scheme to reorder the list will be fairly straightforward. The inverted tree representing the partial order relationship among the policies is determined. Each of the nodes is labeled with the percentage of incoming packets that matches each policy. Start from an initial ordering of lists that is empty. When the new order needs to be determined, simply examine all the policies which are at the top of their branch and select the one with the highest percentage. The selected policy is removed from the partial order and appended to the tail of the new order. The process repeats until all the policies have been added to the new order.

Figure 8.2   Determining Optimal Order of Policies

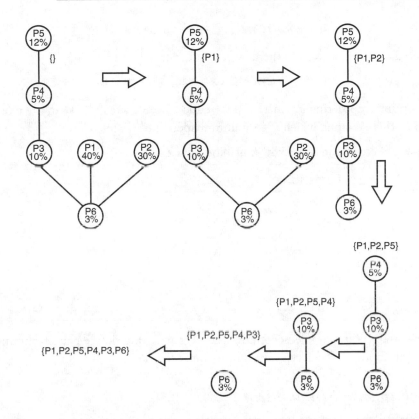

As an example, assume that the measurement of policies has estimated the percentage of packets which match the defined policies as shown in Table 8.2. This information is used to create the list of policies following the steps shown in Figure 8.2. In Step 1, look at the policies on the top of their branches which are {P5, P1, P2} and take the one with the highest percentage, namely P1. This gives you the ordering of {P1}. Then remove this policy from the partial order and repeat the process. In the next step, P2 and P5 are at the top of their branches, in which we select P2 as the one with the higher frequency. This results in an ordering of {P1, P2}. After this step, we are left with only one branch of the partial order, and these policies will be taken in the order in which they occur in the branch. The resulting sequence is {P1, P2, P5, P4, P3, P6}, which is a very different sequence than the one originally based on priorities alone.

You can compare the average number of policies that will be examined for a search in both the new search order of {P1, P2, P5, P4, P3, P6} and the original search order of {P5, P2, P4, ,P1, P3, P6}. This can be done by multiplying the percentage of times a policy is expected to occur by its position in the search order. The expected number of steps in the old search order is

$$40\% * 4 + 30\% *2 + 10\% * 5 + 5\% * 4 + 3\%*1 + 12\%*6 = 3.06$$

The expected number of steps in the new search order is

$$40\% * 1 + 30\% * 2 + 10\% * 5 + 5\% *4 + 3\% * 3 + 12\% * 6 = 1.97$$

Thus, the optimal reordering has managed to reduce the average lookups in the table to 1.97 from 3.06 in this example, which is a significant speed up of 35%.

Table 8.2   Percentage of Packets Matching Policies

Policy	Percentage
P1	40%
P2	30%
P3	10%
P4	5%
P5	3%
P6	12%

The linear search is often implemented in firewalls to provide simple packet filtering and to determine the appropriate encryption rules to apply for IPsec.

Policy Lookup on a Single Field

A linear search is the simplest way to determine the appropriate policy to apply for a packet. Instead of maintaining the policies as a list, one could maintain policies in another data structure, like a tree, and obtain better search efficiency. Tree-based searches can be easily performed in $O(\log n)$ where n is the number of policies being searched upon. In order to present the tree-based search schemes, I will proceed through a sequence of algorithms. In the first step, I will look at searching policies that contain only one type of term in the conditional express. I will examine three types of policies of this nature, one in which finding the right policy requires an exact match between a header field of an incoming packet and the condition specified in the policy expression; the other in which finding the right policy requires checking that the header field of an incoming packet lies among the range specified by the condition part of a policy; and another in which finding the right policy requires searching for the policy with the longest prefix match with the incoming header field. After looking through the steps required for each of the individual fields, I look at schemes to structure the tree when multiple fields make up the conditional part of a policy.

Policy Searches Based on Exact Matches

Consider a set of policies which specifies an exact match as the conditional part of its policy. An example in which this condition often arises is the use of incoming DS field. The DS field of a packet can take a value from 0 to 63. You can specify rules, such as the following: If the DS field value is 3, 5 or 7 the packet is of type class 1, otherwise the packet is of type class 2. In addition to the DS field, you often need to do exact matches on a source port number or destination port number that makes up the conditional expression within the policy.

In the case of the DS Field, the number of choices are small (at most 63) so that it is feasible in many implementations to do a direct lookup into a table of 64 entries to determine the class specified by a policy. However, there are other instances of policy specification where the number of possible conditions would be too large to allow a direct table lookup. An example is the policy where the conditional part consists of a port number.

Consider the set of policy expressions shown in Table 8.3, which shows the conditional part as the source port number and the class to which a matching packet needs to be mapped. There are eight policy rules mapping incoming packets to one of two classes, with a default one that matches everything up to class three.

Table 8.3 Example for Exact Match Search

Policy	Source Port	Class
P1	30	One
P2	32	Two
P3	34	One
P4	39	Two
P5	40	One
P6	45	Two
P7	59	One
P8	Any	Three

There is a variety of algorithms that can be used to search through the preceding list for a matching policy. Several such algorithms have been described in the compilation of computer algorithms by Knuth [KNUTH]. A tree-based approach for searching through these policies requires formulating them into a binary tree such as the one shown in Figure 8.3. The structuring of the policies into the tree structure shown can be done by means of a two-step algorithm shown below:

- Arrange all the policies (except default one) into increasing order of the condition part (source port).

- Take the median policy in this arrangement, and make it the root node of a tree. All policies with condition part smaller than that of the root node go into the left sub-tree, and all policies with condition part larger than that of the root node go into the right subtree.

- Recursively apply the process to the left and right subtrees.

The median policy in a list is the policy in the middle of the list. If there is an odd number of policies in the list, then there is exactly one median policy. If there is an even number of policies in the list, there are two policies that can be called median, and we can select any one of these for the construction process. In a list of 7 policies, the fourth policy is the median one. In a list of 10 policies, one could use either the fourth one or the sixth one.

| Figure 8.3 | Binary Search Tree for Exact Field Match |

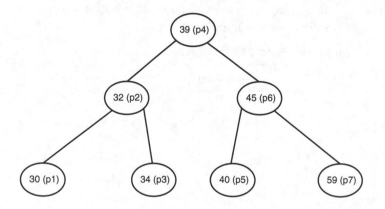

When the policy applicable to an incoming packet needs to be determined, you need to extract the source port number from the incoming packet and search for a match within the tree. The search starts from the root node of the tree. If the field being searched has an exact match with the value in the root node, that is the right policy to apply. Other-wise, if the field being searched is smaller than the value in the root node, the search moves on to the left child of the root node, where this sequence is repeated. If the field being searched is larger than the value in the root node, the search moves on to the right child of the root node, where this sequence is repeated. If no match is found, the default policy is applied.

For the example shown in Figure 8.3, assume that a packet has an incoming source port number of 80. Compare it with the root node which has the value of 39 (P4). Because 80 is larger than 39, move to the right subtree, and compare it with 45 (P6). This is not an exact match, so you move on to the right subtree which is 59 (P7). There is no match found, and no more nodes left to traverse. Hence, there is no match, and the default policy applies. This packet needs to be mapped to class 3.

If the incoming packet has a source port number of 34, the search starts at root with a value of 39 (P4). 34 is smaller than 39, so the search moves on to the left child 32 (P2). This is not a match, but 34 is larger than 32, so the search moves on to the right child 34 (P3). This is an exact match, and the applicable policy, P3, is used. The packet is then mapped on to class 1.

As in the case of the linear search order, you can arrange the tree to be searched more efficiently if the estimate of the percentage of packets each policy would match is known. The structure shown in Figure 8.3 is suitable if each policy is equally likely to be applied, such as when each policy has the same expected percentage. If the percentages are different, it is desirable to keep the policies that are more likely to be accessed near the top. One way to build such a tree is to choose the root of the tree to be the node with the highest percentage. All the nodes with smaller values become the left subtree, and all the nodes with larger values become the right subtree. If during the construction stage you find that there are many nodes that meet the condition for highest percentage accesses, they can be structured using the normal tree construction step described previously.

Table 8.4	Percentage Access for Exact Match Policies	
Policy	Condition	Part Percentage
P1	30	20%
P2	32	40%
P3	34	5%
P4	39	10%
P5	40	5%
P64	5	8%
P7	59	8%
P8	Any	4%

Consider the set of percentage probabilities shown in Table 8.4. The tree construction process is shown in Figure 8.4. At the first step, the root selected is P2 which has the highest percentage of access. This divides the problem into two subtree construction problems, one for the left subtree containing P1 only and the other for the right subtree containing P3 through P7. The left subtree is trivial, so we look at the right subtree. The policy with the highest percentage of access is P4, which becomes the root of the subtree with two subtrees, P3 on the left and P5-P7 on the right. P6 and P7 have the same probability, so we arrange them with P6 being the parent and P7 being the right subtree (as one would in normal construction). This leaves P5 which is made the left child of P6. The steps of the tree construction process are shown in Figure 8.4.

Figure 8.4   Search Tree Construction Example for Exact Matches

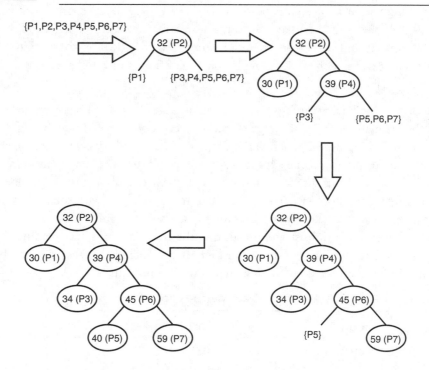

Now you can compare the expected number of steps spent in the policy search process of the original tree structure and the new tree structure. With the original tree structure, which does not take into account the access percentage, the expected number of steps for packets matching P1 (20%), P3 (5%), P5 (5%), or P7 (8%) is 3, packets matching P2 (40%) or P6 (8%) is 2, and packets matching P4 (10%) is 1. The default match with 4% of packets also takes 3 steps. The expected average number of steps is 2.32. For the new tree, packets matching P5 (5%) or P7 (8%) take 4 steps, packets matching P3 (5%) or P6 (8%) take 3 steps, packets matching P1 (20%) or P4 (10%) take 2 steps, and packets matching P2 (40%) takes one step. The default policy can take anywhere between 2 and 4 steps, so let's take the worst case of 4 steps. The expected number of steps in this case is 2.07 steps, an improvement of about 10%.

Such a restructuring of the tree works well if the percentage of packets matching the default policy is not very high. What if the percentage of packets that match the default policy is very high, such as 90%? In that case, you should structure the policy tree so that the necessary steps to determine that none of the policies are applicable are minimized. To do this, store a lower limit and an upper limit at each of the nodes in the tree. The lower limit of a node is the value of the left-most child of the node, and the upper limit is the value of the right-most child of the node. For example, the lower limit for the root node P4 in Figure 8.3 would be 30, and the upper limit would be 59. Similarly, the lower limit for the node P2 would be 20, and the upper limit would be 34. When a matching policy is being searched for, and the value being searched for is less than the lower limit or greater than the upper limit at any node, the default policy is applicable. Only if the value lies within the lower and upper limits do you need to search further down the children of the node. Thus, if you are searching for a policy to match a packet with a source port number of 76 using the tree in Figure 8.3, you can conclude at the root node P1 that the default policy is the one applicable. Similarly, if you try to find a policy for a packet with a source port number of 37, the algorithm traverses the nodes P4 and P2 as usual. However, at P2 the algorithm sees that the value being looked for 37 is higher than the upper limit 34, and decides to apply the default policy instead.

Policy Searches Based on Ranges

In fields, such as source or destination port numbers, policies often specify a range rather than a single value. A range is a short form for expressing several values, and specifies a lower and upper limit for the values it contains. It allows for much more efficient searching if you can locate the range within which the fields of an incoming request lie.

These sets of policies can be constructed into a tree for searching as in the case for searching with exact matches. The structure of the tree should be such that the range of the policies at the root node are "larger" than the ranges of all the policies within the left subtree, and "smaller" than the ranges of all the policies within the right subtree. You need to define what being "smaller" or "larger" means for a range.

Let's assume for the time-being that none of the ranges specified within any of these policies overlap. In this case, the notion of "smaller" or "larger" can be defined as follows: Range A is smaller than range B if the upper limit of range A is smaller than the smaller limit of range B. Similarly, range A is larger than range B if the lower limit of range A is larger than the upper limit of range B. Thus, the port range of 20-60 is smaller than the port-range of 61-80, but larger than the port range of 10-15.

With this notion of ordering among the ranges, searching for applicable policies can be done in a manner very similar to that for exact searches. Consider the set of policies shown in Table 8.5.

Table 8.5	Example for Range Match Search		
Policy	Source Port	Class	
P1	50-80	Two	
P2	100-200	One	
P3	50	Two	
P4	300-400	One	
P5	500-700	Two	
P6	50	One	
P7	900-1000	One	
P8	Any	Three	

These ranges are arranged in a tree as in the case of an exact match search. However, each node of the tree contains a range instead of containing a single number. The range is the conditional part of the policy that is represented at the node. When an applicable policy is being searched for, the value of the header field of the incoming packet (for this example, the source port number) is compared to the range limits specified at the root node. If the header field lies within the range stored at the node, the policy at the node is applied. If the header field is less than the lower limit of the range, the subtree to the left of root node is searched. If the header field is more than the upper limit of the range, the subtree to the right of the root node is searched.

The policy search tree is constructed from a given set of policies similarly to that of the exact match search. You sort the policies in increasing order of the "larger" relation. Then you take the median policy in the ordered list and make it the root of the policy search tree. Entries to the left and right of the root are made into the right and left search subtrees recursively. The policy search tree that corresponds to the set of policies shown in Table 8.5 is shown in Figure 8.5.

Suppose you get a packet with a source port number of 950. You start from the root node P4 and see that you need to go right to node P5. You go further to the right of node P5 to node P7 where you find a matching policy. Similarly, the packet with source port number of 250 traverses the nodes P4, P2, P3 and determines that policy P3 is applicable.

Figure 8.5   Binary Search Tree for Non-Overlapping Ranges Example

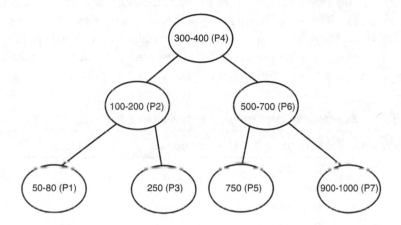

As with exact matches, you can construct the search tree so that policies which match a higher percentage of packets are placed near the root of the search tree. This improves the efficiency of the search process. When the default policy is the one that applies, usually you can assign limits to each of the nodes to halt the search process. This method is identical to that described for the exact search matches. The lower limit at a node is the lowest value among all the lower limits specified at any of the nodes in its left subtree. The upper limit at a node is the highest value among all the upper limits specified at any of the nodes in its right subtree. If a packet arrives with the header field outside of the upper/lower range, the default policy is applicable to it.

In real life, ranges often overlap. If you review the simple set of policy examples illustrated in Table 8.1, you see that the source port range overlap occurs among several policies: P1 and P2 overlap, as do P3 and P5. The policies with a wild card for the port numbers overlap with all the other policies. Therefore, the search scheme must be able to handle the case of overlapping ranges.

The difficult issue with overlapping ranges is that it is not possible to easily state that one range is "lower" than another if they overlap. One way to solve the problem is to break the policies into smaller units so that there is no overlap between them. You can then apply the techniques for searching through non-overlapping ranges to look through the applicable policies.

As an example, consider the set of overlapping policies shown in Table 8.6. Each policy comes with a priority that describes how to break the tie if more than one policy applies to the same packet. This set of overlapping policies can be broken into non-overlapping ranges. The only policy that is not broken in this fashion is the default policy (P5) which applies to all the ranges. Within each range, more than one policy can apply. The set of non-overlapping ranges, and the different policies that are applicable to them, is shown in Table 8.7.

Table 8.6   Example for Overlapping Range Search

Policy Name	Source Port	Priority	Class
P1	200-400	1	One
P2	265	2	Two
P3	4000-6000	1	Three
P4	3000-4000	3	Two
P5	*	0	Four

Table 8.7   Non-Overlapping Regions for Example Policy

Range Name	Source Port	Applicable Policy
R1	200-264	P1
R2	265	P2
R3	266-400	P1
R4	3000-3999	P3
R5	4000	P4
R6	4001-6000	P4

The set of applicable policies at each range can be reduced to be the one with the highest priority. This reduces the problem to that of non-overlapping range one. In Table 8.7, the applicable policy in the case of range R2 is policy P2, and the applicable policy in the case of range R5 is policy P4. If there is no conflict among the policies, exactly one applicable policy must be found for each range. The search tree that corresponds to this set is shown in Figure 8.6. Each node in the table shows the policy ranges which applies, the name of the range as shown in Table 8.7, and the policy that would be applicable within that range (P1 through P4).

Figure 8.6   Example Binary Search Tree for Overlapping Ranges

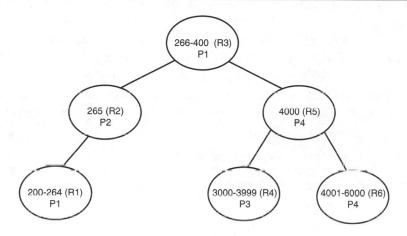

Policy Search with Longest Prefix Match

In many cases, policies are specified so that you need to find the matching entry which has the largest prefix. This situation arises commonly when IP addresses are used as conditions for specifying policies. Another common policy condition which requires a longest prefix search are policies that are specified on Web URLs. The longest prefix search is a type of range search, except that the range which is more specific (matches a longer prefix) needs to be given a higher priority than the range which is less specific.

As an example of a policy that requires longest prefix match, consider a policy that maps URLs into classes. A first policy can map the URL `http://www.foo.com/` into class one, and a second policy can map the URL `http://www.foo.com/cgi-bin/` into class two. When a request with a URL of `http://www.foo.com/images/image1.gif` arrives, it maps onto class one. When a request with a URL of `http://www.foo.com/cgi-bin/` `program1` arrives, it matches both rules, but must be mapped onto class two (as per the second rule) because it matches a larger prefix of the second rule.

As another example of longest prefix matches based on policies, consider two policies, one mapping all packets with source IP address in 10.0.0.0/8 to class one and the other mapping all packets with source IP addresses in 10.2.0.0/16 to class two. A packet with source IP address of 10.4.5.67 only matches with the first policy and is mapped into class one. A packet with source IP address of 10.2.34.35 matches both the policies. However, the field matches the condition in policy 2 in 16 bits while it only matches the condition in policy 1 in 8 bits. Therefore, the second policy takes precedence over the first policy.

The traditional algorithm to search for longest prefix matches is using a Patricia Tree [SEDGEWICK]. A Patricia Tree is a tree containing two types of nodes, external nodes contain the values against which comparisons are made, and internal nodes contain bit positions that are to be examined. Given a value to search for, the algorithm starts from the root of the tree and examines the bits of the value which are specified by the content of the root node. Depending on the result of the comparison, the algorithm selects one of the children subtrees for further processing. When an external node is reached, the value stored at the external node is compared to the input value and represents the longest prefix match, as shown in Table 8.8.

Table 8.8   Example for Longest Prefix Search

Policy Name	Source Address	Class
P1	9.0.0.0/8	One
P2	9.2.0.0/16	Two
P3	10.0.0.0/8	One
P4	10.4.0.0/16	Two
P5	*	Three

This process is best illustrated by an example. Consider the set of policies shown in Table 8.8. The Patricia Tree corresponding to the example is shown in Figure 8.7. Each node of the tree shows the mask that defines the bit positions of the incoming value that need to be examined. Each of the subtrees is labeled with the resulting value which would cause that branch to be followed. At the root of the tree, the positions to be examined are the first 8 bits. If the value contained in these positions is 9, the branch labeled 9.0.0.0 is followed. If the value is 10, the branch labeled 10 is followed. If the value is something different, the rightmost branch is followed. At the nodes on the next level, the next 8 bits are examined. The leaf nodes are shown by a square, and they contain one of the policies that would apply to them.

Consider a packet with the source address of 9.2.34.5. At the first node, it is masked with 255.0.0.0 resulting in the value of 9.0.0.0. This causes the leftmost branch to be followed. At the next stage (node N2), the value is masked with 0.255.0.0, resulting in 0.2.0.0. This results in following the left subtree which is a leaf node. The value in this node, 9.2.* matches the incoming value, and P2 is the applicable policy to apply. A packet with a source address of 11.2.34.5 similarly gets the default policy of P5.

Figure 8.7   Patricia Tree for Longest Prefix Match

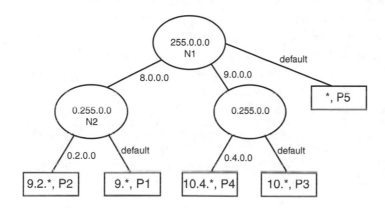

Variations of the Patricia Tree are used in IP routing [SKLOWER]. In fact, if you change the field from source IP address to destination IP address, the problem of finding the right class is the same as a traditional routing table lookup for forwarding IP packets. It follows that the algorithms that are used for high-speed IP packet routing can also be applied for policy classification when IP addresses are a component of the conditional part of a policy expression. A description of some of these techniques can be found in [ROUTING1] and [ROUTING2].

Policy Searches with Multiple Dimensions

So far, the problem of searching for policies using only one field within the conditional part of the policy expression has been reviewed. Because there are many parts that make up the conditional expression, you must develop schemes that can perform searches along each of the different dimensions. In this section, some of these schemes are reviewed. The first scheme is projection search, in which you search along individual fields of a policy, and which combines the resulting searches to obtain the eventually applicable policy. The other scheme uses a hierarchy of single field searches to obtain the same result.

Projection Search

A policy is applicable to a packet only when there is an overlap with the packet headers and the range specified by the policy along all the fields. Therefore, you can find the set of policies that is relevant to a packet by searching for the matching policies along each of the individual fields, and by taking the overlap among the sets of policies determined to be overlapping in each field. Each individual field can be viewed as the projection of the policy along that specific field, resulting in the name *projection search*.

As an example, consider the set of policies shown in Tables 8.9 and 8.10, which uses the policies listed in Table 8.1. We can take the projections of the policies along each of the two fields used in the condition part of the policies and determine two sets of applicable policies, each set being determined by looking at only one field. Finally, an intersection of the resulting set of policies is taken, and the highest priority policy among these sets is selected. The projection of the policies by considering only the port dimension is shown in Table 8.9 and the projection of the policies by considering only the destination IP addresses is shown in Table 8.10.

Table 8.9   Projection of Policies in Table 8.1 Along Source Port Field

Policy Name	Source Port	Priority	Class
P1	200-400	1	One
P2	265	2	Two
P3	4000-6000	1	Three
P4	*	2	One
P5	3000-4000	3	Two
P6	*	0	Four

Table 8.10   Projection of Policies in Table 8.1 Along Destination IP Address Field

Policy Name	Dest IP Address	Priority	Class
P1	9.0.0.0/8	1	One
P2	9.2.0.0/16	2	Two
P3	*	1	Three
P4	10.0.0.0/8	2	One
P5	10.4.0.0/16	3	Two
P6	*	0	Four

Table 8.9 has two default rules that apply to all the port numbers, namely P2 with a priority of 2 and P6 with a priority of 2. Apart from the default rules, the others can be structured into a search tree which is shown in Figure 8.8. You have probably noted the close similarity between Figures 8.6 and 8.8, which are essentially used for the same set of policy examples. When making the structure for the projection search, instead of resolving the conflicts among the policies by using their priorities at each node, simply enumerate all the applicable policies (including the default policies) at each of the nodes in the tree. The reason for retaining all the policies is that some of the applicable policies might not apply when the information from the other dimensions is merged.

Figure 8.8   Projection Search Tree Along Port Field

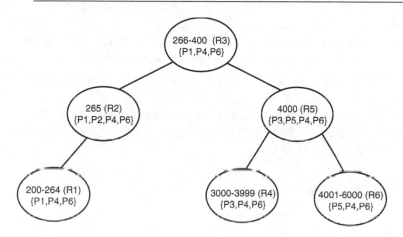

A similar search tree can be constructed for the other dimension, destination IP address, on the basis of Table 8.10. This again has two default rules, and the rest are structured in a search tree which is shown in Figure 8.9. The difference between the search of a single value and projection search is that all the policies that are applicable to the item being searched for are collected. This implies all the policies along the path that was traversed for reaching a policy are collected, including the default paths along each node. Thus, for the destination IP address of 9.2.13.4, take the matching policies along the path, P1, P2, P3, and P6.

Figure 8.9   Project Search Tree Along IP Address Field

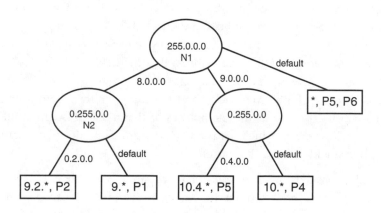

Now use the projection search method to determine the policy that applies to a packet of port 265 and destination IP address of 9.2.13.4. Looking at Figure 8.8, you see that the port dimension states that policies {P1, P2, P4, P6} are applicable to it. Similarly, in Figure 8.9, we see that the policies {P2, P1, P3, P6} apply to it. The common subset of policies that applies is {P1, P2, P6} of which we select the highest priority policy, namely P2. Searching for overlapping policies by making individual searches among the different fields defining the policy and then taking the common subset is amenable to parallel implementation in hardware processors. There are several modifications of this approach, and the optimizations that can lead to better performance in hardware implementations is discussed by Laxman [LAXMAN].

Multitier Table Search

The multitier table search uses the same idea as the projection search—that searching one field is more efficient than searching multiple fields simultaneously. However, while the project search formed the intersection among several rules in parallel, the multitier table search establishes a hierarchy of entries that will be examined in sequence to determine the applicable set of policies. In order to define the multitier table search, define the order in which each of the fields is reviewed. First, find the set of policies that is relevant to the packet by looking at the first field. Then, from the resulting set of policies, reduce the relevant policies by looking at the next field you want to review. Continue the sequence for all the fields in the packet header, and the highest priority policy in the final set is considered applicable.

In order to expedite the search, the rules are preprocessed into a table that is optimized for a fast lookup along individual fields. Except for the field that is being looked at first, multiple lookup tables need to be defined for the other fields. The effectiveness the policy depends on the order in which the fields are selected for the lookup. If you don't expect to find a policy match for most of the packets, and you expect to apply the default policy for them, it is advantageous to select the fields so that the fields with the fewest defined policies are used first in the search order. This allows for a higher possibility of determining that there is no match for a given packet and a better running time on the average. On the other hand, if you expect to define the policies so that a match is commonly expected, you should reverse the order in which fields are looked up. This allows for a quick match early on in the process and reduces the running time.

As an example, consider the set of rules that was shown in Table 8.1. Figures 8.8 and 8.9 showed search trees along two different axes. However, one way to improve the search is by building not one global search table along the second field that one is looking to search, but making a table only among the policies that are applicable at any given node.

Build a search tree very similar to that shown in Figure 8.8 along the first field, the port numbers. Several nodes in Figure 8.8 have multiple policy entries. Build several search trees along the second field (IP addresses), with each search tree only applicable to one node found along the previous field. Several of these trees are shown in Figure 8.10. The search tree nodes corresponding to the second dimensions are shown as rectangular boxes, while the search tree nodes corresponding to the first dimension are shown as circular nodes. When a specific node along a first dimension is considered valid, the corresponding tree to search along the second dimension is pointed to by a curved arrow.

Figure 8.10	Multitier Search Tree for Policies

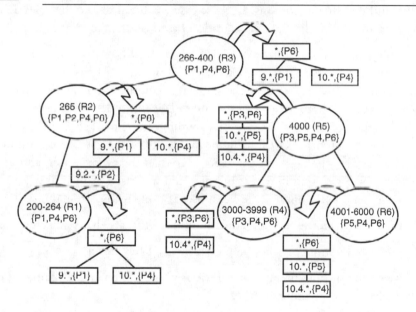

By following the different tables along individual dimensions, the applicable policies for any incoming packet header can be determined. As an example, consider the packet of port 265 and destination IP address of 9.2.13.4. By following the initial search tree with the policies, you reach node R2 by looking along the port field. You then follow the second tier search tree along the rectangular boxes, and see that there is a match with the node labeled 9.2.* and that the applicable policy is P2.

Rule-Based Search

The use of predictive rule-based systems for policy specification and conflict resolution was introduced in Chapter 6, "Policy Validation and Translation Algorithms." Although the use of rule-based systems is not appropriate for conflict resolution, it can be advantageous to determine which policy applies to a given request or packet.

In order to determine the relevant policy to apply, add the rules defining the characteristics of the current packet to the set of policy rules. Then, derive subsequent rules until you determine the right classification of an incoming request. This representation allows for a more flexible matching of the rules than the simple table-driven algorithms.

In many instances, you might want to apply policy rules in the context of application proxies rather than at the packet layer. As an example, consider the classification of packets into different service levels at a Web server. The determination of which communications are higher-priority and which are lower-priority depends on complex rules based on the identity of the user, whether he has made a purchase in the past, the type of Web URL he is requesting, and on other conditions. In these cases, you can define the rules as simple policy definitions and derive the right classification based on the techniques in predicate logic.

As an example, consider a site that has a DiffServ-enabled network connection from its ISP. As a result, the site is able to mark packets belonging to its customers as *expedited forwarding* or *best effort*. The goal of the site is to mark the packets from users who are likely to make purchase transactions to the site as EF, and to let other people who are merely surfing the site and not likely to buy anything to be marked as BE packets. Although this only marks packets flowing from the site to the customer's browser, users who are likely to buy will have a better experience than the average user, and therefore are likely to be happier, resulting in repeat business and increased profitability. The site has the following criteria for determining whether a user is likely to buy something:

- If a user had previously bought something from the site, he is a likely buyer.
- If a user has a non-empty shopping cart, he is a likely buyer.
- If a user had not bought anything previously, and has an empty shopping cart, he is not likely to buy anything.

You can express these rules and the marking criteria using simple predicate logic by using the following rules:

1. PreviousBuyer $\rightarrow$ LikelyBuyer
2. ~EmptyCart $\rightarrow$ LikelyBuyer
3. EmptyCart $\wedge$ ~PreviousBuyer $\rightarrow$ ~LikelyBuyer
4. LikelyBuyer $\rightarrow$ EF
5. ~LikelyBuyer $\rightarrow$ BE

PreviousBuyer is true if the active user has bought something previously from the site, EmptyCart is true if the shopping cart of the current customer is empty, LikelyBuyer implies that we expect the customer to buy something, EF is true if the packets belonging to this customer are going to be marked as expedited, and BE is true if this customer's packets are going to be marked as best effort. We are using the symbols and notations as explained in Chapter 6 in the sidebar "Symbolic Logic." These can be represented in the disjunctive normal form notation as:

P1:   ~PreviousBuyer V LikelyBuyer

P2:   EmptyCart V LikelyBuyer

P3:   ~EmptyCart V PreviousBuyer V ~LikelyBuyer

P4:   ~LikelyBuyer V EF

P5:   LikelyBuyer V BE

To establish the appropriate marking for an active session, the site determines the characteristics of the active users. Suppose that it has determined that the following items characterize an active user at the site:

I1:   ~PreviousBuyer

I2:   EmptyCart

Now follow a deduction logic combining the rules from P1 through P5 and the inputs I1 and I2 to derive the right marking for this user through the following steps:

D1:   ~EmptyCart V ~LikelyBuyer (resolve I1 and P1)

D2:   ~LikelyBuyer (resolve D1 and P1)

D3:   BE (resolve D2 and P5)

Consider another user who has an empty shopping cart, but is a previous buyer. In this case, the two items that characterize the user are as follows:

I3:   PreviousBuyer

I4:   EmptyCart

In order to determine the appropriate marking for this customer, perform the following steps:

D4:   LikelyBuyer (resolve I3 and P2)

D5:   EF (resolve D2 and P5)

Any system of predicate logic can be used to infer the actions to be performed using the specified set of rules and the input characteristics of a user. The use of symbolic logic can permit more complex rules to be written and can simplify sophisticated inferences related to users.

> **Note**
>
> Keep in mind that the evaluation algorithms for the direct evaluation of the conditional expressions contained within policy rules generally run slower than the simple table-driven techniques just discussed. They are not appropriate for use on a packet-by-packet basis.

Policy Validation Algorithms

Before the policy rules are applied at the enforcement point, you need to be sure that the rules are indeed well formed and valid. Because the device is the one that would implement the policy rules, it is useful to validate and double-check its specification prior to the actual enforcement.

If the agents at the different services trust the management tool, the policies do not need to be validated. However, there are several situations in which the policies from the management tool might not be well formed. Most of the scenarios involve failure in the distribution process of the policies. As an example, the management tool might fail in the middle of storing policies within an LDAP directory. This can lead to some of the policies not being defined properly. Consider the case of a management tool writing policies into the repository using the IBM Schema described in Chapter 7. In the example shown there, it needed to create three policy rules and two service categories. If the management tool failed before writing the entries for the service categories, an agent would find that it has policies referencing service categories that are not defined. Other inconsistencies in policies would arise because of multiple managers trying to modify policies at the same time.

The distribution process can provide some safeguards against the potential corruption in the set of policies being delivered. A proprietary management framework can support a distribution scheme which ensures that the set of policies is delivered uncorrupted to each agent. In that case, the agent need not run the validation tests. However, the protocols being standardized, such as LDAP, COPS, or SNMP, do not provide such strong assurances. It is therefore advisable to have agents perform validity checks on the policies they receive.

There are two issues with local validation:

- Determine that there are no conflicts among the different rules.

- Make sure that the policies have not been corrupted after they were put in place by the management tool.

Several factors can cause the corruption of the policies—the invocation of two instances of a management tool within a network by two independent administrators, the crash of a management tool, or the loss of a connection in the middle of a policy distribution phase. Techniques to resolve both of these problems are discussed next.

Local Conflict Detection Algorithms

The set of algorithms described in Chapter 6 to check for conflicts within the general context can be used to check for local conflicts check as well. The set of policies applicable to a device is probably smaller than the set of policies that would apply to all the devices within the network, so the algorithms are likely to run much faster than at the management console. Of course, this also depends on the processing power available at the enforcement point.

At the PEP, there is an alternative method to validate that the set of policies defined at the local node is consistent. In order to perform the classification algorithms efficiently, the PEP needs to preprocess all the policies into data structures that are amenable for efficient searching. These data structures are used to determine the right policy or policies to apply to any specific packet. During the preparation of the data structure for some of those algorithms, it is readily apparent if there are packets to which more than one policy can apply. For most of the policy application algorithms (except for the rules-based approach), the preprocessing step is required. In many cases, a PEP can combine its local conflict detection algorithm with the preparation of the local data structure.

In the case of the simple linear search, the rules need to be placed in an ordered list. If it is not apparent how two rules should be ordered, and the rules are not mutually exclusive, there is a conflict between them. Two rules are mutually exclusive if they specify different nonoverlapping ranges along the same field and thus will never be applicable to the same packet. The PEP needs to break the rule ordering in some fashion. Most PEPs use the technique of placing the more-specific rules before the less-specific rules in the order in which they are to be used for the linear search.

In the case of a tree-based search, you need to apply policies only after a node of the tree has been selected as part of the policy search process. When the tree is constructed, a set of policies is determined to be applicable at each node. If the policy with the highest precedence is not unique at the node, there is a conflict that needs to be broken in some way. An analogous unique policy must be determined at the end of the last field processed in the multitier table search.

When the PEP finds a policy conflict, it must resort to automated means to resolve the conflict. Unlike the policy management tool, no user interfaces are available for the conflict resolution. In most cases, it is best to resolve the conflict in some manner and progress as usual while the policy management tool is notified of the local conflict and an administrator specifies the details of how that conflict should be resolved.

Local Integrity Validation Algorithms

In addition to the policy validation scheme, the PEP needs to validate that it has received all the policies that the management tool specified and that the policies have not been tampered with. The tampering might be deliberate, such as by a malicious intruder, or it might be accidental, such as two parallel invocations of the management tool interfering with each other.

You can protect against deliberate tampering by requiring the policy manager to sign the policies before distributing them to the agent. The signatures can be done using a private secret key that is pre-established between the agent and the management tool. If the private key is shared among all the agents, the other agents need to be trusted in order to ensure that the key is not compromised. On the other hand, if an individual key is defined for each different agent, you need to develop a scheme for managing and distributing the keys to the different agents. The key distribution mechanism needs to be independent of the distribution scheme for policies, because it would be a pre-requisite for the distribution to occur. Note that these keys used for putting signatures on the policies can be different from the keys that are used for authenticating agents and administrators when they are accessing a policy repository. For authentication purposes, it is better to have a separate key per entity trying to access the repository.

A better method is to establish the signature using a public key scheme. In this case, the agent needs a way to validate and determine the management tool's public key. In many cases, a public key infrastructure is needed for other reasons, and a certificate server might be available in the network. If so, the certificate server can be reused for the distribution of the management tool's public key. On the other hand, if a certificate server is not available, the management tool's public key can be pre-configured at each of the agents. Each of the agents needs identical configuration, which can be shipped along with the agent software.

Within an enterprise environment, malicious tampering of the policies is not usually an issue. However, you need to protect against accidental tampering or the cases in which multiple copies of the policy management tool are invoked. In some cases, such an integrity association can be done by ensuring that the policies are delivered as a unit. For example, if the policy management tool communicates directly to the agents for distribution, the policy management tool provides all the policies to the agent using a single transport session. All policies obtained on the same session are treated as one unit. When two sessions are established to the agent simultaneously, the race condition of two management tools trying to configure the same server is readily detected and can be used. The agent can select one of the instances over the other. However, in distribution schemes in which the policy management tool uses an intermediary for policy distribution, such as a COPS server or an LDAP repository, the integrity of policies is not readily apparent by the use of a session. Therefore, the policy management tool must use some method to ensure that the entire set of policies is delivered as a unit.

When an LDAP server is used for policy distribution, you can store information about the units of policies at the LDAP server. One such unit of policy is the group of policies that is referenced by the devices in the same role within the network. The IETF direction toward definition of LDAP schemas is to define the notion of containers that point to the various policies that are pertinent to a device in a specific role. The set of all policies (and associated LDAP entries) that forms a unit of the policy is then available to the agents. If the management tool can specify when the policies in the container were created in a separate LDAP entry, the agent can check the modification attributes on the names policies and double-check that it is indeed retrieving the policies as they were intended to by the management tool. This provides for detecting inadvertent modification of the policies by another management tool in parallel. The modification time attributes for all entries are readily available at most LDAP server implementations. Remember that the modification time attribute does not provide adequate protection against deliberate and malicious attacks to corrupt the policy information stored at a repository.

CHAPTER 9

Policy Application Instances

Thus far in this book, the components that comprise a policy-based network management solution have been presented in isolation. This chapter looks at how all the various components can be combined to provide an integrated solution that can simplify the task of administering an IP network.

Some of the business needs that drive the deployment of different networking technologies were discussed in Chapter 3, "The Generic Provisioning Problem," which also discussed how they could be supported using the different networking technologies. This chapter shows how a policy-based solution is used to administer an IP network in the various environments described in Chapter 3.

The solutions described in this chapter combine the various components described in previous chapters. For each component, where different alternatives exist, you select the one that is most appropriate for the specific problem. Thus, this chapter doesn't present any new algorithms or concepts. However, it does provide a complete solution for many typical problems that can benefit from a policy-based approach. It presents the topics covered previously in this book from a different perspective.

The business needs we consider in this chapter include the issue of supporting SLAs in an enterprise network, enabling IPsec-based extranets for business partnerships among different enterprises, supporting SLAs for an ISP providing network connectivity, providing VPN services by an ISP, and customer management within an application-hosting environment.

Although many of the technologies discussed earlier in this book can be used to support these business needs, we will focus on the technologies of *Differentiated Services* (DiffServ) and IPsec to illustrate the structure of a policy-based architecture. Similar solutions can be designed for other technologies as well.

For each of the application scenarios we examine, four items are presented:

- A high-level policy specification, which is a model that describes the business needs that an organization might want to address

- A low-level policy specification, which is a model that describes the policy rules that correspond to the technology used to satisfy specific business needs

- A scheme to translate the high-level policy specification to the low-level policy specification

- A policy distribution solution that is suitable for use within the specified environment

Remember that the policy specifications and architectures are intended for the purposes of illustration only. They represent one of many possible solutions that can be used to achieve the same goal.

Enterprise SLA Support

One business need that arises in many enterprise environments is the support for performance and availability SLAs for IP networks. The typical performance SLA specifies performance and availability bounds on the different applications. You would define the structure of a tool that would allow an operator to specify the business SLA requirements and, based on that information, automatically configure the various routers and servers in a manner appropriate for supporting the performance SLA.

We will focus on an environment like the one described in Chapter 3, which consists of multiple enterprise site networks connected via a core network. Because we are assuming that DiffServ is deployed in the network, we assume that DiffServ-capable access routers connect the core network to the various site networks. Similarly, DiffServ-capable core .routers are deployed to provide different service classes within the network. We also assume that the servers deployed in the enterprise are capable of DiffServ.

High-Level Policy Specification

Within an enterprise environment as described in Chapter 3, one of the components of the business SLAs enforced in the IT department specifies desired objectives for *application performance*. These objectives typically require bounds on the response time of applications running on the various servers. For example, a performance objective might look like this: "A mail message of less than 100KB should become available to a client in less than half a second." In general, an SLA consists of many such performance objectives that need to be satisfied simultaneously.

Figure 9.1 shows a very simple model that can be used to define the performance component of business SLAs. It consists of defining different types of objects—namely, clients, servers, applications, SLA, performance objectives, and classes of service. This is very similar to the model that was used to illustrate the policy translation logic in Chapter 6, "Policy Validation and Translation Algorithms."

Figure 9.1   High-Level Policies for Enterprise SLAs

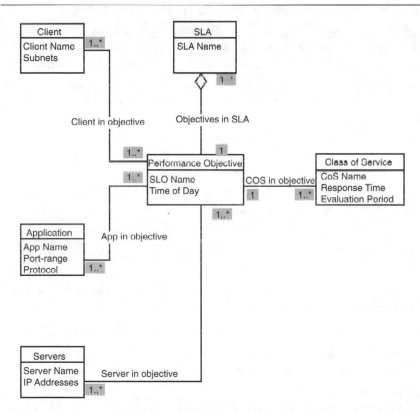

This representation of the model is based on the *Unified Modeling Language* (UML). UML notation is used throughout this chapter. A description of the UML notation can be found in the sidebar called "The Unified Modeling Language." Figure 9.1 is thus the UML representation of a very simple object model used to represent the performance objectives in business SLAs.

As shown in Figure 9.1, an SLA (Service-Level Agreement) is an aggregation of several performance objectives. Each objective defines an association between a client, an application, a server, and a class of service. Semantically, a performance objective states that traffic flows used by a client to access an application running on a specific server be mapped to one of many classes of service. For example, consider a client called Accounting, which accesses an application called SAP running on a server called business-server. A performance objective might state that Accounting's access to SAP running on business-server be given the Gold class of service.

In the object model of Figure 9.1, a *client* represents users in the network. Each client has two properties: a name (`ClientName`) that identifies it uniquely, and the subnet address, identifying the location of the machines used by these users. A *server* is a machine where applications run, and its properties include a name and IP address(es) of its interfaces. We assume that applications run on well-known port numbers or a range of port numbers on each of the servers. Thus, an *application* has the properties of name and IP address(es), a port range, and a protocol. A *class of service* defines a level of performance. Its properties include a name, response time, and an evaluation period. The response time is the expected application response time for any traffic flows that map into this class of service. The evaluation period states how long measurements must be taken in order to determine the response time. For example, the Gold class of service might have a response time of 500ms, for an evaluation period of 1 hour. Any traffic flow that maps into the Gold class of service is required to have a response time of 500ms or less when averaged over intervals of an hour or more.

The *performance objective* provides an association between a client, an application, a server, and a class of service. An objective has an association with exactly one class of service, but the association could be with more than one client, application, or server. An objective could be valid at only specific times of the day, which is one of the attributes shown for the performance objective in Figure 9.1.

These high-level policies capture a very simple notion of the performance component of an SLA that might be used in an enterprise environment. A business SLA can contain other aspects not related to performance objectives.

The Unified Modeling Language

The UML is a pictorial notation for the development of object-oriented models. Although the UML specification in its entirety presents a fairly sophisticated way to represent different types of models, we will use a relatively small subset of the UML capabilities to explain the different object models that will be needed in this chapter.

An object-oriented model for any system describes the objects that make up the system. Each object has some attributes that are its intrinsic properties, and it supports some operations. When there are many objects of a similar nature, they are grouped as belonging to the same class, and each object is referred to as an *instance* of that class. All objects in the same class support a common set of attributes and operations. Objects in one class can have different types of relationships with objects in another class.

The object models shown in this chapter are instances of a *class diagram* in UML. A class diagram shows the different classes that exist in the model and the relationships between these classes. Each class in UML is represented by a rectangle, which may be divided into two or three subrectangles. The top-most subrectangle contains the name of the class, and the subrectangle below it contains the name of all the attributes belonging to any instance of that class. The third (bottom-most) subrectangle shows the operations on a class. However, because I am using object models to represent policies, none of the classes need to have any operations. All the classes in this book have two subrectangles, with the top one showing the name of the class and the bottom one listing the attributes of the class. Figure 9.1 has several class definitions, such as `Client` and `Application`. The `Client` class has two attributes, `ClientName` and `Subnets`.

An association between the classes is shown by means of a connecting line between them. An association between two classes implies that each instance of an object in one of the classes has some relationship to instances of objects in the other classes. The association could be named by a label assigned to the connecting lines. Figure 9.1 shows several associations. For example, there is a "COS in objective" association between a Performance Objective and a Class of Service. An instance of a class may have an association with one or more instances of another class. This multiplicity is shown by a range (or number) near the class. In Figure 9.1, the association between Class of Service and Performance Objective has a 1 near the objective class and a 1..* near the Class of Service. This means that each instance of a Performance Objective is associated with exactly one Class of Service, and that an instance of the Class of Service may be associated with one or more Performance Objectives. Similarly, a Performance Objective can be associated with any number of applications, servers, or clients.

A special type of relationship among classes is the *aggregation relationship*. If an instance of class A consists of multiple aggregates of class B, class A is an aggregate of class B. This relationship is shown by means of a diamond shape at the aggregate end of the association. In Figure 9.1, an SLA is an aggregate of many performance objectives (as you can see from the diamond at the SLA end of the association). As shown in Figure 9.1, an SLA can contain one or more performance objectives. Also, each performance objective can belong to only one SLA.

The notations discussed in this sidebar are adequate for our purposes in this book. This is only a small subset of the full UML language. UML contains notations for showing many other different types of relationships among objects. It also defines ways to represent several other types of diagrams in addition to the class diagrams I am using. For a more detailed description of UML, see texts such as ones by Fowler and Scott [UMLREF] and Page-Jones [UML2].

Low-Level Policy Specification

The low-level policies that would be deployed within the network depend on the technology used to support the business needs within the network. In this example, we assume that the technology consists of DiffServ using the class selector PHBs. See Chapter 2, "Background Information," for a discussion of DiffServ and this PHB.

We assume that the servers and access routers within the enterprise are capable of marking DiffServ packets and that the core routers within the enterprise support the forwarding behavior corresponding to the different classes of services. We further assume that the different classes represent priority levels for packet forwarding and transmission. In this case, the policy definition for the different components within the network consists of the following:

- Each server within the network should mark packets with the correct ToS byte (DiffServ field) that identifies the packets with its appropriate class selector PHB. Its policy definition consists of the rules for marking the packets correctly.

- Each access router within the network has the onus of marking packets with the right ToS byte if the server has not marked it properly. Its policy definition consists of the rules for marking the packets correctly.

- Each core router should forward the packets, giving them a priority in accordance with the marked ToS byte. Its policy definition consists of the priority level to be assigned to each type of ToS encoding.

The Policy Translation Process

In order to generate the low-level policies from the high-level specification using the model shown in Figure 9.1, a policy management tool requires some additional information about the network topology. Specifically, you need information about the routers that are available within the network—whether they are acting as access routers or core routers.

I further assume that the policy management tool comes with the ability for an expert user to specify the implementation of the classes of services into specific DiffServ PHBs. The characteristics of a Gold application, as well as the amount of bandwidth to be allocated to this class, are determined by the expert user. Thus, an expert user may define that you should use the class selector PHBs within the network, with the Gold class of service corresponding to the highest-priority service, the Silver class of service corresponding to the medium-priority service, and the Bronze class of service corresponding to the default service, with a maximum bandwidth limit of 80 percent of a link's capacity to be used by applications in the default class of service. The functions performed by the policy management tool are similar to the steps described in Chapter 6.

The policy management tool can determine the topology of the network to determine the set of access routers that would lie along the path of each of the application flows specified in the set of application flows. An access router is impacted by a policy only when it lies on the path of either the source or the destination subnet. Although routing in the core network is subject to change, the set of access routers that are impacted by a policy can be determined by the physical topology in the network. An access router connects one or more sites to the core network. It is impacted by a policy only if the client or the server machines specified in the application policy are among the sites impacted. Similarly, an end host is impacted only if it is either among the set of clients specified in the policy or among the set of servers specified by the policy.

Having determined the relevant set of policies for each of the servers and access routers, the management tool can use the translation tables provided by the expert user to determine the correct marking behavior for all the servers and access routers. For the core routers themselves, the policy management tool must generate a consistent mapping of the ToS encoding to the right priority level along the routers' forwarding paths.

The Policy Distribution Process

Having determined the appropriate policies for each of the access routers and core routers, the policy management tool distributes the policies to the different routers and servers. In an ideal world, the correct way to do so would be to write the policy representation into an LDAP directory that uses the IETF standard schema to describe the policies. In the ideal scenario, all routers and servers would have the capability to retrieve the policies from the directory, either directly or through an intermediary policy server that performs lookups within the directory. The intermediary box could use COPS to communicate the provisioning policies to the different routers in the network.

In the real world, the ideal situation is unfortunately not realized. Many servers and routers also support the capability to retrieve the policy definitions from the directories, although they might not use the standard schema. In that case, the policy management tool would have to write out the definitions for the servers using the schema that would be understood by the individual servers, the routers, or the policy servers acting as the intermediaries for a set of routers. During the topology discovery process, the policy management tool can identify the types of servers and routers present in the network. It can then determine the right schema to write in the directory in order to enable the enforcement of policies for those devices.

Figure 9.2 shows the different components of the support for the policy architecture in an enterprise environment. It shows three campus networks in an enterprise that are connected by a core network with DiffServ support. DiffServ capabilities are present on the servers, on access routers that connect campuses to the core network, and on core routers that constitute the core network. A management tool populates the directory server with the policies required to support the business SLAs in such an environment. The servers in the network can pull the policy definitions directly from the directory and use that information to configure themselves. The core routers in the network, and one of the access routers, can also perform the same function. Two of the access routers shown in the network do not access the LDAP directory directly. Instead, a policy server acts as an intermediary for them. The policy server then uses the COPS protocol to transfer the policy information to the access routers.

Figure 9.2   Policy Architecture for Enterprise SLAs

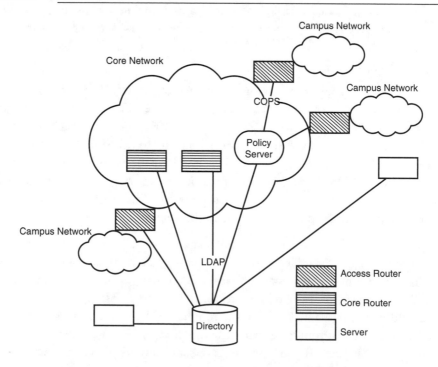

Extranet Support for the Enterprise Environment

As described in Chapter 3, enterprises establish extranets in order to automate their business processes with other enterprises, such as their contractors and suppliers. An *extranet* allows a business partner to access part of the enterprise infrastructure. We assume that the following entities (illustrated in Figure 9.3) are involved in establishing the extranets that are examined here:

- **An extranet client application.** This client application runs in the DMZ of a business partner, which is a supplier to the enterprise in this example. It runs on a machine that supports IPsec. These types of machines are the only entities in the supplier's environment that are allowed to communicate with a set of servers within the enterprise. One or more of these extranet client applications can be present in the supplier's environment. They may be operational on a single extranet client machine or on more than one extranet client machine.

- **An extranet server application.** This application runs in the DMZ of the enterprise and communicates with the extranet client applications that are operational in the supplier's DMZ. The extranet server application runs on extranet server machines. Two such servers (extranet server 1 and extranet server 2) are shown in Figure 9.3.

- **A policy management console.** This is responsible for administering the policies that drive the configuration of the machines running the extranet client applications as well as the extranet server application. These include all the extranet servers present in the enterprise's DMZ, as well as all the extranet client machines in the supplier's or business partner's networks.

- **A policy repository.** This is responsible for keeping track of the different extranet clients that are allowed into the network, as well as the IPsec configuration that is appropriate for them. The repository keeps policy information for the machines running the extranet client application as well as the extranet servers. It needs to be located in the enterprise DMZ.

Figure 9.3   Policy Environment for Enterprise Extranets

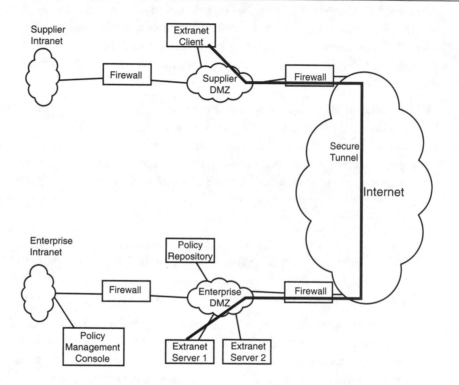

High-Level Policy Specification

The specification for the high-level policies for extranet support is the description of the members of each extranet and the security level that is associated with the extranet communication. Each extranet consists of one or more business partner organizations, one or more applications running on some enterprise servers, and a security class of service.

Figure 9.4 shows a very simple object model that captures the extranet relationships. An *extranet* definition allows a set of business partners to access a set of applications that are running on some servers in the enterprise. A *business partner* may have more than one machine at its site where the extranet client application is operational. Thus, the business partner contains an association with multiple *extranet client* machines. Each extranet client houses the extranet client application and is identified by its name and IP address. The extranet definition allows some machines to become accessible to external business partners. These machines (the *extranet servers*) have a name and an IP address as their attributes. Only some *applications* running on the servers may be made accessible to external business partners. These applications are identified by their name, their other attributes (including the ports they run on), and the protocol these applications use to communicate. An extranet is associated with one or more business partners, one or more extranet servers, and one or more applications. Each extranet definition allows extranet clients belonging to associated business partners to access associated applications that are executing on associated extranet servers.

| Figure 9.4 | High-Level Policies for Enterprise Extranets |

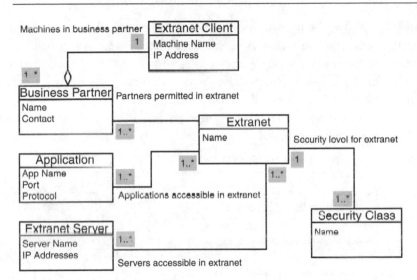

Each extranet is associated with exactly one security class. The security class defines the type of security that needs to be provided to the traffic flows that form part of the extranet definition. The details of the security class are provided in the low-level technology-specific definitions and are described in more detail in the following section.

All the extranet definitions taken together constitute the high-level policy in this environment.

Low-Level Policy Specification

The low-level policy specification of the extranet depends on the technology used to define and support the extranets. Because we are assuming the use of IPsec protocol for supporting extranets, the low-level policy specification consists of defining the characteristics of the secure communication tunnels that will be established using the IPsec protocol suite.

The extranets that are described and supported within the network can be mapped to a set of secure communication channels established between the extranet client applications and the extranet server application. We are assuming that this secure communication channel is established using IPsec. The definition of the secure communication channel needs to be augmented with the parameters that would be required to establish the secure communication channel using IPsec. As described in Chapter 3, this requires that we specify at least four types of information for each of the communication tunnels: the Phase 1 characteristics, the Phase 1 transforms, the Phase 2 characteristics, and the Phase 2 transforms. For simplicity, we can group all these into a network security class and allocate each of the secure communication tunnels into one network security class.

Figure 9.5 shows a simple object model that can be used to represent the low-level IPsec policies using UML notation. An instance of a *security policy rule* maps an instance of a *communication tunnel* to an instance of a *security class*. Using the "if condition then action" representation of the policy rule, the security policy rule uses the associated communication tunnel as the condition part and the associated security class as the action part. The details of the actions to be performed are provided by the other objects associated with an instance of the security class.

Figure 9.5   Low-Level Policies for IPsec

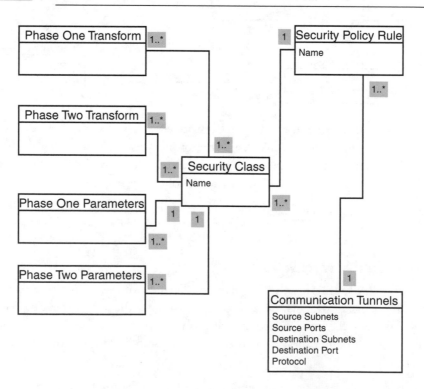

Each instance of a security class is associated with one instance of *Phase 1 parameters* and one or more instances of *Phase 1 transform*. Similarly, it is associated with one instance of *Phase 2 parameters* and one or more instances of *Phase 2 transform*. Each instance of a Phase 1 transform defines a set of acceptable encryption/authentication algorithms that can be used for Phase 1 communication within IPsec. Each instance of Phase 1 parameters contains values of various parameters, such as the duration after which keys for Phase 1 communication must be renegotiated. An analogous explanation holds for the Phase 2 counterpart of the transforms and parameters. Depending on the phase of communication with a remote party, the associated instances of transforms and parameters dictate the operation of the IPsec protocol engine.

Each security policy rule is associated with only one security class, and each communication tunnel is associated with only one security policy rule. However, a security class may be associated with more than one security policy. Similarly, instances of Phase 1 transforms, Phase 1 parameters, Phase 2 transforms, and Phase 2 parameters can be shared across multiple instances of security classes. Please note that the IPsec object model shown in Figure 9.5 is a simple model intended for illustrative use within this book. It is not derived from the *Policy Framework Working Group's* (PFWG) information model [POLICYWG]. At the time this book was published, that model was still in flux. Also, a model derived from it would have been more complex than the one shown in Figure 9.5. Assuming that we wanted to use the current version of the PFWG's information model (refer to Figure 7.3), the security policy rule class should have been derived from the `PolicyRule` class in the PFWG's definition, the secure communication tunnel from the `PolicyCondition` class, and the security class from the `PolicyAction` class. A model derived from the PFWG definition is the recommended direction for actual use within different products. Within the IETF, there is an ongoing effort to define a comprehensive object model for IPsec policies [IPSPREF] that follows the guidelines of the PFWG's information. That model, when completed, will provide a standard information model for low-level policies to be used with IPsec.

The Policy Translation Process

In order to translate the high-level policies expressed in Figure 9.4 to the low-level policies expressed in Figure 9.5, we need to map the definitions of the extranets to a set of secure communication tunnels and then generate the right associations between the communication tunnels and the Phase 1 and Phase 2 parameters and transforms.

As in the case of the enterprise SLA, we presume that an expert user (such as the Chief Security Officer of an enterprise) determines an appropriate definition for a security class. For example, a security class named "secure" might be defined as using the IPsec

Authentication header protocol without encryption of packets, and a security class named "ultrasecure" might be defined as using IPsec Encapsulating Security Payload protocol with both authentication and encryption. These definitions have to be based on an object model as well. Figure 9.6 shows the UML representation of a model that the expert might use. Figure 9.6 defines the security class that was first introduced in Figure 9.4.

Figure 9.6   Security Officer Configuration for IPsec

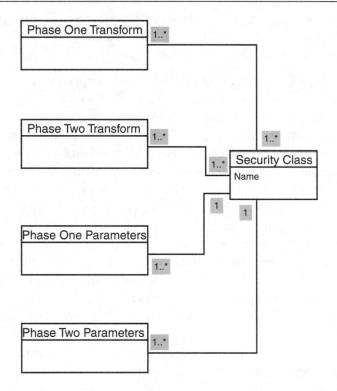

You have probably noticed that the object model used by the expert user (Figure 9.6) is a part of the object model used for the low-level policy definition (Figure 9.5). I deliberately made this choice in order to reduce the different types of models you need in this chapter. However, there is no requirement that the two be similar. In an actual implementation, a vendor may choose to use a model closer to Figure 9.6 for manipulation of security class definitions by the expert user. With the model shown in Figure 9.6, the expert user must deal with a small number of classes and objects. For the actual representation of policies, the implementation might choose to use a schema based on the standard working group specifications. This results in a schema that combines the classes shown in Figure 7.3 with the classes shown in Figure 9.6. Some early thoughts on building a standard representation of IPsec security schemas can be seen in the Internet drafts at the IPsec policy working group [IPSPREF]. That schema is more complex, but it is possible to convert information stored in an object model like that of Figure 9.6 to object models based on the IETF working group specifications.

In order to translate the definition of extranets into secure communication tunnels, the policy translation tool creates one secure tunnel between each participating extranet client application machine and the named participating extranet server application machine. It then determines the appropriate mode in which the security transformation must take place. If the point where IPsec transformations occur is the same machine as the end points of the communication, you can use the transport mode. Otherwise, you need to use tunnel mode.

After the set of secure communication tunnels to be established has been determined, you can proceed with determining the relevant set of tunnels for each firewall and machine involved in the extranet. From the set of relevant tunnels at each device, you can determine the right set of Phase 1 and Phase 2 tunnel descriptions to be used for IPsec configuration (see Chapter 3 for details).

Policy Architecture

The policy architecture for extranet support may take the form shown in Figure 9.7. The policy repository in this case is a Web server that supports a set of cgi-bin scripts. The cgi-bin scripts allow agents running on the machines that host extranet client applications (the extranet clients) or extranet server applications (the extranet servers) to register with the repository and to get notified about any possible policy changes.

Each agent is shipped with the identity of the policy repository and security credentials so that it can authenticate itself to the repository and communicate securely using *Secure Sockets Layer* (SSL). The agents register themselves to the policy repository and provide information on the characteristics of the machine they are running on (such as the IPsec implementation version or the operating system). Each agent also provides a reserved port number on which it is listening for notifications regarding changes in policy.

The policy management console translates the set of extranet descriptions (defined by a user on the basis of the information model shown in Figure 9.4) into the low-level policy specification (based on the information model shown in Figure 9.5). The policy management console then retrieves the characteristics of each of the machines (extranet clients and extranet servers) involved in the defined extranets. As soon as the policy management console knows a device's characteristics, it can generate the configuration or command-line scripts needed for the device in order to support the low-level policy specification. The policy management console then stores the configuration files or command-line scripts at the policy repository using one of the cgi-bin scripts.

Figure 9.7   Policy Architecture for Extranet Support

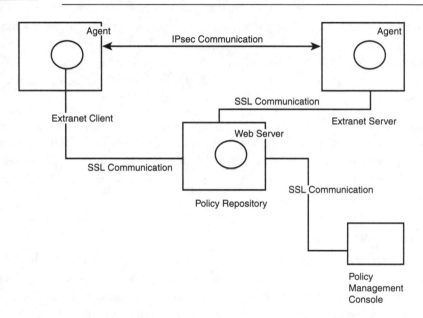

When the policy repository receives an updated configuration for any of the devices, it notifies the agent on the affected device by sending a message to a port reserved for this purpose. Each agent provided information about such a port at the time of its registration. The agents then retrieve the relevant configuration file or command scripts and appropriately configure the local device (be it an extranet server or an extranet client). The agents also report the results of the configuration process to the policy repository. The policy management console can retrieve these reports and validate that the configuration process did in fact complete successfully at each device.

The agents required for extranet configuration usually need to traverse multiple firewalls in order to reach the policy repository. For the environment shown in Figure 9.3, two firewalls lie in the communication path between the extranet client and the policy repository: one at the supplier (business partner) side, and one at the enterprise side. These firewalls must allow the extranet client to communicate with the policy repository and must allow the policy repository to send notifications to the extranet client. If the ports used to listen to notification by the agent on the extranet client are configured statically, it is easy to set up firewall filters to permit such a communication to occur. The Web server used as a policy repository listens on a fixed port (usually 80), so it is relatively straightforward to configure the involved firewalls to permit access to them.

In some cases, the business partner might not want to give outside access to agents that are running on the extranet client machines. The business partner might only want to permit the agent to initiate conversation with the machines in the supplier's network. In this case, the agents can't receive notifications about policy updates and must poll the policy repository periodically to track any changes to their configuration that might occur.

SLA Support for the ISP Environment

As in the case of the enterprise server, the provider of networking services often needs to specify SLAs for its customers. The SLA definition in terms of a network provider usually relates to the latency and throughput of the network that is available to its customers across the network. We assume that the environment for the ISP looks like the one shown in Figure 9.8, where many customers connect to the ISP at its *points of presence* (POPs) via access routers. The figure shows Customer A and Customer B, who use the services of the ISP. Each customer may have several sites connected to the ISP network. In Figure 9.8, Customers A and B each have two sites connected to the ISP. Multiple customers may be connected to the ISP's core network via the same access routers. In Figure 9.8, Site 2 of Customer A and Site 1 of Customer B are connected to the same access router—Access Router 2. Furthermore, the ISP typically has peering arrangements with other ISPs so that it can connect to the global Internet. One such peering is shown in the figure at the Access Router 4. The SLAs that are signed with the customers relate to the one-way network latency between the customer's sites. An example of such an SLA is "All packets between Customer A Site 1 and Customer A Site 2 will be delivered with a latency between the access routers of no more than 500ms."

Figure 9.8   ISP Environment

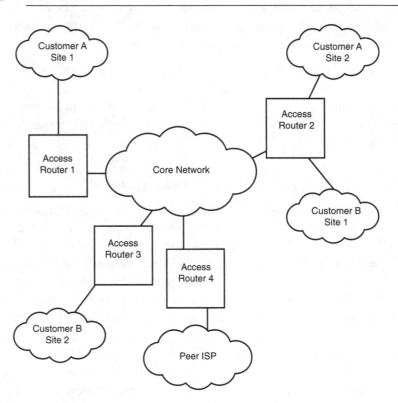

High-Level Policy Specification

Figure 9.9 shows a simple object model that can be used to describe the SLAs in an ISP environment. The basic notion is that of a *customer*, who has many *customer sites*. Each site has an IP subnet address and a name. Each customer has one *SLA contract* with the ISP. Each SLA contract applies to one customer and is an aggregate of multiple *performance objectives*, each being applicable at a different time of the day. Each performance objective is associated with a *class of service*, such as Gold, Silver, or Bronze. The class of service defines the bound on network latency that is to be supported for packets traveling between the customer sites across the ISP's network. The network latency is measured over an evaluation period to assess whether the objectives have been satisfied. The length of the evaluation period is another attribute within the class of service. Each performance objective is associated with exactly one class of service, but many different objectives can be associated with the same class of service. Different performance objectives are needed in an SLA, because a customer might want a different performance level during different times of the day. For example, the customer might want Gold service during business hours but Bronze service during off-peak hours. Thus, a key attribute of a performance objective is the time of day when it is valid. The collection of all the SLA contracts agreed upon by an ISP constitute its high-level policies.

Figure 9.9   High-Level Policies for ISP SLAs

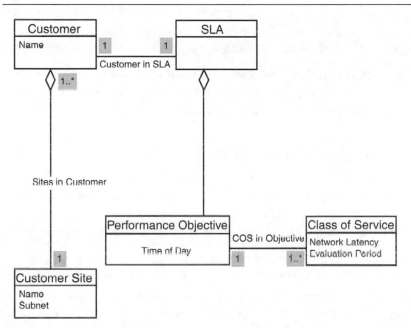

When adding a new customer, a network administrator must simply record the customer's sites and the class of service. If the customer requires different classes of service at different times, multiple performance objectives are created for the customer. A new site can be added to or removed from an existing customer by a network administrator. The policy management tool takes care of modifying the access routers so that they work properly.

Low-Level Policy Specification

The low-level policies are determined by the technology supporting the SLAs within the ISP environment. As mentioned earlier, we are focusing on the use of DiffServ as the technology that enables the service differentiation. Therefore, the low-level policies have many similarities to the low-level policies used in the example with enterprise SLAs. The difference in this example is that there are no servers in the ISP environment.

We assume that the access routers in the ISP network can mark DiffServ packets and that the core routers in the network support the forwarding behavior that corresponds to the different classes of service. We further assume that the different classes represent priority levels for packet forwarding and transmission. In this case, the policy definition for the different components in the network consists of the following:

- Each access router in the network has the onus of marking packets coming from the customer with the right ToS byte. Its policy definition consists of the rules for marking the packets correctly.

- Each core router should forward the packets, giving them a priority in accordance with the marked ToS byte. Its policy definition consists of the priority level to be assigned to each type of ToS encoding.

The Policy Translation Process

We assume that a resource discovery component can determine the set of all routers that are present in the ISP network. If the ISP network has all interface addresses in a given IP subnet address, all routers with interfaces in the ISP subnet play the role of a core router, and all the routers with at least one interface in some other subnet address play the role of an access router.

As in the case of enterprise SLAs, we assume that the policy management tool lets an expert user specify the implementation of the classes of service into specific DiffServ PHBs. The characteristics of a Gold application, as well as the amount of bandwidth to be allocated to this class, are determined by the expert user. Thus, an expert user may define that you should use the class selector PHBs within the network, with the Gold class of service corresponding to the highest-priority service, the Silver class of service corresponding to the medium-priority service, and the Bronze class of service corresponding to the default service.

In order to translate the high-level customer SLAs into the low-level policies, the translation process consists of determining the set of relevant customers at each access router. The access router must have one interface that is in the same subnet as that of the customer. Then, the appropriate ToS marking for the customer can be determined by combining the expert user tables and the class of service assigned to the customer. For each access router, you set a marking policy based on the packets' source addresses. If a packet originates from the specific customer's network, it is marked according to the customer's service class.

For traffic streams that are destined for access router-connected customer sites but that originate from other sites, a destination address-based policy can also be defined. This is to ensure that packets destined for a Gold customer are marked correctly when they enter the ISP's network. Therefore, a destination-based marking policy must be entered for each customer site at all the access routers, and a source address-based marking policy must be entered for all directly attached customer sites at each access router that provides connectivity for the customers who use Differentiated Services.

The core routers are configured to provide a consistent mapping of the ToS encoding to the right priority level along the routers' forwarding paths.

Policy Architecture

Assuming that the ISP routers are COPS-enabled, a possible architecture for policy distribution in the ISP environment is shown in Figure 9.10. The access routers in the ISP's network communicate via COPS with a set of policy servers. The policy servers in turn take their information from an LDAP server. The policy management tool populates the LDAP server with the appropriate configuration and marking rules for the access routers as well as the appropriate behaviors for the core routers. The LDAP server is populated with rules defining the policies using the IETF standard schema definition (ideally), although any schema that is understood by the policy servers themselves would suffice for this purpose.

More than one COPS server can base its decisions on the content of the LDAP policy repository. Each COPS server can control more than one access router. Figure 9.10 shows only the distribution of policies to access routers, but a similar architecture can be used to distribute policies to the core routers.

Figure 9.10   Policy Architecture for ISP SLA Support

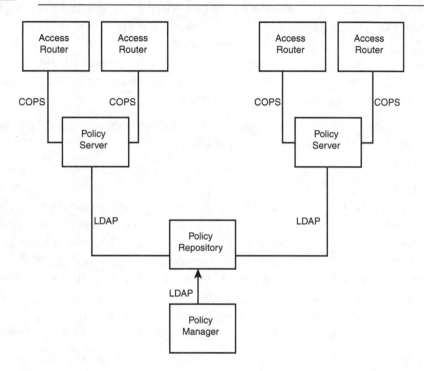

VPN Support for the ISP Environment

In addition to using the ISP as the conduit for access to the Internet, an enterprise may also want to use it as the provider that interconnects its various sites. If an ISP can promise adequate security for this communication, it can provide VPN offerings to its customers.

VPN support over the ISP network can be done in one of two modes of operation. In the first mode, the enterprise trusts that the ISP will perform the appropriate security functions needed for its communication. In the second case, the enterprise doesn't trust the ISP, asking the ISP for only plain IP connectivity and using IPsec-enabled routers under the enterprise's own control. The architecture chosen for enabling this communication might be somewhat different between these two modes of operation.

VPNs from a Trusted ISP

If the ISP is trusted and is providing VPN services, the access routers in control of the ISP can provide encryption and authentication using the IPsec protocol. You must keep in mind that IPsec is only one of the protocols that an ISP may use to provide VPNs. It can also use other schemes, such as providing VPNs using underlying dedicated frame relay or ATM connections.

Figure 9.11 shows an object model that can be used to model VPNs from an ISP perspective. The basic notion is that of a *customer*, who has many *customer sites*. Each site has an IP subnet address and a name. Each customer has one *VPN* contract with the ISP. Each VPN contract covers exactly one customer and specifies exactly one security class to be provided to the customer. A security class might have a name such as UltraSecure, Secure, or ClearText. It defines the type of encryption or authentication that is to be done for packets traveling between the customer sites across the ISP's network. A security class may be associated with more than one VPN. The collection of all the VPNs supported by an ISP constitute its high-level policies.

Figure 9.11 ISP High-Level Policies for Specifying VPN Definitions

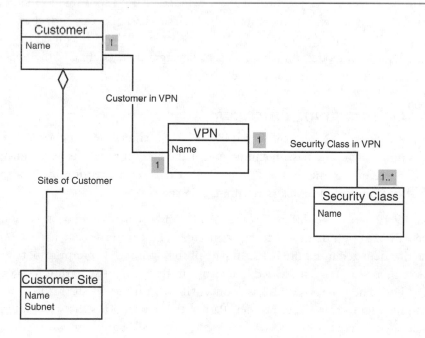

In order to determine the correct access router configuration for a given VPN, the ISP simply treats the VPN as a completely connected mesh connecting all the customer sites belonging to that VPN. The complete mesh approach will work if the size of customer sites in a VPN is less than approximately 1,000. Most IPsec-capable access routers can support close to 1,500 preconfigured IPsec tunnels at any given time. After the right set of tunnels are generated, you can obtain the device configuration for each of the routers under the control of the ISP using techniques similar to those described in the policy translation process for support of extranets in the enterprise environment.

The distribution of policies for configuration of VPNs and IPsec routers can be done following the model shown in Figure 9.10, which uses COPS to push the policies to the IPsec-capable access routers, with the policy server itself reading the policies from a directory server. Other alternative means of distribution are also possible. If the IPsec-capable access routers can read the entries in the policy repository directly, they can obtain the policy information using LDAP and configure themselves in accordance with the retrieved policies.

Given the many common functions between the support of SLAs by an ISP and the offering of the VPN service, you probably are wondering if it is possible to merge the two services. It is indeed possible to combine the high-level VPN policy model as just specified with the ISP SLA model to allow an ISP to provide VPNs with assured performance levels. At the high-level model, this simply means having a policy define both a security class and a performance-related class of service.

VPNs Defined by an Enterprise

As opposed to a VPN service offered by an ISP, an enterprise can choose to establish VPNs on its own. The basic technology that the enterprise uses is very similar to that of the ISP, except that the firewalls that provide the IPsec encryption functions would be placed in a different administrative domain in the two scenarios.

Figure 9.12 shows the different scenarios of a VPN service definition. Consider an enterprise with two sites that need to be connected. The enterprise may choose one of the three scenarios depicted in Figure 9.12. In part of the figure, the enterprise obtains a leased line between its two sites. This leased line results in that enterprise having its own private leased line. The enterprise still has connectivity with the ISP, but this ISP connectivity is used primarily to access the Internet. Part of the figure shows the same enterprise when it has decided to use a VPN service provided by the ISP. The private leased line has been replaced with a virtual link. The firewalls that provide the IPsec encryption functions are under the administrative control of the ISP. The same firewall may provide the encryption and authentication of packets belonging to multiple enterprises. In part of the figure, the firewall is under the administrative control of the enterprise, and it needs to be configured across the ISP network, which is not a trusted network (from the perspective of the enterprise).

Figure 9.12   **VPN Service Definition Scenarios**

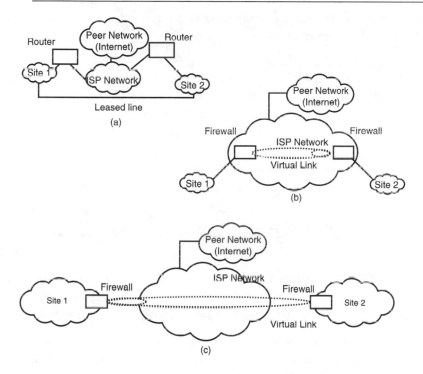

The scenario represented by part of Figure 9.12 is the one that applies when VPNs are defined and administered by an enterprise. The enterprise needs an object model to represent its VPN definitions just like the ISP did. The object model in Figure 9.11 can be used, except that there is only one customer—namely, the enterprise itself. Only one VPN covers all the sites of the enterprise, and it uses one instance of a security class. From the VPN description, the configuration needed for the various firewalls can be generated. The generation process would be identical to that described in the case of VPNs supported by an ISP. However, the distribution of policies might need to be done in a somewhat different manner than that of the ISP environment.

Because secure access to COPS or LDAP servers across an insecure network is not as widely deployed as secure access to Web servers across the open Internet, I think policy deployers will prefer to have a secure policy distribution via the more traditional HTTP-over-SSL combination. At this point in time, that seems easier than trying to access COPS in a secure fashion or trying to access LDAP servers using an SSL connection. Although there is no technical reason for COPS or LDAP communication using SSL to be inherently less secure than HTTP over SSL, more Web servers are deployed in the open Internet using SSL. As a result, many security lapses in implementations of Web servers have been fixed as compared to those in implementations of COPS or LDAP servers.

Using the Web-based distribution scheme, the enterprise would deploy a policy management console to populate a policy repository at one of its sites. The policy repository is a Web server that supports secure communication using SSL. Agents running on the different firewalls cooperating to make up the VPN for the enterprise would access the policy repository using HTTP/SSL. The Web server would authenticate the agents using SSL certificates (or any other mechanism the enterprise has chosen to deploy). It would then distribute the configuration required to establish VPNs to the agents, which would configure the firewalls they are operational on.

Customer Support for the Application-Hosting Environment

In an application-hosting environment, the important aspects related to business needs are adding and removing new customers to and from the server farm. Each such customer would be accepted with assurances about its performance and security needs.

Accepting any new customer into a server farm requires the configuration and provisioning of multiple network devices, including traffic shapers, servers, and firewalls. In order to illustrate the policy management framework, we refer to the structure of a server farm, as shown in Figure 9.13. This type of structure is typically found at the large hosting sites of providers who support multiple customers at the same time. Some of the machines in the server farm are shared across all customers, and others are dedicated to specific customers. Figure 9.13 shows the shared portion of the server farm and the machines belonging to one customer. The latter are enclosed in the dotted-line box. The contents inside the box are replicated for each customer. The shared infrastructure is used for common security, monitoring, and management functions.

Figure 9.13   A Typical Application-Hosting Environment

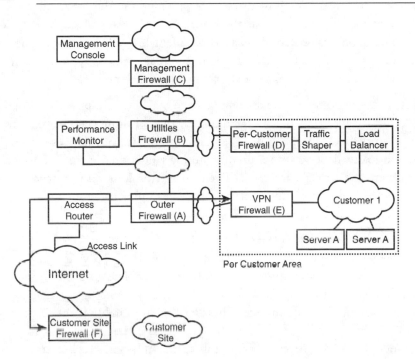

An outer firewall (Firewall A) protects the contents of the server farm from that of the external Internet. Just after the outer firewall is another firewall (the utilities firewall—Firewall B) that protects a utility network segment placed between the outer firewall and the utilities firewall. On the utility network segment, the hosting service provider might run applications such as a performance monitor to evaluate the health of its customers' sites. The utilities firewall protects these applications from any unauthorized access from customers' servers. After the utilities firewall, a customer-specific firewall (Firewall D) separates parts of the site that are dedicated on a per-customer basis. The customer-specific firewalls insulate individual customers from each other. This customer-specific firewall is followed by a *traffic shaper*, which is a rate control device used to regulate the amount of traffic to and from the customer's servers. Immediately after the traffic shaper is a *load balancer*, which allows the spreading of requests to multiple servers hosting applications belonging to the customer. On the other side of the customer-specific network is a VPN firewall (Firewall E), which is IPsec-capable and connects via the Internet to another customer-site VPN firewall (Firewall F). Between these two VPN firewalls, an IPsec tunnel is established to provide secure access for the customer to configure its applications. Such an IPsec tunnel is shown by means of a thick arrow between the firewalls E and F in the figure.

The section between the customer-specific firewall and the VPN firewall is replicated for each different customer hosted by the service provider. On the other side of the utilities firewall, a management subnet hosts the management console of the hosting services provider. This subnet is protected via a management firewall (Firewall C). The management firewall prevents unauthorized access to the management applications from the customer's servers, as well as from any external users on the Internet.

Within such an environment, we assume that the machines are physically installed with the desired hardware and software configuration for each customer. However, after the initial installation of the machines, you need to configure the various devices (servers, firewalls, shapers, and load balancers) to set up the filtering rules, rate limits, and dispatching rules consistent with the service agreement. The next section looks at the structure of a tool that enables the addition of a new server within this infrastructure.

High-Level Policy Specification

The high-level policy specification for the application server provider can be specified as defining only one type of entity—namely, the customer. The customer hosts various applications on its servers. Each application hosted by the customer is associated with a service level, such as Gold, Silver, or Bronze. These levels determine how much bandwidth a customer will receive, as well as how many servers are to be installed and made available to the customer. The policy specification in this case simply maps each customer to a desired service level. Assuming that Differentiated Services is enabled in the network, the service level can also define the value with which the DS field of packets belonging to this customer application should be marked. Additional security classification associated with the customer can specify the type of IPsec connection that needs to be established for the customer's access to the remote site.

In addition to the service level, each customer provides information such as the address of the firewall at the remote customer's site, a contact address, and so on.

Figure 9.14 shows the UML representation of an object model that can be used to model the SLAs between the customers and the application-hosting provider. Each *customer* has several characteristics, such as its name, a contact address, the IP addresses assigned to its servers and other devices, the identity of its load balancer, traffic shaper, and various firewalls. The customer is associated with a customer *site* to which a secure communication tunnel needs to be provided. The site has attributes that identify its name as well as the VPN firewall that is needed to establish secure communication with the site. The SLA associates each customer with a *performance class* and a *security class*. The security class determines the characteristics of the secure communication between VPN firewalls E and F shown in Figure 9.13. The performance class determines the priority of the customer within the farm, how much bandwidth it should be allocated at the traffic shaper, and the minimum and maximum number of resources each customer is entitled to. Each customer in this model has only one site it can connect back over its VPN. Each customer is also mapped to exactly one security class and one performance class.

Figure 9.14   ASP High-Level Policies for Specifying Customers

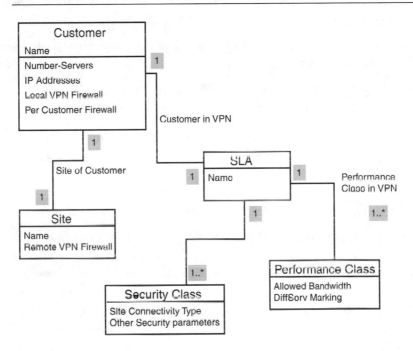

Low-Level Policy Specification

The low-level policy specification in the ASP case contains the configuration information for the following devices:

- The filters at the outer firewall, which must allow packets coming into the various customer servers. Also, they must allow IPsec encrypted packets to come from the customer's intranets to the VPN firewall corresponding to that customer.

- The filters at the utilities firewall, which must allow packets coming into the customer servers and allow monitoring tools access to the utilities subnet. (Some of the utilities must be configured to test the set of customers currently active within the network.)

- The customer-specific firewall, which must be configured to allow access to only the hosted applications from the Internet and to allow full access from the management subnet.

- The management firewall, which must be configured to allow access to customers' servers from the management applications and tools.

- The traffic shaper, which must be configured with the right bandwidth rates that correspond to each of the applications hosted by the customer.

- The load balancer, which must be configured with the right number and addresses of servers assigned to the customer and the application.

- The servers, which must be configured so that they mark the customer's packets in the right manner.

- The VPN firewall on both the ISP and the customer's sites, which must be configured in order to enable secure communication.

The filter rules for various firewalls, the IPsec policies setting up VPN to the customer's site, and the traffic shaper bandwidth controls make up the low-level policies in this environment.

Policy Translation and Distribution

Although a large number of devices need to be controlled in this scenario, the policy translation process is fairly straightforward. For most of the firewall filters, you simply need to generate the list of customer application port numbers that are accessible from the external Internet or from the various devices inside the network. Similarly, the determination of the rates at the traffic shaper is driven mostly by the specification of the customer's service classes.

Consider a customer who hosts an application running on port 80 and is using the IP addresses of 9.2.10.1 and 9.2.10.2. This customer is entitled to an incoming request rate of 1,000 connections per second. Among the various firewalls shown in Figure 9.13, the outer firewall, the management firewall, the utilities firewall, and the per-customer firewall must be configured to allow access to this application on the two machines of 9.2.10.1 and 9.2.10.2. The traffic shaper also needs to be configured at the specific inbound rates. If there are any traffic-shaping devices in other parts of the network, they would need to be configured as well. Furthermore, the VPN firewalls (E and F) must be configured to allow secure communication.

One possible way in which the policy distribution process can work for an ASP environment is shown in Figure 9.15. It shows a policy management console that is active within the management subnet, and two policy repositories. I use a Web-based policy repository to configure the IPsec tunnels between the two VPN firewalls—one at the ASP site and another at the customer site (these are Firewalls E and F in Figure 9.13). I also use an

LDAP directory server for the configuration of individual servers and traffic-shaping boxes for the customer. The traffic shapers, servers, and load balancer obtain their policy information using LDAP, and the VPN firewalls obtain their configuration from the Web server. Both the policy repositories are located in the utilities subnet of the ASP. From each type of the repository, thick arrows in Figure 9.15 show the devices whose policies are located at each of the repositories. Because a detailed description of these types of repositories was provided in previous sections, I will not go into more detail at this point. In the ASP solution it is not necessary to use two different types of repositories. All the device policies could have been stored in either the Web server-based repository or in the LDAP repository. However, showing two different types of repositories provides an example in which different distribution schemes need to be used together.

Figure 9.15   Policy Architecture for the ASP Environment

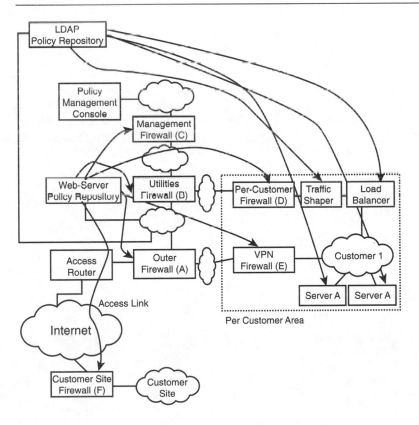

The ASP example is the last one I will examine in this chapter. As a final point, remember that the examples in this chapter are meant to be illustrative rather than exhaustive. By using similar techniques in other scenarios, you can determine the best manner in which to apply policy-based solutions in a different context.

CHAPTER **10**

Advanced Topics

This book has primarily looked at aspects of policy that are related to translating high-level user needs to device-specific configuration. Many interesting and important areas related to policy-based networking are not covered fully in this book. This chapter provides a brief overview of some related information that should be of interest to you.

Topics that we will examine briefly include the problem of monitoring policy compliance within networks, developing adaptive and state-dependent policies, and policy exchanges across different administrative domains. We'll also look at some of the routing policy specifications within the Internet, as well as some disciplines not covered fully in this book that might benefit from the deployment of policy-based techniques.

Policy Monitoring

By using a policy-based provisioning tool, a network administrator takes the first step toward ensuring that the devices within the network are configured in accordance with its business needs. However, it is always desirable to have an independent process to verify that the network is meeting the desired business needs.

You can monitor compliance of low-level policies by ensuring that the configuration of the different devices within the network is what is expected by the policy management tool. A management tool typically revalidates that the policies are indeed implemented at the different devices by examining the device configuration after the tool updates the policy to comply with the new policies. However, monitoring policy compliance at the device configuration level might ensure that the high-level policies are indeed being satisfied. For the two primary business needs that are explored in this book—namely, performance SLAs and security relationships—there are independent ways to validate compliance with the high-level policies. Such monitoring tools must be deployed in any network to validate that high-level policies are being satisfied.

For performance SLAs, compliance may be monitored using a variety of methods. You can collect performance statistics by active means, such as by running a set of dummy transactions to monitor their response time or by sending probe packets within the network to measure a network's round-trip latency. Active methods generate extra traffic within the network. A variety of passive methods also can be used to validate compliance with SLAs. These include running monitoring probes that examine packets in the network, to get estimates of applications' response time, as well as many programs that read the logs generated by applications to ascertain how they are performing. A more detailed discussion of SLA monitoring can be found in Chapter 7 of my book on SLAs, *Supporting Service Level Agreements on IP Networks* [SLAREF].

To monitor high-level security policies, such as the definition of VPNs, extranets, or similar constructs, you can devise packet monitoring techniques that will monitor the packets flowing on the network to validate their compliance with the security policy. Thus, if an extranet has been established with some business partners, you can monitor packets traveling to and from the partner to validate that they are traveling with the correct set of authentication and encryption headers. The detection of a packet with the wrong set of headers would indicate that the policies are not being upheld.

Dynamic and State-Dependent Policies

In many cases, policies need to depend on the current state of the network. For example, an application-hosting provider might want to start classifying packets into high- and low-priority classes only when the utilization of its access links is high. If the access link is running at low utilization, the performance of the different classes of packets is not likely to differ by much, or even be impacted by which policies are put into effect. A similar policy might be needed for security scenarios, where you might want to change the security class for communicating with business partners to a more secure mode if an attempt to infiltrate the network is detected.

Some cases of adaptive policies are relatively easy to handle. If a threshold or trigger is responsible for changing the definition of policies, a rule reflecting this can be placed in the policy repository. Agents running on the devices, or an intermediary Policy Decision Point, can then enforce the right policy when the required triggers are observed to take place. One common trigger that might cause policies to change is the time of day. It would not be uncommon for a business's weekday performance policies to be different than those on weekends. An agent on the device, or on a policy server that can change the configuration on multiple devices, can determine the set of policies that need to be changed, depending on time, and can then enforce compliance with those rules.

One case that is difficult to handle is that of determining an adaptive policy that satisfies the requirements of a high-level policy or business needs. For example, consider an enterprise network in which the service-level commitment is to have a database server operate with a response time of 500 ms. To realize this performance, the supporting policy might be to give the database application's traffic streams preference and accord them high priority via packet marking. However, if the network is running at low utilization, there is no real need to run the application as high-priority. On the other hand, at some threshold of network utilization, the application might need to be classified as high-priority, or it might need to be given a dedicated set of resources. The appropriate threshold and the correct way to adapt with these goals are the subject of active research.

Routing Policy

One policy activity that has been around on the Internet for a while is the concept of routing policies. Although such a policy has little in common with the types of policies we have considered in this book, I would like to cover this topic briefly.

The Internet consists of many independent IP networks that interconnect with each other at peering points. Some of these networks belong to enterprises that do not want to carry packets belonging to other entities through their private networks. Other networks belong to ISPs that are willing to act as transit points to other networks. Different domains within the network have their own policies for how they route packets through the network and which packets they will not accept for routing. These policies, taken together, form the routing policies in the Internet.

The routing policies for the Internet are stored at multiple exchange points in the network. As of the year 2000, five such repositories of routing policies were in operation— three in the U.S., and one each in Canada and Europe. These repositories exchange data with each other to maintain the global routing policies specified by different IP networks that make up the Internet.

The policies are used to specify peering agreements among different ISPs as well as to specify preferred routes to be taken inside the network for different destination subnetworks. The language in which they are specified is RPSL (Routing Policy Specification Language). RPSL is defined in [RPSL]. You can find more details on the usage of RPSL in the Internet in [RPSLUSE].

Other Policy Disciplines

This book has focused heavily on the use of policies to support the disciplines related to Quality of Service and IP security. Most of the policy examples have been related to the use of networking technologies (such as DiffServ) to support SLAs, or the different types of security services (such as VPNs and extranets) that can be offered using IP security policies. Of course, these areas are not the only ones to which policies can be applied. This section looks at some other disciplines.

One aspect of security in which policies can play an important role is access control. Access control determines which people or users are allowed access to different resources (such as files, mailboxes, and Web pages) that are available in the network. Access control policies have a format that is not very different from the filtering policies within firewalls. Access control can be implemented using a variety of techniques. Firewalls provide a basic form of access control at the network level. HTTP authentication mechanisms provide a simple authentication scheme for Web users. Different operating systems' user-authentication schemes offer yet another method for controlling access. An organization might have other schemes (such as Kerberos [KERB]) for controlling access. Clearly, managing a myriad of access control technologies within an enterprise is a complex task. A policy-based approach that maps users' access control requirements to the specific details of the various authentication and access control schemes greatly improves the scalability associated with administration.

Another discipline that can benefit from a policy-based approach is storage area networks (SANs). SANs are systems comprised of multiple file servers and disks that are connected by a high-speed network. Such a network is often based on fiber-channel standards [SAN-REF]. A SAN provides a distributed networked environment, and SANs need policies dictating how the storage needs to be allocated to different machines, as well as schemes that provide security and isolation among different users of the SAN. A policy-based approach provides a good way to manage SANs.

Another area in which you can use policies is address allocation using DHCP [DHCP-REF]. Policies can dictate how sets of IP addresses are to be allocated and for what duration. Similarly, policies can be used for applications, such as Web caching, or for the specification of high-level business processes. In any area where you need to administer consistent behaviors across a large number of heterogeneous systems or devices, and a complex set of technologies or devices needs to be addressed, you can deploy policy-based techniques to simplify the task of managing and configuring that environment.

Over the years, as policy standards mature, we should expect to see a growing use of policy-based administration among an increasing variety of disciplines.

Interdomain Policies

This book has looked at how policies can simplify the task of managing devices in a single administrative domain. In a distributed environment, such as the Internet, a network consists of multiple administrative domains. Within an enterprise environment, as well, some level of autonomy may be desired by different organizations in administering and operating their own networks. Thus, it would be interesting to see how the notion of policies applies across administrative domains.

Two activities related to policies have received some attention within the research community. One activity is related to the aspect of policy discovery. In the case of discovery, a device might want to discover all the different policies that might apply to portions of the network that will be traversed to communicate with another device in the network. This discovery can be used to determine what type of communication to use, or even to determine if communication is feasible at all. The IPsec Policy Working Group within IETF [IPSPREF] is looking at the protocols that can discover IP security policies within the Internet.

The other activity deals with actual negotiations of policies across multiple administrative domains. An example of policy negotiation is the establishment of bandwidth SLAs between different ISPs within the Internet. Many of these ISPs offer connectivity to the same geographical areas, and not all have the same load on their networks at the same time. Thus, it might be possible for an ISP to have an agent negotiate to borrow or lend extra bandwidth to its peers automatically. This bandwidth negotiation might reflect itself in terms of the peering arrangements, routing policies, or DiffServ policies that are implemented at the borders of these devices. Such agents are referred to as *bandwidth brokers*. A summary of prototyping activity that is related to bandwidth brokers can be found at http://www.merit.edu/working.groups/i2.qbone.bb.

REFERENCES

[AMAN] J. Aman et al, "Adaptive Algorithms for Managing a Distributed Data Processing Workload," *IBM Systems Journal*, Vol. 36, No. 2., 1997.

[CACHEL] J. Fritz Barnes and Raju Pandey. "CacheL: Language Support for Customizable Caching Policies," Proceedings of the Fourth International Web Caching Workshop (WCW '99), March 1999, San Diego, California, USA.

[CAHN] Robert S. Cahn, *Wide Area Network Design*, Morgan Kaufmann Publishers, ISBN 1558604588, 1998.

[CHESWICK] W. R. Cheswick and S. M. Bellovin, *Firewalls and Internet Security: Repelling the Wily Hacker*, Addison-Wesley, ISBN 0201633574, 1996.

[COMER] Douglas Comer, *Internetworking with TCP/IP: Principles, Protocols, and Architecture*, Prentice Hall, ISBN 0132169878, 1995.

[DDNS-RFC] P. Vixie et al, *Dynamic Updates in the Domain Name System*, Internet RFC 2136, April 1997.

[DEERING] S. Deering and R. Hinden, *Internet Protocol, Version 6 (IPv6) Specification*, Internet RFC 2460, December 1998.

[DENWEB] The Directory Enabled Networking Ad Hoc Working Group: http://www.murchiso.com/den.

[DHCP-REF] Ralph Droms, PhD, and Ted Lemon, *The DHCP Handbook: Understanding, Deploying, and Managing Automated Configuration Services*, MTP, ISBN 1578701376, 1999.

[DMTFCIM] Specifications page for CIM from the DMTF: http://www.dmtf.org/spec/cims.html.

[DNSIZONE] M. Ohta, "Incremental Zone Transfer in DNS," Internet RFC 1995, August 1996.

[DNSRFC] P. Mockapetris, "Domain Name System," Internet STD 13, RFC 1034, and RFC 1035, November 1987.

[DSWG] The IETF Differentiated Services Working Group: `http://www.ietf.org/html.charters/diffserv-charter.html`.

[EXPECTREF] Don Libes, *Exploring Expect: A Tcl-Based Toolkit for Automating Interactive Programs*, O'Reilly & Associates, ISBN: 1565920902, 1994.

[FERGUSON] Paul Ferguson and Geoff Huston, *Quality of Service: Delivering QoS on the Internet and in Corporate Networks*, John Wiley & Sons, ISBN 0471243582, 1998.

[GONCAL] Marcus Goncalves, *Directory-Enabled Networks*, McGraw Hill, ISBN 0071349510, 1999.

[HMAC] H. Krawczyk et al, *HMAC: Keyed-Hashing for Message Authentication*, Internet RFC 2104, February 1997.

[HUITEMA] C. Huitema, *Routing in the Internet*, Prentice Hall, ISBN 0131321927, 1995.

[IKE] D. Harkins and D. Carrel, *The Internet Key Exchange (IKE)*, Internet RFC 2409, November 1998.

[IPAUTH] S. Kent and R. Atkinson, *IP Authentication Header*, Internet RFC 2402, November 1998.

[IPESP] S. Kent and R. Atkinson, *IP Encapsulating Security Protocol (ESP)*, RFC 2406, November 1998.

[IPSEC] S. Kent and R. Atkinson, *Security Architecture for the Internet Protocol*, Internet RFC 2401, November 1998.

[ISAKMP] D. Maughan et al, *Internet Security Association and Key Management Protocol (ISAKMP)*, Internet RFC 2408, November 1998.

[ISPSPREF] IETF Working Group on IP Security Policy: `http://www.ietf.org/html.charters/ipsp-charter.html`.

[KAOS] R. Darimont, E. Dalor, P. Massonet and A. Van Lamsweerde, "GRAIL/KAOS: An Environment for Goal Driven Requirements Engineering," Proceedings of the 20th International Conference on Software Engineering, Kyoto, April 1998, pp. 58-62.

[KCHAO] A. Kershenbaum and W. Chou, "A Unified Algorithm for Designing Multidrop Teleprocessing Networks," IEEE Transactions on Communications COM-22(11):1762-1772, 1974.

[KERB] Brian Tung, *Kerberos: A Network Authentication System,* Addison-Wesley, ISBN 0201379244, 1999.

[KERSH] A. Kershenbaum, *Telecommunication Network Design Algorithms,* McGraw Hill, 1993.

[KILKKI] Kalevi Kilkki, *Differentiated Services for the Internet,* MTP, ISBN 1578701325, 1999.

[KLIEN1] L. Klienrock, *Queuing Systems: Theory,* John Wiley & Sons; ISBN: 0471491101, 1975.

[KLIEN2] L. Klienrock, *Queuing Systems: Computer Applications,* John Wiley & Sons; ISBN: 047149111X, 1976.

[KNUTH] D. E. Knuth, The Art of Computer Programming (Volume 3): Sorting and Searching Algorithms, Addison-Wesley, ISBN: 0201896850, 1998.

[LASCO] James Hoagland, "Specifying and Implementing Security Policies Using LaSCO, the Language for Security Constraints on Objects," Ph.D. Dissertation, University of California, Davis, March 2000.

[LAXMAN] T. Laxman and D. Stalidis, "High Speed Policy Based Packet Classification Using Multi-dimensional Range Matching," Proceedings of the ACM SIGCOMM 98, Vancouver, Canada, September 1998.

[LDAPREF] Tim Howes, Mark C. Smith and Gordon S. Good, *Understanding and Deploying LDAP Directory Services,* MTP, ISBN 1578700701, 1999.

[LDIFREF] G. Good, "The LDAP Data Interchange Format (LDIF)—Technical Specification," Internet RFC 2849, June 2000.

[LOSHIN] P. Loshin, *IPv6 Clearly Explained,* Morgan Kaufmann Publishers, ISBN 0124558380, 1999.

[MENTOR] A. Kershenbaum, P. Kermani, and G. Grover, "MENTOR: An Algorithm for Mesh Network Topological Optimization and Routing," IEEE Transactions on Communications 29:503-513, 1991.

[MIB2] K. McCloghrie and M. Rose, *Management Information Base for Network Management of TCP/IP-Based Internets: MIB-II,* Internet RFC 1213, March 1991.

[OAKLEY] H. Orman, *The Oakley Key Determination Protocol,* Internet RFC 2412, November 1998.

[POLICYWG] The IETF Policy Framework Working Group: http://www.ietf.org/html.charters/policy-charter.html.

[PONDER] N. Damianou, N. Dulay, E. Lupu, and M Sloman, "Ponder: A Language for Specifying Security and Management Policies for Distributed Systems," Imperial College, UK, Research Report DoC 2001, January 2000.

[POSTEL] J. Postel, ed., *Internet Protocol: DARPA Internet Program Protocol Specification,* RFC 791, DARPA, September 1981.

[RAPWG] The IETF Resource Allocation Protocol Working Group:
`http://www.ietf.org/html.charters/rap-charter.html`.

[RFC1413] M. St. Johns, *Identification Protocol,* Internet RFC 1413, February 1993.

[RFC1414] M. St. Johns and M. Rose, *Identification MIB,* Internet RFC 1414, February 1993.

[ROUTING1] Marcel Waldvogel, George Varghese, Jon Turner, and Bernhard Plattner. "Scalable High Speed IP Routing Lookups," *Proceedings of SIGCOMM'97,* ACM Special Interest Group on Communications (SIGCOMM) Conference; Cannes, France; September 1997.

[ROUTING2] Mikael Degermark, Andrej Brodnik, Svante Carlsson, and Stephen Pink. "Small Forwarding Tables for Fast Routing Lookups," *Proceedings of SIGCOMM'97,* ACM Special Interest Group on Communications (SIGCOMM) Conference; Cannes, France; September 1997.

[RPSL] C. Alaettinoglu et al, *Routing Policy Specification Language (RPSL),* Internet RFC 2622, June 1999.

[RPSLUSE] D. Meyer et al, *Using RPSL in Practice,* Internet RFC 2650, August 1999.

[SANREF] T. Clark, *Designing Storage Area Networks,* Addison-Wesley, ISBN 0201615843, 1999.

[SCHNR] B. Schneier, *Applied Cryptography: Protocols, Algorithms and Source Code in C,* John Wiley & Sons, ISBN 04711289457, 1995.

[SCHW2] M. Schwartz, *Computer Communication Network Design and Analysis,* Prentice Hall, ISBN 01316134X, 1977.

[SEDGEWICK] Sedgwick, Robert. *Algorithms in C.,* Addison-Wesley, Reading, ISBN 0201514257, 1990.

[SKLOWER]Keith Skowler, "A Tree-Based Packet Routing Table for Berkeley Unix," Proceedings of the Winter 1991 USENIX Conference; Dallas, TX; USENIX Association, 1991.

[SLAREF] D. Verma, *Supporting Service-Level Agreements on IP Networks*, MTP, ISBN 1578701465, 1999.

[SLPREF] James Kempf and Robert St. Pierre, *Service Location Protocol for Enterprise Networks*, John Wiley & Sons; ISBN: 0471315877, 1999.

[SNMP] William Stallings, *SNMP, SNMPv2, SNMPv3, and RMON 1 and 2*, Addison Wesley, ISBN 0201485346, 1999.

[SNMPCONF] The IETF SNMP Configuration Working Group: http://www.ietf.org/html.charters/snmpconf-charter.html.

[SOCKSREF] M. Leech et al, *SOCKS Protocol Version 5*, Internet RFC 1928, April 1996.

[STRASSDEN] John Strassner, *Directory Enabled Networks*, MTP, ISBN 1578701406, 1999.

[STRASSNER] John Strassner, *Policy-Based Management*, MTP, ISBN 1578702259, 2000.

[TANNEN] Andrew S. Tannenbaum, *Computer Networks*, Prentice Hall, ISBN 0133499456, 1996.

[TCPMIB] K. McCloghrie, *SNMPv2 Management Information Base for the Transmission Control Protocol Using SMIv2*, Internet RFC 2012, November 1996.

[THAWTE] Thawte Digital Certificate Services: http://thawte.com.

[THOMAS] Stephen A. Thomas, *IPNG and the TCP/IP Protocols: Implementing the Next Generation Internet*, John Wiley & Sons, ISBN 0471130885, 1996.

[TLSREF] T. Dierks and C. Allen, *The TLS Protocol Version 1.0*, Internet RFC 2246, January 1999.

[TME10] Rolf Lendernmann et al, *An Introduction to Tivoli's TME 10*, Prentice Hall, ISBN 0138997179, October 1997.

[TNG] Rick Sturm, *Working with Unicenter TNG*, Que Education and Training, ISBN 0789717654, August 1998.

[TOPOC] C. Topolcic, *Experimental Internet Stream Protocol, Version 2 (ST-II)*, Internet RFC 1190, October 1990.

[UDPMIB] K. McCloghrie, *SNMPv2 Management Information Base for the User Datagram Protocol Using SMIv2*, Internet RFC 2013, November 1996.

[UML2] M. Page-Jones, *Fundamentals of Object-Oriented Design in UML*, Addison-Wesley, ISBN 020169946X, 1999.

[UMLREF] M. Fowler and K. Scott, *UML Distilled*, Addison-Wesley, ISBN: 0201325632, 1997.

[UUNETSLA] UUNET Service-Level Agreement: `http://www.uu.net/lang.en/customers/sla/terms`.

[VERIS] VeriSign Systems: `http://www.verisign.com`.

[WOLFF] Ronald Wolff, *Stochastic Modeling and the Theory of Queues*, Prentice Hall, ISBN: 0138466920, 1989.

Index

Microsoft Technologies

Inside Windows 2000 Server

By William Boswell
1st Edition
1515 pages, $49.99
ISBN: 1-56205-929-7

Taking the author-driven, no-nonsense approach we pioneered with our *Landmark* books, New Riders proudly offers something unique for Windows 2000 administrators—an interesting, discriminating book on Windows 2000 Server written by someone who can anticipate your situation and give you workarounds that won't leave a system unstable or sluggish.

Windows 2000 Active Directory

By Ed Brovick, Doug Hauger, and William Wade III
1st Edition
416 pages, $29.99
ISBN: 0-7357-0870-3

Written by three of Microsoft's key premium partners, with high-level access to people, information, and resources, this book offers a concise, focused, and informative *Landmark* format, filled with case studies and real-world experience for Windows 2000's most anticipated and most complex feature—the Active Directory.

Windows 2000 Essential Reference

By Steven Tate, et al.
1st Edition
670 pages, $35.00
ISBN: 0-7357-0869-X

Architected to be the most navigable, useful and value-packed reference for Windows 2000, this book uses a creative "telescoping" design that you can adapt to your style of learning. The authors give you answers based on their hands-on experience with Windows 2000 and apply their formidable credentials toward giving you the answers you won't find anywhere else.

Windows 2000 Routing and Remote Access Service

By Kackie Charles
1st Edition
400 pages, $34.99
ISBN: 0-7357-0951-3

Ideal for system administrators looking to create cost-effective and secure remote access across the network. Author Kackie Charles uses concrete examples to demonstrate how to smoothly integrate Windows 2000 routing with your existing routing infrastructure, and connect users to the network while maxmizing available bandwidth. Featured coverage includes new authentication models, routing protocols, configuration of the Windows 2000 router, design issues, security, and troubleshooting.

Windows 2000 Deployment & Desktop Management
By Jeffrey A. Ferris
1st Edition
408 pages, $34.99
ISBN: 0-7357-0975-0

More than a simple overview of new features and tools, this solutions-driven book is a thorough reference to deploying Windows 2000 Professional to corporate workstations. The expert real-world advice and detailed exercises make this a one-stop, easy-to-use resource for any system administrator, integrator, engineer, or other IT professional planning rollout of Windows 2000 clients.

Windows 2000 DNS
By Herman Knief, Jeffrey Graham, Andrew Daniels, and Roger Abell
2nd Edition
480 pages, $39.99
ISBN: 0-7357-0973-4

Focusing on such key topics as designing and securing DNS services, planning for interoperation, and installing and using DHCP and WINS services, *Windows 2000 DNS* is a comprehensive guide to the newest iteration of Microsoft's DNS. The authors provide you with real-world advice, best practices, and strategies you will need to design and administer DNS for optimal performance.

Windows 2000 User Management
By Lori Sanders
1st Edition
240 pages, $34.99
ISBN: 1-56205-886-X

With the dawn of Windows 2000, it has become even more difficult to draw a clear line between managing the user and managing the user's environment and desktop. This book, written by a noted trainer and consultant, provides a comprehensive, practical guide to managing users and their desktop environments with Windows 2000.

Windows 2000 Professional
By Jerry Honeycutt
1st Edition
330 pages, $34.99
ISBN: 0-7357-0950-5

Windows 2000 Professional explores the power available to the Windows workstation user on the corporate network and Internet. The book is aimed directly at the power user who values the security, stability, and networking capabilities of NT alongside the ease and familiarity of the Windows 9X user interface. This book covers both user and administration topics, with a dose of networking content added for connectivity.

Planning for Windows 2000

By Eric K. Cone,
Jon Boggs, and Sergio Perez
1st Edition
448 pages, $29.99
ISBN: 0-7357-0048-6

Are you ready for Windows 2000? This book explains the steps involved in preparing your Windows NT-based heterogeneous network for Windows 2000. Rollout procedures are presented in detail as the authors draw from their own experiences and scenarios to explain an otherwise tangled series of procedures. *Planning for Windows 2000* is an indispensable companion to anyone considering migration.

Windows 2000 Professional Reference

By Karanjit Siyan, Ph.D.
3rd Edition
1848 pages, $75.00
ISBN: 0-7357-0952-1

Windows 2000 Professional Reference is the benchmark of references available for Windows 2000. Although other titles take you through the setup and implementation phase of the product, no other book provides the user with detailed answers to day-to-day administration problems and tasks. Solid content shows administrators how to manage, troubleshoot, and fix problems that are specific to heterogeneous Windows networks, as well as Internet features and functionality.

Windows 2000 Security

By Roberta Bragg
1st Edition
500 pages, $39.99
ISBN: 0-7357-0991-2

No single authoritative reference on security exists for serious network system administrators. The primary directive of this title is to assist the Windows networking professional in understanding and implementing Windows 2000 security in his organization. Included are Best Practices sections, which make recommendations for settings and security practices.

Windows NT/2000 Network Security

By Eugene Schultz
1st Edition
440 pages, $45.00
ISBN: 1-57870-253-4

Windows NT/2000 Network Security provides a framework that will promote genuine understanding of the Windows security model and associated capabilities. The goal is to acquaint readers with the major types of Windows security exposures when used in both peer-to-peer and client-server settings. This book teaches readers the specific security controls and settings that address each exposure, and shows them how to evaluate tradeoffs to determine which control (if any) to apply.

Windows NT Performance Monitoring, Benchmarking, and Tuning

By Mark Edmead and Paul Hinsberg
1st Edition
288 pages, $29.99
ISBN: 1-56205-942-4

Windows NT Performance Monitoring, Benchmarking, and Tuning provides a one-stop source for sound technical information on doing everything necessary to fine-tune your network. From benchmarking to analyzing performance numbers to isolating and solving resource bottlenecks, the authors provide a reliable blueprint for ensuring optimal Windows NT performance.

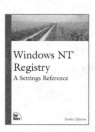

Windows NT Registry: A Settings Reference

By Sandra Osborne
1st Edition
576 pages, $29.99
ISBN:1-56205-941-6

More than a simple troubleshooting or optimization book, this solutions-driven guide shows you how to manage hardware, Windows NT Workstation and other clients, notebook computers, application software, and Internet settings using the Registry in the most efficient and cost-effective manner possible. If you're a network developer, system engineer, server administrator, or workstation technician, you'll come to rely on the expert advice contained in this comprehensive reference.

Windows NT/2000 Thin Client Solutions

By Todd Mathers
2nd Edition
840 pages, $45.00
ISBN: 1-57870-239-9

A practical and comprehensive reference to MetaFrame 1.8 and Terminal Server Edition, this book should be the first source for answers to the tough questions on the TSE/MetaFrame platform. Building on the quality of the previous edition, additional coverage of installation of Terminal Services and MetaFrame on a Windows 2000 Server, as well as chapters on TSE management, remote access, and application integration, are included.

Windows 2000 Virtual Private Networking

By Thaddeus Fortenberry
1st Edition, January 2001
350 pages, $45.00
ISBN 1-57870-246-1

Because of the ongoing push for a distributed workforce, administrators must support laptop users, home LAN environments, complex branch offices, and more—all within a secure and effective network design. The way an administrator implements VPNs in Windows 2000 is different than that of any other operating system. In addition to discussions about Windows 2000 tunneling, new VPN features that can affect Active Directory replication and Network Address Translation are also covered.

Windows 2000 Active Directory Design & Deployment
By Gary Olsen
1st Edition
648 pages, $45.00
ISBN: 1-57870-242-9

This book focuses on the design of a Windows 2000 Active Directory environment, and how to develop an effective design and migration plan. The reader is lead through the process of developing a design plan by reviewing each pertinent issue, and then provided expert advice on how to evaluate each issue as it applies to the reader's particular environment. Practical examples illustrate all of these issues.

Windows 2000 and Mainframe Integration
By William Zack
1st Edition
390 pages, $40.00
ISBN:1-57870-200-3

Windows 2000 and Mainframe Integration provides mainframe computing professionals with the practical know-how to build and integrate Windows 2000 technologies into their current environment.

Windows 2000 Server: Planning and Migration
By Sean Deuby
1st Edition
480 pages, $40.00
ISBN:1-57870-023-X

Windows 2000 Server: Planning and Migration can quickly save the NT professional thousands of dollars and hundreds of hours. This title includes authoritative information on key features of Windows 2000 and offers recommendations on how to best position your NT network for Windows 2000.

Windows 2000 Quality of Service
By David Iseminger
1st Edition
264 pages, $45.00
ISBN:1-57870-115-5

As the traffic on networks continues to increase, the strain on network infrastructure and available resources has also grown. *Windows 2000 Quality of Service* teaches network engineers and administrators to how to define traffic control patterns and utilize bandwidth on their networks.

Windows NT Power Toolkit
By Stu Sjouwerman and Ed Tittel
1st Edition
848 pages, $49.99
ISBN: 0-7357-0922-X

A unique offering from New Riders, this book covers the analysis, tuning, optimization, automation, enhancement, maintenance, and troubleshooting of both Windows NT Server 4.0 and Windows NT Workstation 4.0. *Windows NT Power Toolkit* includes comprehensive coverage of all service packs and security updates, IE5 upgrade issues, recent product additions, third-party tools and utilities.

Windows NT Terminal Server and Citrix MetaFrame
By Ted Harwood
1st Edition
46 pages, $29.99
ISBN: 1-56205-944-0

This technical reference details all aspects of planning, installing, administering, and troubleshooting Microsoft Terminal Server and Citrix MetaFrame systems. MetaFrame greatly enhances the usability of NT as a thin-client solution, but the heterogeneous networking issues involved in its integration will be a significant source of information pain. *Windows NT Terminal Server and Citrix Metaframe* is one of only two books available on this technology.

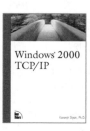

Windows 2000 TCP/IP
By Karanjit S. Siyan, Ph.D.
2nd Edition
920 pages, $39.99
ISBN 0-7357-0992-0

Focusing on ways to administer networks using Microsoft TCP/IP, this book is for professionals who want to read about best practices on using the technology. Without spending time on basics that readers already understand, *Windows 2000 TCP/IP* presents advanced solutions and is a must-have for any system administrator.

Windows NT Domain Architecture
By Gregg Branham
1st Edition
312 pages, $38.00
ISBN: 1-57870-112-0

As Windows NT continues to be deployed more and more in the enterprise, the domain architecture for the network becomes critical as the complexity increases. This book contains the in-depth expertise that is necessary to truly plan a complex enterprise domain.

Windows NT/2000 Native API Reference
By Gary Nebbett
1st Edition
528 pages, $50.00
ISBN:1-57870-199-6

This book is the first complete reference to the API functions native to Windows NT and covers the set of services that are offered by the Windows NT to both kernel- and user-mode programs. Coverage consists of documentation of the 210 routines included in the NT Native API, and the functions that will be added in Windows 2000. Routines that are either not directly accessible via the Win32 API or offer substantial additional functionality are described in especially great detail. Services offered by the NT kernel—mainly the support for debugging user mode applications—are also included.

Windows NT Applications: Measuring and Optimizing Performance
By Paul Hinsberg
1st Edition
288 pages, $40.00
ISBN: 1-57870-176-7

This book offers developers crucial insight into the underlying structure of Windows NT, as well as the methodology and tools for measuring and ultimately optimizing code performance.

Windows NT Device Driver Development

By Peter Viscarola and W. Anthony Mason
1st Edition
704 pages, $50.00
ISBN: 1-57870-058-2

This title begins with an introduction to the general Windows NT operating system concepts relevant to drivers, then progresses to more detailed information about the operating system, such as interrupt management, synchronization issues, the I/O Subsystem, standard kernel mode drivers, and more.

DCE/RPC over SMB: Samba and Windows NT Domain Internals

By Luke Leighton
1st Edition
312 pages, $45.00
ISBN: 1-57870-150-3

Security people, system and network administrators, and those writing tools for them all need to be familiar with the packets flowing across their networks. Authored by a key member of the Samba team, this book describes how Microsoft has taken DCE/RPC and implemented it over SMB and TCP/IP.

Windows Script Host

By Tim Hill
1st Edition
448 pages, $35.00
ISBN: 1-57870-139-2

Windows Script Host is one of the first books published about this powerful tool. The text focuses on system scripting and the VBScript language, using objects, server scriptlets, and ready-to-use script solutions.

Delphi COM Programming

By Eric Harmon
1st Edition
500 pages, $45.00
ISBN: 1-57870-221-6

Delphi COM Programming is for all Delphi 3, 4, and 5 programmers. After providing readers with an understanding of the COM framework, it offers a practical exploration of COM to enable Delphi developers to program component-based applications. Typical real-world scenarios, such as Windows Shell programming, automating Microsoft Agent, and creating and using ActiveX controls, are explored. Discussions of each topic are illustrated with detailed examples.

Applying COM+

By Gregory Brill
1st Edition
450 pages, $49.99
ISBN: 0-7357-0978-5

By pulling a number of disparate services into one unified technology, COM+ holds the promise of greater efficiency and more diverse capabilities for developers who are creating applications—either enterprise or commercial software—to run on a Windows 2000 system. *Applying COM+* covers the features of the new tool, as well as how to implement them in a real case study. Features are demonstrated in all three of the major languages used in the Windows environment: C++, VB, and VJ++.

Exchange & Outlook: Constructing Collaborative Solutions

By Joel Semeniuk and Duncan MacKenzie
1st Edition
576 pages, $40.00
ISBN 1-57870-252-6

The authors of this book are responsible for building custom messaging applications for some of the biggest Fortune 100 companies in the world. They share their expertise to help administrators and designers use Microsoft technology to establish a base for their messaging system and to lay out the tools that can be used to help build those collaborative solutions. Actutal planning and design solutions are included along with typically workflow/collaborative solutions.

Windows NT Shell Scripting

By Tim Hill
1st Edition
400 pages, $32.00
ISBN: 1-57870-047-7

A complete reference for Windows NT scripting, this book guides you through a high-level introduction to the Shell language itself and the Shell commands that are useful for controlling or managing different components of a network.

Win32 Perl Programming: The Standard Extensions

By Dave Roth
1st Edition
640 pages, $40.00
ISBN:1-57870-067-1

Discover numerous proven examples and practical uses of Perl in solving everyday Win32 problems. This is the only book available with comprehensive coverage of Win32 extensions, where most of the Perl functionality resides in Windows settings.

Windows NT/2000 ADSI Scripting for System Administration

By Thomas Eck
1st Edition
700 pages, $45.00
ISBN: 1-57870-219-4

Active Directory Scripting Interfaces (ADSI) allow administrators to automate administrative tasks across their Windows networks. This title fills a gap in the current ADSI documentation by including coverage of its interaction with LDAP and provides administrators with proven code samples that they can adopt to effectively configure and manage user accounts and other usually time-consuming tasks.

Windows NT Automated Deployment and Customization

By Richard Puckett
1st Editon
300 pages, $32.00
ISBN: 1-57870-045-0

This title offers time-saving advice that helps you install, update and configure software on each of your clients, without having to visit each client. Learn how to control all clients remotely for tasks, such as security and legal software use. Reference material on native NT tools, registry edits, and third-party tools is included.

Internet Information Services Administration
By Kelli Adam
1st Edition
192 pages, $29.99
ISBN: 0-7357-0022-2

Administrators who know IIS from previous versions need this book to show them in concrete detail how to configure the new protocols, authenticate users with the new Certificate Server, and implement and manage the new e-commerce features that are part of IIS 5. This book gives you all of that: a quick read that provides real-world solutions, and doubles as a portable reference.

SMS 2 Administration
By Darshan Doshi and Mike Lubanski
1st Edition
448 pages, $39.99
ISBN: 0-7357-0082-6

SMS 2 Administra-tion offers comprehensive coverage of how to design, deploy, and manage SMS 2.0 in an enterprise environment. This book follows the evolution of a software management system from the initial design through the implementation life cycle, to day-to-day management and usage of the system. Packed with case studies and examples pulled from the author's extensive experience, this book makes this complex product seem almost simple.

SQL Server System Administration
By Sean Baird and Chris Miller, et al.
1st Edition
352 pages, $29.99
ISBN: 1-56205-955-6

Assuming that the reader is familiar with the fundamentals of database administration and has worked with SQL Server in some capacity, this book focuses on the topics of interest to most administrators: keeping data consistently available to users. Unlike other SQL Server books that have little relevance to the serious SQL Server DBA, *SQL Server System Administra-tion* provides a hands-on approach that administrators won't find elsewhere.

SQL Server 7 Essential Reference
By Sharon Dooley
1st Edition
400 pages, $35.00
ISBN: 0-7357-0864-9

SQL Server 7 Essential Reference is a comprehensive reference of advanced how-tos and techniques for developing with SQL Server. In particular, the book addresses advanced development techniques used in large application efforts with multiple users developing Web applications for intranets, extranets, or the Internet. Each section includes details on how each component is developed and then integrated into a real-life application.

Open Source

MySQL
By Paul DuBois
1st Edition
800 pages, $49.99
ISBN: 0-7357-0921-1

MySQL teaches readers how to use the tools provided by the MySQL distribution, covering installation, setup, daily use, security, optimization, maintenance, and troubleshooting. It also discusses important third-party tools, such as the Perl DBI and Apache/PHP interfaces that provide access to MySQL.

Web Application Development with PHP 4.0
By Till Gerken, et al.
1st Edition
416 pages, $39.99
ISBN: 0-7357-0997-1

Web Application Development with PHP 4.0 explains PHP's advanced syntax including classes, recursive functions, and variables. The authors present software development methodologies and coding conventions, which are a must-know for industry quality products and make software development faster and more productive. Included is coverage on Web applications and insight into user and session management, e-commerce systems, XML applications, and WDDX.

PHP Functions Essential Reference
By Landon Bradshaw, Till Gerken, Graeme Merrall, and Tobias Ratschiller
1st Edition
500 pages, $35.00
ISBN: 0-7357-0970-X
February 2001

This carefully crafted title covers the latest developments through PHP 4.0, including coverage of Zend. These authors share their knowledge not only of the development of PHP, but also how they use it daily to create dynamic Web sites. Covered as well is instruction on using PHP alongside MySQL.

Python Essential Reference
By David Beazley
1st Edition
352 pages, $34.95
ISBN: 0-7357-0901-7

Avoiding the dry and academic approach, the goal of *Python Essential Reference* is to concisely describe the Python programming language and its large library of standard modules, collectively known as the Python programming environment. This informal reference covers Python's lexical conventions, datatypes, control flow, functions, statements, classes, and execution model—a truly essential reference for any Python programmer!

GNU Autoconf, Automake, and Libtool

By Gary V. Vaughan, et al.
1st Edition
400 pages, $40.00
ISBN: 1-57870-190-2

This book is the first of its kind, authored by Open Source community luminaries and current maintainers of the tools, teaching developers how to boost their productivity and the portability of their applications using GNU Autoconf, Automake, and Libtool.

Linux/UNIX

Linux System Administration

By M Carling, James T. Dennis, and Stephen Degler
1st Edition
368 pages, $29.99
ISBN: 1-56205-934-3

Today's overworked sysadmins are looking for ways to keep their networks running smoothly and achieve enhanced performance. Users are always looking for more storage, more services, and more Speed. *Linux System Administration* guides the reader in the many intricacies of maintaining a secure, stable system.

KDE Application Development

By Uwe Thiem
1st Edition
190 pages, $39.99
ISBN: 1-57870-201-1

KDE Application Development offers a head start on KDE and Qt. The book covers the essential widgets available in KDE and Qt, and offers a strong start without the "first try" annoyances which sometimes make strong developers and programmers give up.

Linux Firewalls

By Robert Ziegler
1st Edition
496 pages, $39.99
ISBN: 0-7357-0900-9

This book details security steps that a small, non-enterprise business user might take to protect his system. These steps include packet-level firewall filtering, IP masquerading, proxies, tcp wrappers, system integrity checking, and system security monitoring with an overall emphasis on filtering and protection. The goal of *Linux Firewalls* is to help people get their Internet security measures in place quickly, without the need to become experts in security or firewalls.

Linux Essential Reference

By Ed Petron
1st Edition
368 pages, $24.95
ISBN: 0-7357-0852-5

This title is all about getting things done by providing structured organization to the plethora of available Linux information. Providing clear and concise instructions on how to perform important administration and management tasks, as well as how to use some of the more powerful commands and more advanced topics, the scope of *Linux Essential Reference* includes the best way to implement the most frequently used commands, manage shell scripting, administer your own system, and utilize effective security.

UnixWare 7 System Administration
By Gene Henriksen and Melissa Henriksen
1st Edition
560 pages, $40.00
ISBN: 1-57870-080-9

In great technical detail, this title presents the latest version of SCO UnixWare and is the definitive operating system resource for SCO engineers and administrators. SCO troubleshooting notes and tips are integrated throughout the text, as are tips specifically designed for those who are familiar with other UNIX variants.

Developing Linux Applications with GTK+ and GDK
By Eric Harlow
1st Edition
512 pages, $34.99
ISBN: 0-7357-0021-4

This handbook is for developers who are moving to the Linux platform, and those using the GTK+ library, including Glib and GDK using C. All the applications and code the author developed for this book have been released under the GPL.

GTK+/Gnome Application Development
By Havoc Pennington
1st Edition
528 pages, $39.99
ISBN: 0-7357-0078-8

More than one million Linux users are also application developers. *GTK+/Gnome Application Develop-ment* provides the experienced programmer with the knowledge to develop X Windows applications with the popular GTK+ toolkit. It contains reference information for more experienced users who are already familiar with usage, but require function prototypes and detailed descriptions.

Grokking the GIMP
By Carey Bunks
1st Edition
342 pages, $45.00
ISBN: 0-7357-0924-6

Grokking the GIMP is a technical reference that covers the intricacies of the GIMP's functionality. The material gives the reader the ability to get up to speed quickly and start creating great graphics using the GIMP. Included as a bonus are step-by-step cookbook features used entirely for advanced effects.

GIMP Essential Reference
By Alex Harford
1st Edition
400 pages, $24.95
ISBN: 0-7357-0911-4

As the use of the Linux OS gains steam, so does the use of the GIMP. Many Photoshop users are starting to use the GIMP, recognized for its power and versatility. Taking this into consideration, GIMP Essential Reference has shortcuts exclusively for Photoshop users and puts the power of this program into the palm of the reader's hand.

Solaris Advanced System Administrator's Guide
By Janice Winsor
2nd Edition
587 pages, $39.99
ISBN: 1-57870-039-6

This officially authorized tutorial provides indispensable tips, advice, and quick-reference tables to help you add system components, improve service access, and automate routine tasks. this book also includes updated information on Solaris 2.6 topics.

Solaris System Administrator's Guide
By Janice Winsor
2nd Edition
324 pages, $34.99
ISBN: 1-57870-040-X

Designed to work as both a practical tutorial and quick reference, this book provides UNIX administrators complete, detailed descriptions of the most frequently performed tasks for Solaris. Learn how to employ the features of Solaris to meet these needs of your users, and get tips on how to make administration easier.

Solaris Essential Reference
By John Mulligan
1st Edition
304 pages, $24.95
ISBN: 0-7357-0023-0

A great companion to the solarisguide.com website, *Solaris Essential Reference* assumes readers are well-versed in general UNIX skills and simply need some pointers on how to get the most out of Solaris. This book provides clear and concise instructions on how to perform important administration and management tasks.

Networking

Cisco Router Configuration &Troubleshooting
By Mark Tripod
2nd Edition
330 pages, $39.99
ISBN: 0-7357-0999-8

A reference for the network and system administrator who finds himself having to configure and maintain existing Cisco routers, as well as get new hardware up and running. By providing advice and preferred practices, instead of just rehashing Cisco documentation, this book gives networking professionals information they can start using today.

Understanding Directory Services

By Beth Sheresh and Doug Sheresh
1st Edition
390 pages, $39.99
ISBN: 0-7357-0910-6

Understanding Directory Services provides the reader with a thorough knowledge of the fundamentals of directory services: what Directory Services are, how they are designed, and what functionality they can provide to an IT infrastructure. This book provides a framework to the exploding market of directory services by placing the technology in context and helping people understand what directories can, and can't, do for their networks.

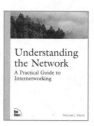

Understanding the Network: A Practical Guide to Internetworking

By Michael Martin
1st Edition
690 pages, $39.99
ISBN: 0-7357-0977-7

Understanding the Network addresses the audience in practical terminology, and describes the most essential information and tools required to build high-availability networks in a step-by-step implementation format. Each chapter could be read as a standalone, but the book builds progressively toward a summary of the essential concepts needed to put together a wide-area network.

Understanding Data Communications

By Gilbert Held
6th Edition
620 pages, $39.99
ISBN: 0-7357-0036-2

Gil Held's book is ideal for those who want to get up to speed on technological advances as well as those who want a primer on networking concepts. This book is intended to explain how data communications actually work. It contains updated coverage on hot topics like thin client technology, x2 and 56Kbps modems, voice digitization, and wireless data transmission. Whatever your needs, this title puts perspective and expertise in your hands.

LDAP: Programming Directory Enabled Applications

By Tim Howes and Mark Smith
1st Edition
480 pages, $44.99
ISBN: 1-57870-000-0

This overview of the LDAP standard discusses its creation and history with the Internet Engineering Task Force, as well as the original RFC standard. LDAP also covers compliance trends, implementation, data packet handling in C++, client/server responsibilities and more.

Gigabit Ethernet Networking

By David Cunningham and Bill Lane
1st Edition
560 pages, $50.00
ISBN: 1-57870-062-0

Gigabit Ethernet is the next step for speed on the majority of installed networks. Explore how this technology will allow high-bandwidth applications, such as the integration of telephone and data services, real-time applications, thin client applications, such as Windows NT Terminal Server, and corporate teleconferencing.

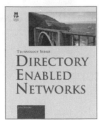

Directory Enabled Networks

By John Strassner
1st Edition
752 pages, $50.00
ISBN: 1-57870-140-6

Directory Enabled Networks is a comprehensive resource on the design and use of DEN. This book provides practical examples side-by-side with a detailed introduction to the theory of building a new class of network-enabled applications that will solve networking problems. DEN is a critical tool for network architects, administrators, and application developers.

Supporting Service Level Agreements on IP Networks

By Dinesh Verma
1st Edition
270 pages, $50.00
ISBN: 1-57870-146-5

An essential resource for network engineers and architects, *Supporting Service Level Agreements on IP Networks* will help you build a core network capable of supporting a range of service. Learn how to create SLA solutions using off the shelf components in both best-effort and DiffServ/IntServ networks. Learn how to verify the performance of your SLA, as either a customer or network services provider, and use SLAs to support IPv6 networks.

Quality of Service in IP Networks

By Grenville Armitage
1st Edition
310 pages, $50.00
ISBN: 1-57870-189-9

Quality of Service in IP Networks presents a clear understanding of the architectural issues surrounding delivering QoS in an IP network, and positions the emerging technologies within a framework of solutions. The motivation for QoS is explained with reference to emerging real-time applications, such as Voice/Video over IP, VPN services, and supporting Service Level Agreements.

Designing Addressing Architectures for Routing and Switching

By Howard Berkowitz
1st Edition
500 pages, $45.00
ISBN: 1-57870-059-0

One of the greatest challenges for a network design professional is making the users, servers, files, printers, and other resources visible on their network. This title equips the network engineer or architect with a systematic methodology for planning the wide area and local area network "streets" on which users and servers live.

Wireless LANs: Implementing Interoperable Networks

By Jim Geier
1st Edition
432 pages, $40.00
ISBN: 1-57870-081-7

Wireless LANs covers how and why to migrate from proprietary solutions to the 802.11 standard, and explains how to realize significant cost savings through wireless LAN implementation for data collection systems.

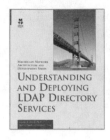

Understanding and Deploying LDAP Directory Services

By Tim Howes,
Mark Smith, and Gordon
Good
1st Edition
850 pages, $50.00
ISBN: 1-57870-070-1

This comprehensive tutorial provides the reader with a thorough treatment of LDAP directory services. Minimal knowledge of general networking and administration is assumed, making the material accessible to intermediate and advanced readers alike. The text is full of practical implementation advice and real-world deployment examples to help the reader choose the path that makes the most sense for his specific organization.

Switched, Fast, and Gigabit Ethernet

By Sean Riley and Robert
Breyer
3rd Edition
615 pages, $50.00
ISBN: 1-57870-073-6

Switched, Fast, and Gigabit Ethernet, Third Edition is the one and only solution needed to understand and fully implement this entire range of Ethernet innovations. Acting both as an overview of current technologies and hardware requirements as well as a hands-on, comprehensive tutorial for deploying and managing switched, fast, and gigabit ethernet networks, this guide covers the most prominent present and future challenges network administrators face.

Wide Area High Speed Networks

By Dr. Sidnie Feit
1st Edition
624 pages, $50.00
ISBN: 1-57870-114-7

Networking is in a transitional phase between long-standing conventional wide area services and new technologies and services. This book presents current and emerging wide area technologies and services, makes them understandable, and puts them into perspective so that their merits and disadvantages are clear.

Local Area High Speed Networks

By Dr. Sidnie Feit
1st Edition
655 pages, $50.00
ISBN: 1-57870-113-9

There is a great deal of change happening in the technology being used for local area networks. As Web intranets have driven bandwidth needs through the ceiling, inexpensive Ethernet NICs and switches have come into the market. As a result, many network professionals are interested in evaluating these new technologies for implementation. This book provides real-world implementation expertise for these technologies, including traces, so that users can realistically compare and decide how to use them.

Designing Routing and Switching Architectures for Enterprise Networks

By Howard Berkowitz
1st Edition
992 pages, $55.00
ISBN: 1-57870-060-4

This title provides a fundamental understanding of how switches and routers operate, enabling the reader to use them effectively to build networks. The book walks the network designer through all aspects of requirements, analysis, and deployment strategies, strengthens readers' professional abilities, and helps them develop skills necessary to advance in their profession.

The DHCP Handbook

By Ralph Droms
and Ted Lemon
1st Edition
535 pages, $55.00
ISBN: 1-57870-137-6

The DHCP Handbook is an authoritative overview and expert guide to the setup and management of a DHCP server. This title discusses how DHCP was developed and its interaction with other protocols. Learn how DHCP operates, its use in different environments, and the interaction between DHCP servers and clients. Network hardware, inter-server communication, security, SNMP, and IP mobility are also discussed. Also, included in the book are several appendices that provide a rich resource for networking professionals working with DHCP.

Network Performance Baselining

By Daniel Nassar
1st Edition
736 pages, $50.00
ISBN: 1-57870-240-2

Network Performance Baselining focuses on the real-world implementation of network baselining principles and shows not only how to measure and rate a network's performance, but also how to improve the network performance. This book includes chapters that give a real "how-to" approach for standard baseline methodologies along with actual steps and processes to perform network baseline measurements. In addition, the proper way to document and build a baseline report will be provided.

The Economics of Electronic Commerce

By Soon-Yong Choi, Andrew Whinston, Dale Stahl
1st Edition
656 pages, $49.99
ISBN: 1-57870-014-0

This is the first electronic commerce title to focus on traditional topics of economics applied to the electronic commerce arena. While all other electronic commerce titles take a "how-to" approach, this focuses on what it means from an economic perspective.

Intrusion Detection

By Rebecca Gurley Bace
1st Edition
340 pages, $50.00
ISBN: 1-57870-185-6

Intrusion detection is a critical new area of technology within network security. This comprehensive guide to the field of intrusion detection covers the foundations of intrusion detection and system audit. *Intrusion Detection* provides a wealth of information, ranging from design considerations to how to evaluate and choose the optimal commercial intrusion detection products for a particular networking environment.

Understanding Public-Key Infrastructure

By Carlisle Adams and Steve Lloyd
1st Edition
300 pages, $50.00
ISBN: 1-57870-166-X

This book is a tutorial on, and a guide to the deployment of, Public-Key Infrastructures. It covers a broad range of material related to PKIs, including certification, operational considerations and standardization efforts, as well as deployment issues and considerations. Emphasis is placed on explaining the interrelated fields within the topic area, to assist those who will be responsible for making deployment decisions and architecting a PKI within an organization.

Network Intrusion Detection: An Analyst's Handbook

By Stephen Northcutt and Judy Novak
2nd Edition
480 pages, $45.00
ISBN: 0-7357-1008-2

Get answers and solutions from someone who has been in the trenches. Author Stephen Northcutt, original developer of the Shadow intrusion detection system and former Director of the United States Navy's Information System Security Office, gives his expertise to intrusion detection specialists, security analysts, and consultants responsible for setting up and maintaining an effective defense against network security attacks.

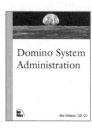

Domino System Administration

By Rob Kirkland
1st Edition
860 pages, $49.99
ISBN: 1-56205-948-3

Need a concise, practical explana-tion about the new features of Domino, and how to make some of the advanced stuff really work? *Domino System Administration* is the first book on Domino that attacks the technology at the professional level, with practical, hands-on assistance to get Domino 5 running in your organization.

Other Books By New Riders

Networking Quality of Service and Windows
Operating Systems
1-57870-206-2 • $50.00 US / $74.95 CAN
Policy-Based Management
1-57870-225-9 • $55.00 US / $81.95 CAN • Available
March 2001
Quality of Service on IP Networks
1-57870-189-9 • $50.00 US / $74.95 CAN
Designing Addressing Architectures for Routing
and Switching
1-57870-059-0 • $45.00 US / $69.95 CAN
Understanding & Deploying LDAP Directory
Services
1-57870-070-1 • $50.00 US / $74.95 CAN
Switched, Fast and Gigabit Ethernet, Third
Edition
1-57870-073-6 • $50.00 US / $74.95 CAN
Wireless LANs: Implementing Interoperable
Networks
1-57870-081-7 • $40.00 US / $59.95 CAN
Local Area High Speed Networks
1-57870-113-9 • $50.00 US / $74.95 CAN
Wide Area High Speed Networks
1-57870-114-7 • $50.00 US / $74.95 CAN
The DHCP Handbook
1-57870-137-6 • $55.00 US / $81.95 CAN
Designing Routing and Switching Architectures for
Enterprise Networks
1-57870-060-4 • $55.00 US / $81.95 CAN
Network Performance Baselining
1-57870-240-2 • $50.00 US / $74.95 CAN
Economics of Electronic Commerce
1-57870-014-0 • $49.99 US / $74.95 CAN

SECURITY

Intrusion Detection
1-57870-185-6 • $50.00 US / $74.95 CAN
Understanding Public-Key Infrastructure
1-57870-166-X • $50.00 US / $74.95 CAN
Network Intrusion Detection: An Analyst's
Handbook, 2E
0-7357-1008-2 • $45.00 US / $67.95 CAN
Linux Firewalls
0-7357-0900-9 • $39.99 US / $59.95 CAN
Intrusion Signatures and Analysis
0-7357-1063-5 • $39.99 US / $59.95 CAN • Available
February 2001
Hackers Beware
0-7357-1009-0 • $45.00 US / $67.95 CAN • Available
March 2001

LOTUS NOTES/DOMINO

Domino System Administration
1-56205-948-3 • $49.99 US / $74.95 CAN
Lotus Notes & Domino Essential Reference
0-7357-0007-9 • $45.00 US / $67.95 CAN

PROFESSIONAL CERTIFICATION

TRAINING GUIDES

MCSE Training Guide: Networking Essentials,
2nd Ed.
1-56205-919-X • $49.99 US / $74.95 CAN
MCSE Training Guide: Windows NT Server 4,
2nd Ed.
1-56205-916-5 • $49.99 US / $74.95 CAN
MCSE Training Guide: Windows NT Workstation
4, 2nd Ed.
1-56205-918-1 • $49.99 US / $74.95 CAN
MCSE Training Guide: Windows NT Server 4
Enterprise, 2nd Ed.
1-56205-917-3 • $49.99 US / $74.95 CAN
MCSE Training Guide: Core Exams Bundle, 2nd
Ed.
1-56205-926-2 • $149.99 US / $223.95 CAN

MCSE Training Guide: TCP/IP, 2nd Ed.
1-56205-920-3 • $49.99 US / $74.95 CAN
MCSE Training Guide: IIS 4, 2nd Ed.
0-7357-0865-7 • $49.99 US / $74.95 CAN
MCSE Training Guide: SQL Server 7
Administration
0-7357-0003-6 • $49.99 US / $74.95 CAN
MCSE Training Guide: SQL Server 7
Database Design
0-7357-0004-4 • $49.99 US / $74.95 CAN
MCSD Training Guide: Visual Basic 6 Exams
0-7357-0002-8 • $69.99 US / $104.95 CAN
MCSD Training Guide: Solution
Architectures
0-7357-0026-5 • $49.99 US / $74.95 CAN
MCSD Training Guide: 4-in-1 Bundle
0-7357-0912-2 • $149.99 US / $223.95 CAN
A+ Certification Training Guide, Second
Edition
0-7357-0907-6 • $49.99 US / $74.95 CAN
Network+ Certification Guide
0-7357-0077-X • $49.99 US / $74.95 CAN
Solaris 2.6 Administrator Certification
Training Guide, Part I
1-57870-085-X • $40.00 US / $59.95 CAN
Solaris 2.6 Administrator Certification
Training Guide, Part II
1-57870-086-8 • $40.00 US / $59.95 CAN
Solaris 7 Administrator Certification
Training Guide, Part I and II
1-57870-249-6 • $49.99 US / $74.95 CAN
MCSE Training Guide: Windows 2000
Professional
0-7357-0965-3 • $49.99 US / $74.95 CAN
MCSE Training Guide: Windows 2000 Server
0-7357-0968-8 • $49.99 US / $74.95 CAN
MCSE Training Guide: Windows 2000
Network Infrastructure
0-7357-0966-1 • $49.99 US / $74.95 CAN
MCSE Training Guide: Windows 2000
Network Security Design
0-73570-984X • $49.99 US / $74.95 CAN
MCSE Training Guide: Windows 2000
Network Infrastructure Design
0-73570-982-3 • $49.99 US / $74.95 CAN
MCSE Training Guide: Windows 2000
Directory Svcs. Infrastructure
0-7357-0976-9 • $49.99 US / $74.95 CAN
MCSE Training Guide: Windows 2000
Directory Services Design
0-7357-0983-1 • $49.99 US / $74.95 CAN
MCSE Training Guide: Windows 2000
Accelerated Exam
0-7357-0979-3 • $69.99 US / $104.95 CAN
MCSE Training Guide: Windows 2000 Core
Exams Bundle
0-7357-0988-2 • $149.99 US / $223.95 CAN

FAST TRACKS

CLP Fast Track: Lotus Notes/Domino 5
Application Development
0-73570-877-0 • $39.99 US / $59.95 CAN
CLP Fast Track: Lotus Notes/Domino 5
System Administration
0-7357-0878-9 • $39.99 US / $59.95 CAN
Network+ Fast Track
0-7357-0904-1 • $29.99 US / $44.95 CAN
A+ Fast Track
0-7357-0028-1 • $34.99 US / $52.95 CAN
MCSD Fast Track: Visual Basic 6, Exam #70-
175
0-7357-0019-2 • $19.99 US / $29.95 CAN

MCSD FastTrack: Visual Basic 6, Exam #70-
175
0-7357-0018-4 • $19.99 US / $29.95 CAN

SOFTWARE ARCHITECTURE & ENGINEERING

Designing for the User with OVID
1-57870-101-5 • $40.00 US / $59.95 CAN
Designing Flexible Object-Oriented Systems
with UML
1-57870-098-1 • $40.00 US / $59.95 CAN
Constructing Superior Software
1-57870-147-3 • $40.00 US / $59.95 CAN
A UML Pattern Language
1-57870-118-X • $45.00 US / $67.95 CAN

 # How to Contact Us

Visit Our Web Site

www.newriders.com

On our Web site you'll find information about our other books, authors, tables of contents, indexes, and book errata.

Email Us

Contact us at this address:

nrfeedback@newriders.com

- If you have comments or questions about this book
- To report errors that you have found in this book
- If you have a book proposal to submit or are interested in writing for New Riders
- If you would like to have an author kit sent to you
- If you are an expert in a computer topic or technology and are interested in being a technical editor who reviews manuscripts for technical accuracy

- To find a distributor in your area, please contact our international department at this address.

nrmedia@newriders.com

- For instructors from educational institutions who want to preview New Riders books for classroom use. Email should include your name, title, school, department, address, phone number, office days/hours, text in use, and enrollment, along with your request for desk/examination copies and/or additional information.
- For members of the media who are interested in reviewing copies of New Riders books. Send your name, mailing address, and email address, along with the name of the publication or Web site you work for.

Bulk Purchases/Corporate Sales

If you are interested in buying 10 or more copies of a title or want to set up an account for your company to purchase directly from the publisher at a substantial discount, contact us at 800-382-3419 or email your contact information to corpsales@pearsontechgroup.com. A sales representative will contact you with more information.

Write to Us

New Riders Publishing
201 W. 103rd St.
Indianapolis, IN 46290-1097

Call Us

Toll-free (800) 571-5840 + 9 + 7477
If outside U.S. (317) 581-3500. Ask for New Riders.

Fax Us

(317) 581-4663

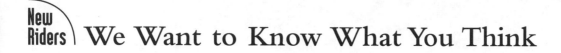

We Want to Know What You Think

To better serve you, we would like your opinion on the content and quality of this book. Please complete this card and mail it to us or fax it to 317-581-4663.

Name _____

Address _____

City_____State_____Zip _____

Phone _____

Email Address _____

Occupation _____

Operating System(s) that you use _____

What influenced your purchase of this book?
- ❏ Recommendation
- ❏ Cover Design
- ❏ Table of Contents
- ❏ Index
- ❏ Magazine Review
- ❏ Advertisement
- ❏ New Rider's Reputation
- ❏ Author Name

How would you rate the contents of this book?
- ❏ Excellent
- ❏ Very Good
- ❏ Good
- ❏ Fair
- ❏ Below Average
- ❏ Poor

How do you plan to use this book?
- ❏ Quick reference
- ❏ Self-training
- ❏ Classroom
- ❏ Other

What do you like most about this book?
Check all that apply.
- ❏ Content
- ❏ Writing Style
- ❏ Accuracy
- ❏ Examples
- ❏ Listings
- ❏ Design
- ❏ Index
- ❏ Page Count
- ❏ Price
- ❏ Illustrations

What do you like least about this book?
Check all that apply.
- ❏ Content
- ❏ Writing Style
- ❏ Accuracy
- ❏ Examples
- ❏ Listings
- ❏ Design
- ❏ Index
- ❏ Page Count
- ❏ Price
- ❏ Illustrations

What would be a useful follow-up book to this one for you?_____

Where did you purchase this book? _____

Can you name a similar book that you like better than this one, or one that is as good? Why?

_____

_____

How many New Riders books do you own? _____

What are your favorite computer books?_____

_____

What other titles would you like to see us develop? _____

_____

Any comments for us? _____

_____

_____

_____

Policy-Based Networking: Architecture and Algorithms, 1-57870-226-7

www.newriders.com • Fax 317-581-4663

Fold here and tape to mail

- -

New Riders Publishing
201 W. 103rd St.
Indianapolis, IN 46290